KEITH MILLER
THE GOLDEN NUGGET

By the same author:
John Reid's Kiwis
Bradman, Benaud and Goddard's Cinderellas
The Quiet Australian—the Lindsay Hassett Story
Simpson's Safari
Time of the Tiger—the Bill O'Reilly Story
Sir Frank—the Frank Packer Story
Captains Outrageous? Cricket in the Seventies
An Illustrated History of Australian Cricket
Great Moments of Australian Sport
The Courage Book of Australian Test Cricket
An Illustrated History of Australian Tennis
The Champions

With Keith Miller
Cricket Caravan
Catch
Straight Hit
Bumper
Gods or Flannelled Fools?
Cricket Typhoon
The Keith Miller Cricket Companion
Fours Galore

With John Waite
Perchance to Bowl

With Victor Richardson
The Vic Richardson Story

With George Hele
Bodyline Umpire

'Killah Dillah Millah' looks the part as he surveys the scene at the Epsom Derby in 1956 (*Photo—London* Daily Express)

KEITH MILLER
THE GOLDEN NUGGET

R. S. WHITINGTON

RIGBY

To Geoffrey Green, John Davey, Bob Condon, Alec Bain, and, of course, to my brother Alex and sister-in-law Jan— what a sextet!

Editor: Reg Edmonds

National Library of Australia
Cataloguing-in-Publication entry

Whitington, R. S. (Richard Smallpeice), 1912–
Keith Miller: the golden nugget.
ISBN 0 7270 1424 2.
1. Miller, Keith, 1919– . 2. Cricket players—Biography. I. Title.

796.35'8'0924

RIGBY PUBLISHERS LIMITED • ADELAIDE
SYDNEY • MELBOURNE • BRISBANE • PERTH
NEW YORK • LONDON • AUCKLAND
First published 1981

Typeset by ProComp Productions Pty Ltd, Adelaide, South Australia
Printed by Hedges & Bell Pty Ltd, Maryborough, Victoria

Acknowledgments

I am extremely grateful to Denis Compton, Ray Lindwall, and Jim Russell for each contributing a foreword to this book about our mutual friend Keith Miller.

Foreword

The scene is Lord's, 1943. A charity match had been arranged between an England side and the Dominions, to give the London people some relief from thoughts of air-raids. Luck smiled upon me that day and I felt set for a big score. Finally the ball was thrown to a tall, dark, brush-back-haired fellow who had been racing round the boundary like a young gazelle and whose gigantic throws, with an almost nonchalant whip of the wrist and forearm, had drawn whistles of admiration from the crowd. He was the fifth bowling change.

Not knowing what to expect I turned to the wicketkeeper Stan Sismey and asked: 'What does this chap do, Stan?'

The answer was comforting. 'Oh, he's not really a bowler,' said Stan, 'I expect he wants a bit of exercise, but you might find him a bit quick.'

A bit quick! The bowler took only a short run, but when he let the ball go, my hair nearly stood up on end. That was the fastest ball bowled to me since I played against Ernie McCormick, of the 1938 Australian team in England.

Such was my introduction to Keith Miller. Stan Sismey, incidentally, was not trying to pull my leg. At that time Keith was not considered a bowler. In 1939, for instance, he played for Victoria in every State match and did not bowl a ball.

Two years passed. Then I was invited to play for East Bengal—I was on Army service in India—against the Australian Services team who were on their way home from England. Suddenly the game was interrupted by a vast crowd of Indian rioters marching towards the wicket. The leader walked up to me, possibly because I was batting, and solemnly declared: 'Mr Compton, you very good player—but you must go.'

I tried to argue, but he merely repeated, with even more emphasis: 'No, Mr Compton, you very good player—but you must go.'

There was nothing left but to adjourn the match. Keith and I walked off the field together, laughing over the incident almost as much as deploring the hold-up in the game.

I should have known what to expect: the first time I went out to bat against Keith during the 1946–47 tour of Australia he greeted me with: 'Now Mr Compton, you very good player—but you must go.'

Since then whenever either of us was making runs in a big match the other was almost bound to pronounce the old Indian's verdict.

All this, of course, is part of that enormous by-play on the cricket field of which the spectator unfortunately knows very little. We are not always as serious as we look from a hundred metres away.

As you can imagine Keith and I are very firm friends—have been for nearly forty years—and I am delighted to be given the opportunity to write a short foreword to this biography by his even-longer-time friend Dick Whitington.

I have always found Dick a very fair-minded critic, outspoken—as indeed he should be—but always honest and sincere in his opinions and I cannot imagine a more appropriate author for a biography of Keith.

DENIS COMPTON

Foreword

Keith Miller—what can I say about him? Whatever it is will certainly be biased.

Keith and I became pals from the first day we met in 1946, and remain friends to the present day—although I am about to put that friendship to the test because of a week's promotional tour together for the first time in many years.

But getting back to Keith. I think he is the greatest cricket all-rounder of my time, and that includes Gary Sobers (biased, I said).

Keith had that talent to rise to the occasion when the team was up against it; also, he was a matchwinner when his side was on top. Off the field Keith was a terrific mixer. Very unassuming, he could talk to anyone at any time on any thing—especially about aeroplanes or racehorses.

A great bloke!

By the way, we have had that week away and are still friends. He hasn't changed.

RAY LINDWALL

Foreword

We were sitting in the Press luncheon room at Wimbledon in June 1977, Richard Whitington and I, sitting with our strawberries and cream and half watching an unexciting centre court singles on TV. The colour on the TV set was more brilliant than the tennis, so we lingered on the strawberries and talked about cricket.

'How many books have you written?' I asked Richard.

'About seventeen,' he said, 'as well as those, of course, which I wrote in collaboration with Keith.'

I demolished another strawberry and then commented, 'In all the years you've been writing cricket books, a few with Keith, it has always surprised me that you've never written one about him —the most colourful player I've ever known?'

Some people would use the term 'looking like a stunned mullet' to describe the expression on the face of Richard Whitington, but I simply record that he appeared to go into mild shock.

'For God's sake!' he said. 'I never thought of it.'

And there at Wimbledon as tennis-chronicling typewriters chattered out the importance of an unimportant centre court match, *Keith Miller, The Golden Nugget* was conceived.

The gestation period took a little longer than the regular clinical time but, now that I have seen the healthy, vigorous child, have digested the many facts and figures, anecdotes and sharp criticisms that Dick researched and remembered during that time, I am glad that it did.

To find myself sitting in publishing's grandstand beside such cricketing greats as Denis Compton's and Ray Lindwall's forewords for this book gives me the feeling of a bad bung taken to a cricket match by two knowledgeable superiors. As a modest cricket fan I am just one of the hundreds of thousands who watch with delight and amazement the skills of the performers, the thespians in the great theatre of cricket.

Reading the breadth of statistics and analyses produced by the author reminds me of Arthur Mailey telling me that his then soon-to-be-published book *10 for 66 and All That* 'would sell at least 7584 copies'.

I was bemused at such an apparently accurate sales prediction and asked how he arrived at this precise figure. 'Because,' he said, 'there are 7584 people in the English-speaking world who buy *every* book on cricket published.'

Perhaps you who are reading *Keith Miller, The Golden Nugget* now are one of those thousands; but the enjoyment I got from reading it in manuscript convinces me that there will be many more thousands who will join you.

One of my favourite television shows is called *The Odd Couple*, the continuing saga of two apparently ill-matched, batching, divorced men, yet with an empathy between them that can only be classified as 'Quality X'. In thinking of the Miller–Whitington writing partnership I detect 'X'. I have always thought of them as 'The Odd Couple': Richard, with the precise, clipped speech—the Anglophile from Adelaide; Keith, the epitome of the happy-go-lucky, swashbuckling Australian—first of Melbourne, then of his more temperamentally attuned Sydney.

Yet the understanding of Keith's faults and at times failures, at other times his reaching for the sky with thundering successes of bowling, batting, and fielding, shows Richard as a great student of human nature.

I first met Keith in 1953 when my paper, the Melbourne *Sun* sent me to London to do cartoons and stories on the Coronation of Queen Elizabeth II. To give value for the money expended by them on my trip I also did some illustrated 'funnies' (a newspaper term for humorous colour stories) on various sports. I was already reasonably well known as a tennis writer, but cricket meant my getting to know some of the players at first hand. Keith Miller always struck me as possibly an approachable bloke so I went to the Park Lane Hotel, where the Australians stayed, and awaited their return from some minor match or other.

As the cars pulled up Keith came breezing through with the rest of the team and one could feel his presence charismaing (if there is such a word) out of the group.

'Sure,' Keith said as I explained my mission. 'Why don't you join some of the boys and me for a beer?'

I imagined we would soon be sitting in the plush surroundings of the elegant Park Lane Hotel cocktail bar sipping sedately and I followed them as they swung across the lobby, along a corridor, and out through a rear exit to the seamy lane. We passed a few garbage cans, crossed the narrow lane, and suddenly there we were in the bar-room of a typical small London pub. 'What'll you have?' Keith asked. 'They've got Fosters here.'

And that was my introduction to Keith Ross Miller. It was also my introduction to Arthur Morris, Jimmy de Courcy, and Gil Langley and, during the next month or so covering Test and County matches, we always seemed to gravitate together for our after-match beers. Through them I was able to meet Alan Davidson (who later became my next-door neighbour in Strathfield), Lindsay Hassett, Ian Craig, and many of the others. Occasionally Sid Barnes joined us.

I had known Richard Whitington for some years at Sydney's White City Tennis Club through our mutual friend Adrian Quist. And when lovable Arthur Mailey let me down badly at Nottingham when he gave the hotel room he had booked for me to his Editor-In-Chief, David McNicoll, a late arrival (Who could blame him?) I found myself with no place to sleep. Nottingham was booked out.

It was Richard who took pity on me and assured me on my arrival at the ground that I should not worry. 'I'm staying at the Station Hotel,' he said, 'and I'm sure I can get you in there.'

But when the day's play had ended, and we applied for accommodation, the sad truth was that the hotel was fully booked out. The management would put me first on the waiting list in case there was a cancellation, they said, but when we returned to the desk after dinner not one obliging person had cancelled.

'I know it sounds pretty ghastly,' Dick said, 'but I've got a big double bed in my room and if you'd like to take one side of that it could be better than sleeping in the park.'

I nodded with some unease.

We agreed that a large bolster, sitting on top of a wardrobe, might well be placed between us to preserve the privacy that two married men could reasonably require. So we retired after putting through a call to room service for two tray breakfasts to be delivered in the morning.

The night was uneventful and we snored our way to daylight when a knock awoke us and in came the breakfast tray lady, a dear old thing straight out of Coronation Street.

''Ullo loves,' she said. ''Ave a nice night?' The stunned mullet look I spoke of earlier had nothing on our Mrs 'Arris as she heard two male, gruff voices assure her that we certainly had done so.

I'm sure that Nottingham is no different to the rest of the world when it comes to what was going on in the moral-living lady's mind, but she probably hadn't actually seen it before. It took her one sniffing, grumping, cup-and-saucer-rattling minute to dispose of such goings-on and she left the room in, I'm sure, righteous disgust.

Later that morning I was able to obtain a single room and I enjoyed the Test match (except that Alec Bedser took 14 wickets for a song).

That evening I retired to my room and again telephoned room service, this time to request that one breakfast be delivered to me. On the dot of 7.30 next morning came a knock, followed by the door opening (they had no keys in that hotel, I'm sure), and the entry of our Mrs 'Arris again.

My face must have unforgettable qualities for the good lady instantly remembered me. This time, however, her expression was one of greater understanding and some sympathy. As she set my breakfast tray down she inquired coyly, 'Oh, 'ullo. 'Ave yous two 'ad a row?'

Well, Mrs 'Arris, if you are one of the 7584 regular buyers of cricket books, or, like me, just one of the many thousands who are more selective and are reading this one now, I assure you we didn't ''ave a row'!

Richard and I have remained firm friends over many years, as have Keith Miller, Arthur Morris, Jimmy de Courcy, Alan

Davidson, and the rest.

A few months ago I sat in London's Talk of the Town with Bill Salter, the theatre-restaurant marketing manager, and some colleagues. Our fellow-guests were Keith Miller and his son Denis (named after Denis Compton). The stir as Keith walked into the crowded room was electrical. Everyone, yes everyone, in that place knew Keith Miller, and voices called him from all around the room.

Such is the charisma of the 'Golden Nugget' twenty-three years after his retirement from cricket.

I mention this anecdote to highlight the human qualities of both Richard and Keith in dealing with a bloke like me who sits on the Sydney Cricket Ground Hill from time to time, but who enjoys the intimacy that a book like *Keith Miller, The Golden Nugget* presents of one of the greatest cricketers of all time.

JIM RUSSELL

(Creator of The Potts cartoon strip)

Contents

1
Reluctant Alexander

Back in 1968, when Sir Garfield Sobers was well on his way to his eventual unparalleled Test match record of 93 matches, 8032 runs (365 not out highest score, 26 centuries) at 57·78, 235 wickets at 34·03, and 109 catches, Sir Donald Bradman was quoted in the *Sydney Morning Herald* as having classified the West Indian as 'unquestionably the greatest all-round cricketer of all time'.

Having read this opinion of Don's I decided to join that fine Australian opening batsman of the 1940s and 1950s, Arthur Morris, for lunch over a bottle of his pet claret at the New South Wales Cricketers Club on the fifth floor of Sydney's Cricket House, and ascertain his reaction—to the opinion, not the claret.

It was an overcast June or July day in Sydney, far more fitted for Melbourne. Rain was pouring diagonally down and there was then surprisingly little shelter for pedestrians along the section of George Street that separates Hunter and Bridge streets. Groups of fugitives from the elements were huddling together under the few verandahs and in the doorways of buildings, glancing up dispiritedly at the sombre sky and then darting out.

Eventually I reached the verandahs of the line of shops which adjoin Cricket House, and while passing the entrance to Stan McCabe's Sports Store I saw a little man in a speckled grey suit standing with his back to a counter beside a rack of the latest model cricket bats—Autographs, Stuart Surridges, and Gray-Nicholls.

I had to look twice before I recognised the shrunken figure leaning against the counter as that of the batsman who, at Sydney in 1932, at Johannesburg in 1935, and at Nottingham in 1938, had played three of the most heroic and dramatic innings in the whole history of Test cricket: his 187 not out against Larwood and Voce's 'bodyline'; his 189 not out which caused the opposing Springbok captain, Herbie Wade, to appeal against the light on the ground that 'McCabe's strokes were endangering his fieldsmen'; and his 232 out of 290 in 235 minutes (the last 72 out of 77 in 28 minutes) against England which was described as 'heroic loneliness' by Sir Neville Cardus, as 'insolent brilliance' by opponent Bill Edrich, and as 'the finest innings I have ever watched' by that greatest of all English bowlers, Sydney Barnes. During that innings of 232 Don Bradman had called his teammates from the dark of the dressing-room to the Trent Bridge balcony with the words, 'Come and look at this, you may never see its like again'. After it Don said to Stan, 'I'd have given a great deal to be able to play an innings like yours'.

Yes, I had to look twice that day, for 1968 was the year in which Stan McCabe, or 'Napper', as he was known because of his receding hair and facial resemblance to Napoleon, was to die a few weeks later on 25 August at the age of sixty. And he had become a shrunken and shrivelled little caricature of a man. There was a look of a different brand of heroism in his wistful, blue eyes then, as they mustered a wan, yet welcoming, smile and I entered that doorway to join him.

'Did you read what Don said in the paper this morning?' he demanded, restoring my faith in mental telepathy.

'Yes, I'm on my way to lunch with Arthur Morris up at the club, to discover what he thinks of it. What do you, Stan?'

'I fancy Don's forgotten Keith Miller *and* Wally Hammond,' he replied. 'Wally was the greatest cricketer I ever played against and I'd have bet on Keith Miller beating Gary in a solo, single-wicket match. Maybe I'm a bit prejudiced though. Wally and Keith were not only great champions; they also carried themselves like champions and this meant a lot to me.'

'And *you* never saw the best of Keith; saw him as he was in England in 1945 and in the West Indies in 1955, Stan,' I stressed.

'I saw enough,' he replied. 'And I've read what *Wisden* said about that 185 in 165 minutes he scored for the Dominions against England at Lord's in August of 1945, about "that most masterly innings played for a generation" as *Wisden*'s correspondent described it. Keith, at the peak of his ability as a batsman and a bowler, was the finest all-rounder I have watched and I'm not under-rating Gary. The trouble with Keith was that he was apt to lose interest in things when his team was winning too easily. He needed a crisis to rouse him and his "killer instinct". If he'd been as ambitious, possessed the consistent application and dedication that Don, himself, Len Hutton, and Bill O'Reilly had, he'd have scored about 5000 runs and taken about 300 wickets in Test matches.'

I was happy to agree because I *had* seen that 'most masterly innings of a generation' at Lord's; I *had* watched Keith's other two lonely centuries there for Lindsay Hassett's Services Team against England in 1945; I *had* watched his three sentinelling centuries for Australia in the 1955 series against the West Indies in the Caribbean—in a series in which, partnering Lindwall in those 'Cricketing cauldrons' of Jamaica, Trinidad, Barbados, and what then was British Guiana, Keith had also taken 20 wickets from 188·2 overs at 32·45 *at the age of thirty-five*. And these against teams which included those magnificent batsmen Sir Frank Worrell, Everton Weekes, Clyde Walcott, the ill-starred 'Collie' Smith, *and* the young Gary Sobers.

'Don never saw the best of Keith as a batsman,' Stan continued. 'And for Don, seeing was always believing. That, I think, is why he classed Keith as a great fast bowler, but apt to be over-rated as a batsman.'

'Don needed Keith more as a bowler than as a batsman when he was captaining Australia in 1946–47 and 1948,' I said. 'He had all the batting he needed in Sid Barnes, Arthur Morris, himself, Bill Brown, Lindsay Hassett, Neil Harvey, Colin McCool, Ray Lindwall, and Don Tallon.'

'That's right,' Stan agreed, 'but I'm keeping you from your lunch with Arthur.'

Had I known that, within six weeks, Stan would be dead I would have stayed with him that winter day till his staff returned from *their* lunch. For he looked a very sick and lonely man that grey, sombre afternoon of 1968 in Sydney.

Whose opinion of Miller was one to accept—Don's or Stan's?

Keith Miller represented Australia in 55 Tests; Sobers played in 98. Keith's Test career was delayed for six years by the Hitler war while he advanced from twenty to twenty-six—vitally important years. Keith played in his first official Test match in 1946 when he was twenty-seven, retired in 1956 when he was thirty-six. Gary Sobers began his uninterrupted Test career in 1953 when he was seventeen, retired in 1973 when he was thirty-seven.

Miller's 55 Tests were played against England (29), West Indies (10), South Africa (9), India (5), New Zealand and Pakistan (one each). Sobers' 93 Tests for the West Indies were played against England (36), Australia (19), India (18), New Zealand (12), and Pakistan (8). His other five Tests, if they should be called Tests, were played for the Rest of the World.

Sobers' Test record score of 365 not out was compiled against Pakistan and 13 of his 26 Test centuries came against India, New Zealand, and Pakistan.

So there is much (including Ray Lindwall's foreword) to support McCabe's opinion, especially as it was given in 1968—five years before Gary retired. But Don based *his* views partly, I feel sure, on the fact that Sobers was a 'five-in-one cricketer': a great batsman, great fieldsman, and a fine and versatile bowler who could become an Alan Davidson, Derek Underwood, or 'Chuck' Fleetwood-Smith at will, and maintain Test-standard control in all three of these roles.

Keith for the most part had only three strings to his bow, though in his first Test again England at Brisbane in 1946 and in the Durban Test of 1949 he proved just how dangerous he could be while delivering seam and spin at half his normal pace. Though Keith only captained Australia in part of one Test (during Ian Johnson's absence through illness in the First Test of 1955 at Kingston, Jamaica) he showed himself then and in many matches for New South Wales to be a finer leader than Sobers ever did in Australia in 1968–69.

But, as Keith himself has expressed his complete agreement with Bradman on this question, I won't press it any further—except to say that, like McCabe, I'd back Keith in a solo, single-wicket encounter because I believe him more likely to dismiss

Gary economically with a new ball than vice versa. And to point out that Keith Miller's all-round Test record is still superior to that of all other cricketers except Sobers', as the following figures reveal:

(1) Australian all-rounders:

	Tests	*Innings*	*Runs*	*Average*	*Wickets*	*Average*
Miller	55	87	2958	36·97	170	22·97
Giffen	31	53	1238	23·35	103	27·09
Noble	42	73	1997	30·25	121	25·01
Armstrong	50	84	2863	38·68	87	33·59
Gregory	24	34	1146	36·90	85	31·15
Benaud	63	97	2201	24·45	248	27·03
Davidson	44	53	1328	25·00	186	20·58
Lindwall	61	84	1502	21·15	228	23·05

(2) All-rounders of other countries:

	Country	*Tests*	*Innings*	*Runs*	*Average*	*Wickets*	*Average*
Rhodes	England	58	98	2325	30·19	127	26·96
Hammond	England	85	140	7249	58·45	83	37·83
Mankad	India	44	72	2109	39·28	162	31·47
Bailey	England	61	91	2290	29·74	132	29·74
Goddard	South Africa	41	78	2516	34·46	123	26·22
Woolley	England	64	98	3283	36·07	83	33·91
Greig	England	58	93	3599	40·43	141	32·20

When Miller retired in 1956 he and Wilfred Rhodes of England were the only two players of any country who had scored 2000 or more runs and taken 100 or more wickets in Test matches. Miller's figures (batting and bowling) were comfortably superior to Rhodes'.

Almost all the players whose figures are shown above would have stood the test of what I regard as the true definition of a Test all-rounder—a cricketer who deserved selection for his country, either as a batsman or a bowler and not just because of the sum of his batting and bowling ability.

The term all-rounder has often been loosely used, in my opinion, and is perhaps more carelessly used nowadays than ever before. This is partly because newspapers have style books for their sports writers and sub-editors. Most of these style books are compiled by journalists, many of whose knowledge of sport is minimal.

I well remember an occasion at the Sydney Cricket Ground in the mid 1950s when Richie Benaud had yet to mature as a Test match player. In the style book of Australian Consolidated Press (one compiled, I fancy, by David McNicoll) Benaud was proclaimed as 'all-rounder Benaud' and the style book *had* to be obeyed. It conserved newsprint at a time when costs were spiralling.

The day after I had conformed to instructions Richie executed an execrable stroke at a crucial stage in a Test match and was caught for a pittance from a skier. 'Benaud an all-rounder! Bosh and bunkum!' called an S.C.G. member *at* me on the top tier of the M. A. Noble Stand as I was on my way to lunch that next day. I wonder what the character thinks now? The compiler of that particular style book, McNicoll or not, *was* right about Richie, if a little premature in his assessment.

Finally, before escaping from statistics—Keith himself has always said, 'They never meant much to me', and they take no account of the varying conditions and laws under which they are achieved—it is convenient and important to include here the record Keith compiled in 52 Sheffield Shield matches for Victoria and New South Wales.

Batting: 74 innings, 206 not out highest score, 3803 runs at 57·62.

Bowling: 832·7 overs, 108 maidens, 2849 runs, 110 wickets at 25·90.

Under Ben Barnett for Victoria before the second World War, and under Arthur Morris' and his own leadership for New South Wales after it, Keith was able to devote far greater attention to his batting than to his fast bowling—and this was not to be the case when he played under Bradman for Australia from 1946 to 1948.

But great as was his statistical record Keith may be remembered more vividly for his impact upon international cricket as a character and a personality.

Were he playing today he would stand out far more dramatically and appealingly than even Dennis Lillee or Ian Botham. He must have been the first cricketer Kerry Packer sought to sign for his professional troupe in 1977 had he been at his peak.

Early in 1971 I was enjoying a chat at the Melbourne Cricket Ground's Tavern bar with that perhaps most whimsical and wittiest of all Australian cricketers, Ernie McCormick, when he asked a most significant and relevant question.

Maybe you are too young to have known of Ernie McCormick? According to that outstanding Australian Test umpire of the 1930s, George Hele, Ernie was for three overs faster than Harold Larwood. He was also a veritable foundry for anecdotes. When leaving the field on his English debut at Worcester in May 1938, after delivering 13 no-balls before lunch, Ernie was tackled by an English reporter. 'How do you feel, McCormick? You must be worried?'

'No, I'm fine. Umpire's hoarse,' McCormick replied.

Later on that tour, while golfing in Derbyshire, Ernie sliced a tee shot into thick undergrowth and asked his caddy to go look for the ball. Ten anxious minutes passed and Ernie decided to help with the search. 'Found it yet, Caddy?' he called.

'Yes, just trodden on it, Sir.'

'Fine. Well now come and have a look for me.'

In the 1950s, when Sir Robert Menzies used to organise matches at Canberra's Manuka Oval, McCormick was conscripted one weekend for Sir Robert's Eleven, as what might be termed an afternoon light afterthought. Batsman-journalist-author Jack Fingleton often played host to members of Sir Robert's teams during their stay in the Australian capital. On this occasion he had his house full with Hassett, Morris, Loxton, Johnson, and company when McCormick arrived. There wasn't a bed to spare. Jack parked Ernie on a mattress on the floor under a grand piano. Next morning, anxious to make amends, Jack took him a breakfast tray. 'Sorry about this. How did you make out?' he asked.

'Fine,' replied McCormick. 'I'll never sleep under an *upright* model again.'

But back to that significant and relevant question of his. During our session together at the M.C.C. Tavern bar that evening in 1971, Ernie asked, 'How long is it since you've heard a new anecdote about a Test cricketer?'

'Let's see, when did Freddie Trueman retire?' I queried.

'In 1963, after taking 307 wickets in Tests—about 300 more than I did.'

'About then,' I replied.

Well, there are many notable anecdotes—amusing and otherwise—concerning Keith Miller and they are as revealing about him as those just recounted are of Ernie McCormick.

That is why that superb mimic the late and much lamented Jimmy Burke so often chose Keith as a subject for his impersonations (as also did his other teammates Bobby Simpson and Ray Flockton).

Perhaps Burke's most memorable imitation of Keith was of his delivery of a speech at a mayoral farewell to Keith's New South Wales team in a country town in the mid-1950s. After the mayor had had his say Miller, surrounded by his teammates on the stage of the hall, advanced to the microphone, ran his fingers through his luxuriant and unruly black hair, and replied approximately as follows:

'My Lord Mayor, er, Your Worship, Your er, er, Ladies and gentlemen of er, er, of this magnificent town of ah, ah, ah, er, er, er. Never anywhere have I or my players received so marvellous and hospitable a welcome as here in this famous New South Wales town of ah, ah, ah, er, er, er. You cannot imagine just what a delight and an honour it has been for us to be here in this splendid town, ah, er, city of ah, ah, er, er, er . . . I have played cricket in many parts of the world, as you may know, but never have I received such kindness as during the past few hours in your superb city of ah, ah, ah, er, er, er . . .'

At this stage Keith, forgetting the microphone, turned desperately around to Alan Davidson and Richie Benaud and then, in one of those stage whispers that can be heard at the back of a hall, exclaimed, 'For Christ's sake, Richie, what's the effing name of this effing town?'

According to Ray Flockton and Bobby Simpson, Keith, when captaining New South Wales on the field, was the antithesis of that meticulous and 'scientific' England skipper of the 1970s, that Sherlock Holmes of cricket (he only needed a deerstalker), Michael Brearley. As young players in the early 1950s, both Flockton and Simpson were keen to collect as many clues regarding captaincy as possible. Who better to enlighten them than their new State captain, Keith Miller, they decided. And waited upon events.

The enlightenment was startling in the extreme. Following on to the Sydney Cricket Ground like the two last of Brown's famous cows in Miller's tracks, Ray and Bobby had reached the edge of the strip of pitches when they heard the 'great man' call, 'Where's the ball?' Someone threw it to him. 'I'll bowl. You bastards should know your positions by now. Scatter.'

The word, or rather words, were not 'scatter'. But 'scatter' will do. This is a book for boys as well as men.

Yes, there are plenty of anecdotes about Keith Ross Miller, many of them *extremely* revealing. We shall come to many more of them along the way.

For Keith, as we shall see, possesses that magic trait 'star-quality' to an extraordinary degree. Over to Ian Woolridge (London *Daily Mail*, 17 October 1977): 'We have very definite ideas here about what Australian sportsmen should look like. They should look like Keith Miller, massively handsome, strolling effortlessly through life with a "G'day" to the gatemen at Ascot and a "Hello Charles" to some top-hatted aristocrat who's just called him "Keith", and with such cavalier style that thousands queued overnight outside Lord's merely to watch the way he came down the pavilion steps. Neville Cardus called Keith "the Australian in excelsis" and, by God, he was right.'

And over to Sir Donald Bradman (*Farewell to Cricket*, Hodder and Stoughton, 1950): 'Keith Miller is one of the most volatile cricketers of any age. A long, rangy, athletic type, he loved to drive the ball with tremendous power, tried to hit sixes with abandon. Many of them prodigious. He would have been a far better player had he curbed this propensity and shown more judgement in his hitting. He is a dangerous bowler with the new ball, swinging it both ways at not much short of Lindwall's pace. In 1948 in England he was the best slip fieldsman in the world.

'Altogether he was a crowd-pleasing personality of the Jack Gregory type, whose limitations were caused mainly by his own failure to concentrate.'

Years later Sir Donald was accused of disliking Keith. 'Dislike Keith Miller,' he retorted. 'How could anyone help but liking Keith?'

Back in 1967, while helping Vic Richardson to write his *Vic Richardson Story*, I described Vic in a separate chapter as the 'John Barrymore of cricket'. The analogy applies equally well to Miller, who possessed all the stellar qualities—panache, magnetism, menace, power, glamour, confidence, and courage. He wore them all like a cloak—as naturally as Alexander Dumas Senior's character D'Artagnan wielded his sword.

When the more than 182-centimetre tall, raven-maned, streamlined yet powerfully built and ruggedly handsome Miller came out on to a cricket field as one of a team, even of a team led by Bradman, he was immediately the cynosure of attention. When he strode out alone as a batsman he reminded you of Jack Dempsey crossing to the centre of the ring for the opening round of a world title fight or of matador Luis Dominguin advancing to his bull.

When Miller took the ball from his captain and measured his run, when he took guard from an umpire and surveyed the field and the horizons beyond it, you came alive and alert in your seat. An aura of challenge and expectancy had transformed the scene. This was why you were present—why you had paid your money at the gate. Would he bowl down Len Hutton or Denis Compton's middle stump with his first ball? Would he strike Jim Laker's first delivery out of the ground?

You never knew; because for Miller, the bowler, and Miller, the batsman, just about anything was possible. He was a creature of whim, a marionette of mood. Almost everything he did was utterly spontaneous and unplanned. This was because deep in his heart he was (still is) on and off a horse-racing track, a gambler. And, because, when fully aroused and inspired, he was a cricketing genius. 'Talent does what it can; genius what it must,' as the Earl of Lytton said.

Ralph Barker and Irving Rosenwater's book *Test Cricket England v Australia* (William Heinemann, London, 1969) contains a selection of the biggest hits ever made in these matches. Extending from 1880 at Kennington Oval to 1964 at Lord's, the twenty-five recorded smites include three by Miller.

'1946–47 Adelaide—K. R. Miller (141 not out on the fourth morning) hit a 6 off the first ball of the day (a no-ball by D. V. P. Wright) the ball landing among the members' friends in the enclosure on the square-leg boundary.

'1948 Headingley—K. R. Miller (58) hit a ball from J. C. Laker which pitched at the foot of the trees at the Kirkstall Lane end.

'1950–51 Sydney—K. R. Miller (145 not out) off-drove fast bowler J. J. Warr over the sightscreen to the foot of the Noble Stand.'

The preceding page of Barker and Rosenwater's book contains the following paragraph:

'K. R. Miller (Australia) hit at least one over-the-boundary six on seven of the nine Test grounds on which he played—Lord's, The Oval, Old Trafford, Headingley, Sydney, Adelaide, and Brisbane.'

These were struck in Tests between England and Australia. It would be interesting to know just how many other grounds saw similar Miller strokes in games between Australia and other countries. Unfortunately there is only one Irving Rosenwater and, so far, he has not produced corresponding statistics covering the whole canvas of Test cricket. Give him time—now he has finished his excellent and monumental biography of Bradman.

After watching Miller's performances as a batsman and rookie fast bowler for Lindsay Hassett's Services Team and a Dominions XI in England in 1945, England's 'Emperor of Games' Charles Burgess Fry, who topped the scholarship list at Wadham College, Oxford, the year that subsequent Chancellor of England Lord Birkenhead came fourth, who captained England against Australia and South Africa in the Triangular Series of 1912, who gained a triple blue (cricket, athletics, and soccer) at Oxford, and who is one of three batsmen who have scored six centuries in succession in first-class cricket waxed lyrical about Keith and his cricketing prospects.

In his column in a London morning paper Fry wrote: 'Miller is a young cricketing Alexander, a player and a personality who will set out in search of new worlds to conquer in the years following the Hitler war and establish a unique niche for himself in the annals of Test cricket.'

In Sir Neville Cardus' *Cricket All The Year* (Collins, 1951) we find the following comment on Keith's share in that 'Victory summer' during which at Lord's Cricket Ground alone he scored 568 runs in eight innings with three centuries at an average of 94·68:

'In England in 1945 Miller was the embodiment and emblem of the game's resurrection from the ruin and the graveyard of the war. The sight of him, young and gay and reckless but with the Australian's lines of experience and realism in the face, his vital care-free air and the sense he spread about him of resurgent life, no matter how damaged the world—he expressed the feelings of thousands.'

As a player Keith perhaps never quite lived up to that prediction of Fry's, but he *did* as a personality. Consequently, when he was so surprisingly omitted from the Australian team originally chosen to tour South Africa in 1949–50, the sport-loving public of Johannesburg, Durban, Cape Town, and Port Elizabeth and their Press were deeply resentful. So much so that, after 'Big' Bill Johnston figured in a car accident in Durban in October, South Africa (Press, public, and cricket officialdom) practically demanded that the Australian selectors send Keith to replace him. They had been denied a sight of Don Bradman in 1935–36. Now Miller in 1949–50. It was *too* much.

And thirty years later in 1979 the sixty-seven-year-old former gateman and residential supervisor of the Sydney Cricket Ground, Alan Caffery, named Keith as the 'most popular player (cricketer, Rugby Union, Rugby League, Soccer, Australian Rules player, or athlete) who had ever performed at Sydney's citadel of sport'.

Alan Caffery, recently retired and, following seven operations, lacking the use of one leg, had been on the staff of the S.C.G. for more than thirty years. He had watched and met such champions as Sir Donald Bradman, Stanley McCabe, Bill O'Reilly, Sir Leonard Hutton, Sir Frank Worrell, Sir Garfield Sobers, Denis Compton, Richie Benaud, Lindsay Hassett, Alan Davidson, Alec Bedser, Bobby Simpson, Ray McLean, Norman O'Neill, and Greg Chappell. He had watched and met Britain's, South Africa's, and New Zealand's greatest Rugby players of the 1950s, 1960s, and 1970s. But, for him and all the members of his staff, Keith was 'the most popular—the most liked'.

Keith, throughout his career, has found the time to greet and chat regularly with the characters in the wings of big and other cricket. He has taken the chance to get to know them individually and personally—be they gatemen, doorkeepers, dressing-room attendants, bartenders, sightboard and scoreboard operators, or curators. He always remembers their names when he encounters them and takes a genuine interest in their problems.

In the late 1970s, as a television commentator, he neglected no opportunity—between the overs of a Test match or during interruptions in play—to bring them into the overall picture, make them and the importance of their work known to his millions of viewers. Sir Laurence Olivier, I understand, adopted the same attitude to the underlings in the theatre.

But back to Charles Fry's prediction of 1945—which brings us to what so many who watched him at his best still describe as 'the mystery of Miller'. Why did Keith, despite his outstanding record, fail to fulfil the high expectations held for him following his performances in England in 1945 and in Australia in 1946–47?

That he did so fail is more than strongly suggested in the late A. G. 'Johnnie' Moyes' 'estimate' of him in his *Australian Cricket—A History* (Angus & Robertson 1959). Moyes, as we shall see, was Keith's initial editor when in 1947 he took up journalism as his profession. Together they helped to produce that fine but ill-starred Australian monthly *Sporting Life Magazine* and 'Johnnie' was very fond of Keith.

Nonetheless he has written: 'Miller's place among the great all-rounders is not easy to determine, as we must consider not merely figures but the strength of the opposition, the pitches, the laws in operation, and various other factors, but there cannot be two opinions about his tremendous natural ability. Whether he consistently made full use of it is a different question.

'Not so often as might have been expected did he make as many as 50 runs and take 5 or more wickets in a Test against England—I use that as a yardstick—but he had the ability to produce a few sensational overs at a critical time and turn the course of a game. In that period of inspiration the wind blew from the west with real antagonism and the batsmen had an uneasy feeling as the bowler unleashed his venom and destructiveness. It is as a bowler rather than as a batsman that he will chiefly be remembered.

'Yet in his finest days with the bat,' Moyes continues, 'Miller looked almost regal. He was both cultured and majestic but far too often became the plebeian as he stretched, stumbled, and fell into human error and ungraceful postures. Uncertainty at the start of an innings and a lack of consistency due to the inability to exercise restraint often told against him. In full cry after runs he was often magnificent, but he was not as reliable as he might have been on the big occasion or when the side was in trouble.

'As a bowler Miller was also a bundle of contradictions. Only once against England did he take 10 wickets in a match, but once he had 9, once 7 and twice 6, and I doubt if any post-war bowler was feared so much. With a short run, hair falling all over his eyes, making full use of his height and of his left arm and shoulder, Miller's right arm could be a wheel of pestilence and war, but suddenly the inspiration would vanish; the vicious in-swinger would be lost; the fires of ambition would die down and a round-armer of pre-revolution days (prior to 1860s) or perhaps a leg-break or bosey would follow. Then he would kick the ball away as though he had no more use of it. A man of moods was Miller who, like others, did not relish being hit for fours and would clap his hands for the ball and often send down a fast bumper rising under the armpits or knocking the cap sideways, Ponsford fashion. He was gifted above the ordinary, able at times to rise to the heights, a slip fielder of rare skill—and yet so disappointing with the bat.'

During his British Commonwealth record term Prime Ministership of Australia, Sir Robert Menzies kept only two pictures in his office in Canberra. One of them was a small, glowing, landscape masterpiece by Tom Roberts, the other a photograph of Keith Miller finishing a cover-hit. The one on the dust cover. Sir Robert described the latter far more effectively than I can hope to do in his foreword to Keith's and my fourth book *Bumper*: 'The feet beautifully placed, the lithe body balanced yet leaning out of balance with the shot. The blade through over the left shoulder, the head triumphant, the eye looking at the boundary. It is not only the greatest action photograph of a cricketer I have ever seen; it is in two dimensions a beautiful piece of sculpture, and it would have provoked immense joy in ancient Athens.'

No 'ungraceful posture' or 'plebeian stumbling' here it would seem.

I, like Keith, worked under Moyes on *Sporting Life Magazine* and know Johnnie always strove to be fair in his comments—fair as he saw things. He also had a profound knowledge of cricket (he was chosen to represent Australia in South Africa on the cancelled tour of 1914–15). He was tremendously close to Don Bradman, whom he chose as the godfather of one of his sons. I have always felt that Johnnie's views were somewhat coloured by Don's. And Don, you will remember, had said in 1948, 'Miller was a great fast bowler, but apt to be over-rated as a batsman'.

There is, however, much truth in Moyes' 'estimate'. His word-picture of Keith in action with the ball is graphic.

I have always wondered, however, why he failed to criticise some of Australia's other great all-rounders—notably Giffen, Noble, and Jack Gregory (on the score of inconsistency).

Miller as a player, it is true, often *did* disappoint his greatest admirers, particularly those among them who had watched him in England in 1945. But what a magnificent disappointment. Just how we could do with one such now. Cardus wrote in defence of Miller early in the 1950s: 'There is room surely in cricket today for at least one player who comes to the game most days willing to let himself go in it, without inhibitions . . . If there is the slightest likelihood that Test matches may tend to check the impulses of Miller and curb his flights into a risky void now and again, let Test matches be anathema, and done away with.'

Of Jack Gregory, in that history of Australian cricket, Moyes wrote: 'In Tests against England he made 941 runs at 34·85 with one century and against South Africa he averaged 51·25. Against England he took 70 wickets at 33·77 and against South Africa 15 at 18·93. Add his superlative slip fielding which often bordered on the miraculous and you have a picture of the complete cricketer.'

Miller's figures in 29 games against England (that 'yardstick') are: 1511 runs with three centuries at 33·57, and 87 wickets at 22·80. Maybe Moyes failed for once to consult his record books?

Of Noble Moyes wrote: 'The most accomplished all-round cricketer Australia has produced. Against England in Tests he scored 1905 runs and took 115 wickets—the only other Australian to perform this double being George Giffen. Noble was a superb captain.'

No criticism here either. Only high praise.

The reason could be partly that Gregory, whom I saw in 1924–25, and Noble, of whom I've heard a deal from Moyes, *always* appeared to be trying—in Gregory's case, his guts out. Miller did not. Let's try and discover why.

The difference between Gregory and Miller, according to Stan McCabe was that Jack 'just loved being out on a field playing cricket'.

Jack cried in the Australian dressing-room at Brisbane in 1928 when, after he had fallen trying to catch a batsman near the far popping crease off his own bowling, he injured his knee and was told by the doctor he would never play cricket again; and 'Keith often got bored, even with his own brilliance and lost all interest in proceedings'.

Why *did* the post-war Miller become bored so often, even during Test matches? He was not at all bored while playing for Victoria before the war. On the contrary, he was furious when dismissed for 108 against South Australia; dismissed caught from what he believed to have been a bump ball of Grimmett's and umpired back to the pavilion.

I never saw Keith look bored during any of the five Victory Tests in England in 1945. And he didn't have time to look bored while racing to 185 not out in 165 minutes with seven 6s and 13 4s for the Dominions XI against England in August of that first peacetime summer during what *Wisden* described as 'the most masterly innings seen for a generation'.

The occasional disinterest began during the English autumn of 1945 and continued during the Services Team's arduous tour of India—Bombay, Lahore, Bombay, Poona, Calcutta, and Madras—from October to December of 1945 following five months' cricket in England. It vanished back home in Australia from mid-December to February 1946 but re-appeared after the Second Test at Sydney of 1946–47 against Walter Hammond's England side and kept sporadically raising its head thenceforth—except in the West Indies in 1955.

Let's see if we can find the explanation.

Why was it that a player possessed of such prodigious talent should have become so apathetic (on occasion) about displaying it?

I can advance a host of reasons. Some of them spring from extraneous sources, others are bound up inside Miller himself.

Firstly, because I am no psychiatrist, and because even for Dr Freud analysing Miller would have been a problem, let us examine some of the extraneous causes.

They began in England about the middle of the 1945 summer when South African fast bowler, tank commander, and author of *Brazen Chariots*, Bob Crisp, kept pestering Lindsay Hassett to use

Keith as a fast bowler with the new ball in the Victory Tests. Eventually Lindsay, against his better judgment, agreed and those in the Lord's Long Room who watched Keith's first onslaught upon those then infants of the game, John Dewes, the Hon. Luke White, and that subsequent secretary of the Cricket Council and Test and County Cricket Board, Donald Carr, and then saw him bowl Len Hutton when on 104 of a total of 254, exclaimed, 'This is the fastest and most menacing bowling we have seen since last we saw Harold Larwood.'

In the two England innings of that unofficial Test, Miller delivered 34 overs to take 6 for 86, and Bill Edrich was another of his victims. I shall never forget the sight of the hapless Jimmy Workman, substituting for the injured Stan Sismey as our wicket-keeper, leaping like an Australian Rules football star in his desperate efforts to intercept Miller's bumpers some twenty metres behind the stumps. Keith Carmody, our second string wicket-keeper, was also in our team for that match, but Hassett quite rightly never considered using him in this specialist position.

On the final morning England captain Walter Hammond, who was suffering from a bout of that 'disease of the great', fibrositis, hobbled into our dressing-room, crossed to Hassett, and said, 'Lindsay, I can't stand watching Workman keeping to Miller any more. He reminds me of a scarecrow. There is only one thing preventing you from giving Carmody the gloves. That is my permission and you have it.'

England had lost 6 for 129 in its second innings and led by only 189; Hammond had been pronounced unfit to bat, so it was a very sporting gesture on Wally's part.

Hassett gave Miller 23 overs in the Fourth Victory Test and 20 in the Fifth. In these he compiled scores of 118 and 77 not out but, though given first use of the new balls, captured only one wicket at a cost of 130 runs.

In the remaining first-class games of that tour, Miller was again used as our opening bowler and it became noticeable that, as a batsman, he abandoned his practice of consistently keeping his strokes along the turf and began crash-hitting his drives over the boundaries at Lord's, Trent Bridge, and Scarborough—taking what for him was the easy way.

I have mentioned his unforgettable 185 not out scored in 165 minutes with seven 6s for the Dominions XI against England at Lord's and will describe it when we assume chronological sequence. But now might be the time to intrude an incident in September of that summer that reveals Keith's changing approach.

Facing that accurate new-ball bowler and army colonel J. W. A. Stephenson, whose meticulously waxened black moustache caused him to be called the 'Leo Carillo of cricket', Keith was beaten all-ends-up by a leg-cutter that grazed his off bail in another match at Lord's.

Over to the handsome and dignified Stephenson: 'Forgetting my army discipline, I showed my chagrin at so narrowly missing this highly-prized wicket. "That was a good-un, Keith," I said. Keith came out to meet me, patted the spot where the ball had landed, tossed back that mane of his, and grinned. I bowled him an almost identical ball. He pull-drove it across the flight full on to the tower of the Tavern, narrowly missing the clock, then smiled and called, "That was an even better-un Colonel".'

Another example of Miller's increasingly casual approach to his cricket that English autumn came on the final day of the Australian Services Team's game against Nottinghamshire at Trent Bridge.

Long before play ended for the day it became obvious that no result could be obtained. Notts' most hostile bowler had been the then 36-year-old Bill Voce. But thirteen years had passed since the 1932–33 bodyline summer and Voce could not sustain his hostility for more than a few overs. He, the only challenge that had aroused Keith's interest, vanished from the attack just after tea.

Keith's third batting partner was greeted on the edge of the wicket area. 'This is all getting effing boring. Let's have some fun,' Keith suggested.

'How?'

'Well, we'll call "yes" when we mean "no" and vice versa. We'll completely bamboozle the fieldsmen.'

Miller's perhaps-unique plan worked for a time while some 35 runs were added. Then Keith called 'no' when he meant 'no' and his unfortunate partner was left stranded in mid-pitch.

'It *was* fun, while it lasted,' Keith insisted to his departing comrade.

'Yes—*while it lasted*,' agreed his colleague, a little lugubriously.

After almost five months of cricket, including five Victory Tests against England and that game between the Dominions XI, captained by the West Indies' 'Old Electric Heels' Learie Constantine, and England, the Australian servicemen, A.I.F. and R.A.A.F., learnt that the Australian Board of Control and the Australian Government had arranged for them to return home via India and conduct a series of games there, including three more Test matches.

Most of the R.A.A.F. players chosen for the tour of India had been away from their homes and families for more than four years. The A.I.F. members had returned to Australia from the Middle East and Papua–New Guinea for a time before being dispatched to England in June of 1944. Naturally the R.A.A.F. players were envious when army Captain Albert Cheetham was granted permission to miss the tour of India and return direct to Australia to accept an executive position in an insurance company in Adelaide. Miller could be pardoned for additional disappointment when that other Services Team new bowler Graham Williams was allowed to accompany Cheetham to begin a lucrative job with another Adelaide company.

It was obvious to Keith that he would now fall for the task of opening our attack in the heat and on the heart-breaking pitches of Bombay, Calcutta, and Madras. And the man chosen to assist him was that former New South Wales pace bowler Mick Roper—Roper now weighed above 95 kilograms and in pace was little more than medium.

Rested during the voyage on the *Samaria* from Liverpool to Bombay, however, Keith was back in his normal good spirits when our Indian tour host Kumar Shri Duleepsinhji, that former England batsman and now Maharaj of Ranjitsinhji old Princely State Nawanagar, greeted us on Bombay's Ballard Pier next to the Gateway to India.

Hospitality at the palatial Brabourne Stadium, headquarters of the Cricket Club of India and chosen venue for the First Test, could hardly have been more generous, or our accommodation more luxurious. Our bedrooms faced out on to the cricket ground and one of our tailend batsmen, Corporal C. F. T. Charles 'Fox

Terrier' Price, used to linger in bed until his Christian-Indian bearer-batman warned him our seventh wicket had fallen.

In those last years of the 'British Raj' in India there were reported to be more millionaire members of the C.C.I. than there were at Manhattan's Metropolitan Club. Miller, the star of our side, was fêted by many of them during our week in Bombay, introduced to princes and their princesses, maharajahs and their maharanees.

After play ended for the day a portable dance floor was laid on the grass before the palatial pavilion and a superb Indian jazz band played late into the night. Drinks and supper were brought to guests by white-caparisoned and diagonally red-sashed waiters, while we relaxed in our cushioned wicker armchairs. One of the waiters had a *blue* sash. 'Why blue?' I asked him.

'That mean I am the boss. When *I* say, *they* do,' he explained.

All very fine and great fun while it lasted, but, after ten days, Lindsay Hassett, his vice-captain Keith Carmody and their thirteen players were dispatched on the Frontier Mail train on the three-day journey via Agra, New Delhi, and Amritsar to Lahore, capital of the Punjab, for their match against the Northern Zone.

Bidding us farewell at the railway station our host 'Duleep' warned us not to eat fish or drink tap water during our fortnight away from Bombay before the first of the three Tests. Our team treasurer Captain Jack Mallyon had already become the first victim of the tour and suffered agonies in his room at the C.C.I. Even so we forgot 'Duleep's' warning.

This remarkable, Arabian Nights of a tour will be described later so suffice it now to say that the arduous tour of India helped to dampen Keith Miller's enthusiasm for cricket at a vital stage of his career. No longer was he the 'young and gay' figure Sir Neville Cardus had painted in England in 1945. Even in October and November of that year he was coming to have a chip on his shoulder, a chip about authority and the manner in which international cricket was being conducted and played. And the disgruntled Mick Roper, his close friend and constant companion in India, did little to reduce it.

Roper's, Miller's, indeed the resentment of the entire Services team, including that of its manager, Australian Cricket Board of Control member, Keith Johnson, was not reduced when, despite its drawn series with an almost full-strength England and its unlucky one-all loss to an Indian side that would have defeated the one Lala Amarnath was to bring to Australia in 1947 by an innings, found only two of its members—Hassett and Miller—in the side the Board sent to New Zealand in the autumn of 1946. *And* when the Board appointed Bill Brown captain of that combination.

None the less Miller and Hassett performed outstandingly on that New Zealand tour and Keith, having established himself as a certainty for the following summer's Tests against England, sailed off to Massachusetts to marry Peg Wagner.

Miller, as we shall see, was to begin his official Test career late in 1946 under Bradman by scoring a 79 and taking 9 for 77 at Brisbane. He was to follow this with a 40 (out of 659) and the vital dismissal of Hutton in Sydney, with 33 and 34 at Melbourne, 141 at Adelaide, and 23 and 34 not out back in Sydney.

Second to Bradman on the batting averages with 384 at 76·80 and second on the bowling averages to Lindwall with 16 wickets at 20·87 for the series, he was to confirm his class as an all-rounder: as the finest all-rounder in the world in what, you will recall, Johnnie Moyes regarded as 'the yardstick' of judgment—an Anglo-Australian series.

But he, like a host of Australians on and off the field, did not enjoy watching Bradman wreak his revenge for the old wounds he received against Jardine in 1932–33 and Hammond (that 903 for 7 declared, at The Oval) in 1938, by captaining and batting England into the dust.

And Keith's inner feelings gradually began to show.

Now for a glimpse of that inner Miller, that post-war inner Miller, which caused those feelings to emerge.

Some men *have* to play at being heroes; others have no need to do so. This was seen during the war—men who had proved their courage to themselves had no need to demonstrate it to others. Miller, probably to his own astonishment, had proved *his* courage during three years of aerial combat as a night fighter-bomber pilot over enemy-occupied Europe.

Indeed one of his wing-commanders told me at a dinner in London in 1945 that Keith was 'the bravest and most willing pilot under my command'.

I shall deal later with some of Keith's exploits as a Mosquito fighter-bomber pilot. Enough now to say that constantly playing the hero on a cricket field, even a Test cricket field, can hold less attraction for one who has done this for three years in total war while bombing German airfields and enemy gun emplacements along the coasts of Holland and France.

This I believe helps to explain why, despite his possession of what is known as the 'killer' instinct, Keith grew to be tempted to exhibit it less and less frequently.

So does the fact that Australia at cricket held a unique ascendancy over the rest of the world—England, South Africa, India, New Zealand, and the West Indies—during the years from 1946 to 1952.

So does the fact that Keith has always held a deep sympathy for the underdog and was not over-keen to hammer teams, especially ones which contained his wartime friends and comrades Denis Compton, Bill Edrich, Walter Hammond, Cyril Washbrook, and Len Hutton and his post-war friends Godfrey Evans and Alec Bedser, of England; Lala Amarnath, Vijay Hazare, and Vinoo Mankad, of India; Dudley Nourse, 'Tufty' Mann, Billy Wade, and Jack Cheetham of South Africa; and Frank Worrell, Everton Weekes, and lovable 'Old Man River' Alf Valentine of the West Indies into the ground. Unless it was essential to do so in Australia's cause.

So does the fact that few great cricketers of history have shown less concern for their own batting and bowling averages and analyses than did Miller. 'I never thought much about statistics,' he confessed in 1979 on TV.

So does the fact that Keith, like the young Ian Craig of the 1950s, grew gradually to enjoy the life that goes with international cricket as much, if not more, than the cricket itself. As he travelled the world Keith developed a host of friends, ranging from Prince Philip, Duke of Edinburgh, and Princess Margaret, from Earls Mountbatten and Tedder, via Hallé Orchestra conductor Sir John Barbirolli, cricket writer Sir Neville Cardus, barrister Sir Norman Birkett, and jockeys Lester Piggott and 'Scobie' Breasley to those counterparts of old Alan Caffery, the stagehands of the great cricketing grounds of England, South Africa, the West Indies, and India-Pakistan.

Keith, because of his manliness and the directness and forthrightness of his character, has always been attractive to men. And for him, as for Denis Compton, Lindsay Hassett, Arthur Morris, Tom Graveney, and Godfrey Evans to name but a few, camaraderie over a drink or a dinner after play has always been a favourite feature of life.

Keith has never been as single-minded about his cricket as were for example Bradman, Hutton, and Jackie McGlew. As Geoffrey Boycott is today. He lacked the ambition of Bradman and Hutton, of Grimmett and Hammond and Hobbs.

Perhaps because triumphs came so easily to him, consistent application and dedication of the kind he produced in England in 1945 and again near the end of his career in the West Indies in 1955, were the exception rather than the rule.

Naturally there were times when he loved to shine, to command the stage, but this urge was rarely sustained. His approach to cricket far more resembled that of the immortal Victor Trumper and the much-loved Stanley McCabe than that of Bradman, Hutton, Bill Lawry, Bobbie Simpson, and Boycott, of Gary Sobers and Richie Benaud, and, in more recent times, of Vivian Richards and Greg Chappell.

In technique Keith, to me, was an amalgam of Barry Richards and Peter May as a batsman, of a far-shorter-run Dennis Lillee and Freddie Trueman as a bowler, and of Paul Sheehan and Victor Richardson in the field.

As a captain he reminded me, when at his best, of Vic Richardson more than any other leader I have known.

As a person he also has a lot of Vic Richardson in him. He fought authority when he thought it was acting unwisely or unjustly. He stood up even to Bradman when he thought fit.

But the most remarkable resemblance between Keith and Vic was the way in which they always seemed to be in command of the situation even when in the company of such formidable personalities as former Prime Minister Sir Robert Menzies and the Duke of Edinburgh; how they always seemed the ones who were the more relaxed.

High praise, all this, I acknowledge; but no exaggeration. Add to it his complete loyalty as a friend. Another reason, surely, for immortality. For if friendship, the making and maintaining of friends, is not such a reason, *what is?*

With poet Rupert Brooke, Keith can say, does indeed say in his very way and habit of life, of living: 'There is nothing in the world like friendship. And there is no man who has had such friends as I, so multiform, so prone to laughter, so strong in affection, and so permanent, so trustworthy . . . so apt both to make jokes and to understand them.'

With Brooke, Keith can also say: 'I will have friends about me continually all the days of my life and in whatever lands I may be. So we shall laugh and eat and sing and go great journeys . . .'

Keith Miller possibly has never read Rupert Brooke. Maybe has never even heard of him. But he has no need to, for he can share, *does* share, all or almost all of these claims and thoughts with him. He knows that friendship, like love, has to be *made*, if it is to be maintained. And he *is* a truly magnificent friend.

As Sir Robert Menzies used to say, 'the world belongs to those who can laugh'. Well, Keith Miller has usually been able to laugh and help others to do so.

I well remember his famous panacea for worry, 'It will all be the same in 100 years.'

And how once, when I was worrying unnecessarily about something or other, he asked, 'Do you remember what you were worrying about on this day last year?'

'No,' I confessed.

'And on this day next year, you won't remember what is worrying you now.'

Try it—it works. It also explains Keith Miller. *And* his cricket.

2
How it all began

Psychologists say heredity, early environment, upbringing, and the influence and example of childhood heroes are apt to direct the destinies of human beings.

I am sceptical, however, about the impact of heredity—especially since researching the ancestry of Leonardo da Vinci, Michelangelo, Galileo, Charlie Chaplin, and Groucho Marx. *And* that of Keith Ross Miller.

The family trees of all six of them are stunted in the extreme.

Nor, confining oneself to cricket, can one find explanation from heredity for the prowess of Trumper and Grace, of Hobbs and Macartney, of Bradman and Hammond, Compton and Sobers, Lillee and Thomson, or Vivian and Barry Richards.

The main thing that inimitable 'googler' of the 1920s, Arthur Alfred Mailey, used to recall about his father was that 'he was so poor that Arthur, his mother and the other five members of this Irish family took it in turns to breakfast upon the tops of Mailey Senior's hard-boiled eggs'.

'My father,' wrote Arthur in his *10 for 66 and All That*, 'didn't know the first thing about cricket . . . And, as far as I know, nobody on either side of my family had played *any* game. Prenatal influence certainly cannot be blamed for my cricket career, because my mother seemed to spend all her time cooking over an open fireplace or washing clothes in the backyard, sixteen feet by sixteen in area.'

Those four generations of Gregorys—Dave, Sid, Jack, and

Ross—and Ian, Greg, and Trevor Chappell, the grandsons of Victor Richardson, are but rare exceptions that underline the rule.

Certainly research has revealed nothing in Keith Miller's parentage or lineage to account either for his tremendous natural talent or the vagaries in his expression of it. His father Leslie and his mother Edith were chiefly of Scottish descent. And how many Scotsmen have become even presentable cricketers—kilted or otherwise?

Keith Ross Miller was born on 28 November 1919, a third son and fourth child, in Sunshine, a middle-class western suburb of the solid and conservative city of Melbourne. A suburb called Sunshine, come to think of it, is a most appropriate launching pad for one who was to spend so many hours in the sun and bring so much light into the hearts of so many millions about the British world.

The names Keith and Ross, too, are most apposite for a boy who was to become an outstanding second World War fighter-bomber pilot and a bowler of what batsmen of his day called 'fliers' and of what their successors now term 'bouncers' and 'bombs'.

For those names of Keith's are derived from two intrepid Adelaide aviators, Sir Keith and Sir Ross Smith, who happened to be pioneering the airway from London to Essendon in a Vickers Vimy bi-plane during the final stages of Edith Miller's fourth pregnancy.

Keith and Ross are also very Scottish, of course. There are towns I fancy, or at least villages, by those names in or below the Highlands.

The game of cricket, like Ancient Greece and Ancient Rome (like Ancient England now, for that matter), is something of an empire. And, like an empire, it has its legends—the legends of the boyhoods of its most famous sons.

Instead of Hercules, his lion, and his Garden of the Hesperides, we have William Gilbert Grace and his fathers and brothers and the games they played in Gloucestershire—using apples from the family orchard for balls, a stray stick for a bat, and the door of the cider vat for a wicket. Instead of Achilles, we have young Donald George Bradman and his golf ball, cricket stump, and circular water tank on *his* Acropolis at Bowral.

Instead of Socrates, we have that wiliest of all bowlers Clarence Victor Grimmett and his retriever, the faithful fox terrier Joe, who served instead of ten fieldsmen while his master traipsed interminably up to a solitary stump to deliver leg-breaks, 'straight-throughs', and later 'wrong-uns' at an old wooden box—firstly in Dunedin, New Zealand, then in Sydney, Melbourne's Prahran, and finally in Adelaide.

I say instead of Socrates because of all the world's bowlers—slow, fast, or medium—'Grum', that 'Scarlet Pimpernel', and 'Gnome', as he was also known, must rank as the senior philosopher. He needed to be one to keep on bowling so cheerfully and indefatigably and invincibly at champions like Hobbs and Sutcliffe and Leyland, like Ponsford and Macartney and Bradman, Hammond and Hendren, George Headley, Herbie Taylor and Dudley Nourse, *and* keep his sanity and what now is known as 'cool'.

Strangely enough, there are few if any legends about the young Keith Miller—our cricketing 'Alexander', as I have ventured to call him. So let's try and build one or two.

Keith says his father and his elder brothers, Les and Ray, helped to create his initial interest in cricket. 'They used to play plenty of backyard cricket with me and gave me helpful hints.' Normal but hardly memorable. So I quizzed him further. Miller can be like a brick wall under interrogation at times—especially about very personal things. But gradually the mask and gag were removed.

The Millers moved from Sunshine to a new home at 16 Denver Crescent, Elsternwick, a few kilometres southward from central Melbourne, in 1924 when Keith was four years old. Here there was a back lawn and (in that pre-Hills' hoist era) a clothes line. Here young Miller used to beg, borrow, or steal his sister Gladys' stockings, place a cricket ball in them, hang them on the clothes line, and keep hitting at the ball with a sawn-off bat. He could hardly have managed this, come to think of it, with a Hills' hoist. The stockings and ball must have become tangled in the parallel wires.

The neighbours in Denver Crescent kept complaining about the 'bang, bang, bang' of bat upon stockinged ball, but Keith was a determined youngster and, when suggestions were made that he should practise elsewhere, he ignored them.

'If the fellow on one side of our house could rev up a motorbike at some sleeping hour every morning, and the neighbours on the other side could pinch all the cricket balls when the stockings gave way, I certainly was not going to stop my harmless little bit of recreation,' Keith reasonably argued to himself. 'Perhaps those were the first seeds of the self-reliance, or plain cussedness, which later helped to build my character,' he added some fifty-five years later.

He really was opening his shoulders now and somehow I managed to keep the ball rolling.

'My father and my brothers, both of whom were club cricketers, began teaching me the rudiments of cricket with a tennis ball on that back lawn. They believed that if a youngster starts batting against a soft ball he will get neither hurt nor frightened when it hits him and that he will quickly learn to get his body behind the ball.'

There was, however, one serious drawback on the Elsternwick 'village green'—a miscreant who could have changed the course of cricket history, or grievously reduced it. This character dwelt ogrishly, somewhat like young Davie Copperfield's bugbear Bill Sykes, either in 14 or 18 Denver Crescent. And whenever Keith skied a tennis ball over his fence he would rush out of his house and confiscate it before the Millers had a chance to retrieve it.

'He was brilliant in his way,' Keith says, 'for sometimes he would be out and on to the ball before it had stopped bouncing. He was ruthless, too, for he kept all the balls. I reckon he must have collected hundreds of them.'

Maybe he was the treasurer of a tennis club? But what risks he was taking! Surely he cannot have realised he could have smothered a second World War Jack Gregory, a right-handed Gary Sobers, almost at birth.

Miller's 'kindergarten education' was administered at the Sunshine State School. After the family moved across the city, he went to the Elsternwick equivalent. Here he received a 'great deal of help' with his cricket from a master named Jack Gainey. A member of the First A.I.F., Gainey had been badly gassed in Flanders. Later he was to become a member of the Victorian State Government.

Another character at that Elsternwick institution of learning, named George Stirling, though not a sports master also gave Keith 'lots of help'.

The most inspiring early influence so far as his cricket is concerned, however, came from the exploits of a close neighbour of the Millers in Elsternwick—from none other and no lesser than the great William Harold Ponsford, whom somebody aptly has called the 'John the Baptist for the coming of Don Bradman'.

'I didn't actually know "Ponnie" then,' Keith says, 'but he was my earliest idol and he lived in Orrong Road, about a quarter of a mile from my home. I would often walk past his house just in the hope of catching a glimpse of the great man. When my sister Gladys married and went to live in Glenhuntly "Ponnie", by some coincidence, also took the vows and set up house in the same street—Laura Street, Glenhuntly.'

Do boys, or girls for that matter, choose their own heroes and heroines? Or are they chosen or ordained for them? It is an intriguing question and I ask it because my own father drew up a list of heroes and heroines for me. They were: Cricket—Victor Trumper; Tennis—Norman Brookes; Singing—Enrico Caruso and Amelita Galli-Curci; Dancing—Nijinsky and Anna Pavlova. For Father, up until his dying day in January of 1954, there *were* no other 'greats'. Even that young Lochinvar of the 1920s, that 'Bowral Boy' Don Bradman, could make no impression upon Father—argue as we did till both of us were red in the face.

No, not even 'The Don' with that dramatically brilliant 66 of his against Larwood, Voce, and Hedley Verity at the Adelaide Oval in the Third Test of 1932–33, made any noticeable impression. Victor Trumper remained the '*non pareil*'.

Even that most melodious of German lyric tenors Richard Tauber 'had no voice'. Australia's own 'Queen of Song', Dame Nellie Melba, had 'a squeaky delivery' when compared to Galli-Curci. And nobody except Anna Pavlova, who used to feed the finches in Father's aviary at Unley Park, not even Ulanova or Dame Margot Fonteyn, could dance 'The Dying Swan'.

And way back in the 1920s fathers were always right.

However this may be, the boy Keith Miller chose a pretty solid and reliable hero in William Harold Ponsford. He did so, though, most probably because of his geographical proximity. There was a galaxy of cricketing champions to choose from in those days.

Among them were Victoria's and Australia's gargantuan captain and all-rounder Warwick Armstrong, that spectacular 'Kangaroo of the Creases'; Jack Gregory, remembered today as the 'Keith Miller of the first World War'; that perhaps finest of all history's fast bowlers, Victoria's, Australia's, and later Lancashire's E. A. 'Ted' McDonald; and the 'Governor-General of batsmanship' Charles Gordon Macartney.

'Ponnie' lived just around a few corners, *was* a Victorian, and *was* doing rather better than well with that beloved 'Big Bertha' bat of his, both for his State and Australia—he sufficed.

Ponsford had begun building his cathedral of cricket fame in the summer of 1922–23 when Keith was rising four years old. He invaded the national and international scene somewhat spectacularly by scoring 429 for Victoria against Tasmania when he was twenty-two. This then was the highest individual score compiled in a first-class match. It beat England's Archie MacLaren's 424 for Lancashire against Somerset at Taunton in 1895.

In his first Sheffield Shield innings of that summer Ponsford scored 108 (those of you who believe in coincidences remember that score) against (remember again) South Australia. A year later he made 110 and 110 not out in one match against that inveterate enemy, New South Wales.

In 1924–25, when Keith was five, this glutton for runs made 110 in his first Test innings against England and followed it with 128 in his second Test at the Melbourne Cricket Ground a fortnight later.

It was early January and holiday time in Melbourne then, and Leslie Miller, Senior, of Elsternwick, naturally took his three sons in a tram along Melbourne's Champs-Elysées, St Kilda Road, to Prince's Bridge and then in another tram along Flinders Street and Wellington Parade to Jolimont to watch Ponsford dealing with the great Maurice Tate.

Infectious stuff this and there was more to follow. Indeed Ponsford, not Hammond or Bradman, was the pioneer of the mammoth-scoring age—and was the first merciless and implacable Australian destroyer of bowlers' analyses.

In December of 1927 when Keith had just turned eight

'Ponnie', still wearing his cap at so jaunty an angle that it would have shamed John Bromwich, produced scores of 133, 437, 202, and 316 towards a month's return of 1146 at 229·20 an innings for Victoria. The 316 completed a record string of eleven centuries in consecutive first-class matches in Australia and the 437 established Ponsford as the only cricketer who had (or yet has) twice reached the 400 mark in a first-class match innings.

This then was the batsman the young Miller chose as his idol. And, be it again remarked and remembered, whose outstanding characteristics were his seemingly insatiable ambition and extraordinary consistency.

From Elsternwick State School Keith moved to Melbourne High School in his early teens. Here one of the form masters was William Maldon Woodfull, the captain of the Carlton Cricket Club, of Victoria, and of Australia—as well as being Ponsford's batting partner in State and international matches.

A born leader of men, a man of impeccable integrity and great physical courage (as he was to reveal during the 'Bodyline' bowling crisis of the summer of 1932–33), Woodfull had become one of the best-loved and respected cricket captains Australia has owned. As a batsman he was known as 'The Unbowlable' and as a schoolmaster he was more than a match for any unruly members of his class, for he administered the brand of discipline youngsters were then happy to accept. Even young Miller, I gather.

Surprisingly, though, Woodfull at that stage 'took little interest in the school team'. Or so Miller says. Keith needed stimulation and encouragement at that stage. He was, in his own words, 'physically a little peanut of a boy, shaping more to be a jockey than a cricketer. In fact I wanted to be a jockey, another Jim Pike.'

This new ambition of his was all the more dangerous because the Miller home was not far distant from the famous Caulfield Racecourse and Keith regularly used to go and watch the track gallops there of a morning.

The captain of the Melbourne High School cricket team at that time was another Keith—Keith 'Bluey' Truscott, later to be killed after earning undying fame as a fighter pilot in the Battle of Britain. Truscott, hearing of Keith's new ambition, escorted his namesake along to cricket practice at the St Kilda Cricket Ground,

Ponsford's club. The St Kilda Cricket Club at that time fielded five teams. Unfortunately (*everything* takes time and effort), the now 14-year-old and still midget Miller could not gain selection for any of those teams.

One day at the St Kilda nets Hector Oakley, an established Sheffield Shield batsman, lost patience while facing the tiny fellow's bowling. 'Son, take that ball and hand it to someone who can bowl,' he called.

'We're the only two here Mr Oakley,' Keith retorted—rather boldly, in all the circumstances.

This was to be his parting gesture at St Kilda, however. He joined the Elsternwick Club, where his debut for the First Eleven was 'not exactly distinguished'. Play, owing to the Melbourne climate, was only possible on the first day of the two-Saturday-afternoon game. Elsternwick's opponents batted throughout the first afternoon and Keith had no chance in this department of the game. Elsternwick's selectors dropped him from the next match on the grounds that 'he was too slow in the field'.

His luck was due to change, however, and his persisting determination was to be rewarded. One of the Elsternwick players, Arthur Lord, gave Keith 'a deal of help' with his batting and another player named Bill Nichols had a cricket net rigged in his backyard about an excellent pitch.

Here of a Sunday morning E. V. 'Hughie' Carroll, a Victorian State batsman and coach of the South Melbourne Cricket Club, helped with the practices. Carroll eventually recommended Keith to the South Melbourne Cricket Club committee and he accepted an invitation to join it.

'Using a cut-down bat because of my lack of height and weight,' says Keith, 'I went straight into the first team and "Hughie" put the finishing touches to my technique.'

On arrival at the South Melbourne nets Keith was delighted to find another midget—one who was to remain so—Lindsay Hassett. His joy knew no bounds when he met yet a third dwarf named Cyril Parry. Parry's growth also was permanently retarded. Even much later when keeping wicket for South Australia he stood little taller than the stumps.

South Melbourne's captain at that time, perhaps significantly in retrospect, was the Victorian fast bowler Frank Moreton.

Top: Keith Miller (*second from right*) stands with his navigator Jim Brown (*second from left*) and two mechanics in front of his Mosquito of 169 Squadron at Great Massingham, Norfolk, England. *Bottom:* Jim Brown, the navigator, stands beside the plane that Keith belly-landed after its starboard engine caught fire (*Photos—Keith Miller*)

Yardley is brilliantly caught by Miller off the bowling of Johnson in the Fifth Test at The Oval in 1948 (*Photo—Central Press Photos*)

Another of its players was that rather faster bowler and champion Australian Rules footballer, Laurie Nash, who was to kick 18 goals in the last three quarters of a game between Victoria and South Australia and at the end of it to complain, 'I'd have kicked a lot more if those blighters at centre and half-forward had passed me the ball occasionally'.

Also at South Melbourne were Ian Johnson, eventually one of the club's six Australian Test captains, and that attractive, left-handed opener, Ian Lee.

South Melbourne's final game of that 1934–35 season was played against Carlton, the club which William Woodfull captained. Naturally Keith was keen to succeed against his schoolmaster. And he did. Batting with the score 30 for five wickets, he turned the adverse tide with an innings of 61 and was awarded a silver cup for his 'sterling performance'. It was the Carlton Club who donated the trophy and its captain presented it—presented it in his and Keith's Melbourne High School classroom.

And so during the winter of 1935 young Miller abandoned his ideas of becoming a champion jockey. This was as well because, between November 1935 and November 1936, the months separating his sixteenth and seventeenth birthdays, he grew from less than 150 centimetres to more than 180 centimetres in height. At the peak of his cricketing career Keith weighed about 102 kilograms and even Jim Pike's finest mount, the mighty Phar Lap, at the peak of *his* career, must have jibbed at carrying that.

While still at Melbourne High School Keith was selected in the Victorian Second Eleven to play against Tasmania at the M.C.G. Bill Ponsford had scored 429 there against Tasmania in 1922–23 when he was twenty-two; Keith compiled 181 against it in his first innings in interstate cricket in 1938–39 when he was nineteen.

During the 1939–40 summer, eleven days before his twentieth birthday, Miller played his first Sheffield Shield match—like Ponsford, against South Australia in Adelaide.

'You caught me in slips off that "chucker" Harold Cotton, remember?' Keith said while I was conducting some of the research for this biography. 'I fancy I made 4 and then 7, bowled Grimmett, for a match aggregate of 11.' Eleven (4 and 7) is right. Keith can always remember his failures. Check on him about his triumphs, however, and you will be greeted with embarrassed silence.

'About the only satisfaction I gained from that match in Adelaide,' he went on, 'was when I ran out Don Bradman for 76. I suggest that anyone who could run out "The Don" when he was 24 short of a century could not be "too slow in the field".'

Bill Ponsford's first Sheffield Shield century, a score of 108, remember, came against South Australia in Melbourne in 1922–23. On New Year's Eve and New Year's Day of 1939–40, after fielding while Bradman amassed 267, Keith scored 108 against the same State. 'I'd learned by then always to play forward to Grimmett,' he explained.

After Keith's innings Bradman said he was most impressed, and Clem Hill, recognised as the greatest left-handed batsman of the Golden and Augustan Ages (and in 1939–40 handicapper for one of Melbourne's racing clubs), forecast a big future for him as a batsman.

3
Incredible coincidence

Most young Australians of the early 1980s, those of my acquaintance anyway, cannot imagine how their counterparts of the late 1930s managed to brace themselves for and match the ordeal of helping to resist the westward explosion of Adolf Hitler's wehrmacht and luftwaffe, following the events of April–May 1940.

Looking back over more than half a lifetime I find it impossible to explain this myself. Just how *did* we find the nerve, or in most cases resignation, to confront that forbidding and depressing challenge?

Most young Britishers, Americans, Europeans, and Australians of that time hated war as deeply as do their counterparts of today. They detested the very thought of it. They had recently fought their way through the great Depression, or helped their parents to do so. The world, except for Hitler, Mussolini, and Stalin, looked fair indeed. 'Insanity Fair', author Douglas Reed called it.

Indeed, the young and youngish men of the late 1930s possibly feared the mechanics and resented the consequences of total war even more than do the young and youngish men of today. There was no easy, *en masse* way to annihilation in 1940. The cold, grey steel of the bayonet, not 'the bomb', was the ogre and spectre then —and the threat of 'gas'.

The idealism of 1914 no longer existed—the idealism and the patriotism captured and immortalised by poet Rupert Brooke in:

Now, God be thanked Who has matched us with His hour

And caught our youth, and wakened us from sleeping,
With hand made sure, clear eye and sharpened power
To turn as swimmers into cleanness leaping . . .

Honour has come back again, as a king, to earth,
And paid his subjects with a royal wage;
And Nobleness walks in our ways again;
And we have come into our heritage.

And victory over Hitler's Germany seemed impossible, except to Winston Churchill. The young of the late 1930s had read of and had seen on stages and cinema screens all the filthy, unglamorous garbage of war. They held no illusions; harboured little hope. But they still had their self-respect and they flocked to the enlistment queues in their thousands—even when all wishful-thinking had collapsed in the face of Germany's blitzkreig invasion of Belgium, Holland, and France.

One of the first of the thousands of volunteers was the handsome, debonair, just twenty-year-old Keith Miller. Another was his pal Johnny Hosking, who, according to Keith, 'had visions of becoming either a bosun or an admiral'.

'I decided to stick with Johnny, who wanted to go to sea,' says Keith. 'As a result I very nearly joined the Navy. We talked it over and filled in applications to join up as stokers. We went along to the recruiting office and the man in charge took our application forms. He read mine first and said, "O.K., you're in". And then he read Johnny's. We had a shock—he wouldn't take Johnny.

'If you can't take my mate, you can't have me, I said, and picked up the forms from the desk, tore them up, and walked out with Johnny behind me. I went around to the Air Force recruiting centre and applied to join. Hosking had just heard of Lawrence of Arabia. He went into the Army.'

This was in June of 1940. The Royal Australian Air Force, however, did not call on Keith until January of 1942. In the meantime he worked in the spare-parts section of a motor firm, had a term of employment with a customs and shipping agent, and then joined the Vacuum Oil Company.

During that first, genuine, wartime winter of 1940 he played Australian Rules football for the Victorian Football League club St Kilda, mainly at full-back. 'St Kilda must have been pretty weak at that time,' Keith says, 'because either in 1940 or 1941 I played full-back, centre half-back, centre, centre half-forward, and full-forward for them.'

During the Australian summer of 1940–41, no first-class cricket was conducted but matches were played to raise funds for the war effort. Miller scored 8 and 24 for Victoria–Queensland Combined against New South Wales at Brisbane in November. In mid-December he scored 63 and 16 for Victoria against South Australia in Melbourne and, during the first week of January 1941, he got 29 for Stan McCabe's XI against Don Bradman's XI at Melbourne—in what then seemed likely to be his last innings, Don scored 0 and 12.

After his call-up in January of 1942 Keith was stationed at an R.A.A.F. training station at Mallala about 50 kilometres north of Adelaide. During his time there he gained his wings. He also represented the combined West Adelaide and Glenelg Australian Rules side, West–Glenelg, as centre half-forward in the grand final which they lost by 11 points to combined Port Adelaide and West Torrens.

Nine months after his call-up by the R.A.A.F. Keith was transferred to the Miles Standish Training Camp, south of Boston in Massachusetts, U.S.A. He left Port Melbourne in the 38 000-ton *West Point* in September 1942 as a Flight Sergeant.

Keith was a confirmed lover of classical music even as a 22-year-old and he attended concerts by the Boston Symphony Orchestra in the famous Music Bowl alongside the Charles River.

During one visit to Boston he met 'a girl, a secretary in the Massachusetts Institute of Technology', who, as he undramatically puts it in his book *Cricket Crossfire*, 'later, after the war, was to become my wife'.

This momentous meeting, as Keith explained to me early in 1980, was both accidental and fortuitous.

'I know it normally happens the other way about,' he said, 'but I met my wife through her father. His name was Carl Wagner and he was sipping dry martinis at the bar of Boston's Avery Hotel.

'I was drinking beer with my R.A.A.F. friend Bill Young who came from William Street, Broken Hill—from 572 William Street, Broken Hill, to be exact. How's that for memory almost forty years later?

'Anyway, I was intrigued by the olive plonked in the white liquid in Carl Wagner's glass. I'd not seen a dry martini before. Or a wet one for that matter.

'Carl exploded the mystery and, seeing the Australian shoulder badges on our uniforms, told us his wife Mamie came from Hull, in England.

'I tried a dry martini, or two, and, discovering we were heading for Britain, Carl said, "You must come out and meet my English wife". So we got a cab to Beacon Hill, which is near the Boston State House, and I met not only "Mamie" but her and "Papie's" daughter Peg.

'That's what an olive in a glass can do for you.'

It was during his voyage from New York to Greenock in Scotland in the *Queen Elizabeth*, after his training as a night fighter Mosquito pilot at Miles Standish, that Keith developed another kind of love—a passion for gambling: crown and anchor, poker, and two-up—that compensated for the scant sleeping accommodation and the oppressive atmosphere below deck on the giant, blacked-out, and unescorted liner.

Keith fell in love with England and her wartime people almost upon his arrival there early in 1943. Told that the English were 'creeping about looking miserable' because of the bombing, he found this 'utter nonsense'.

When he came to Bournemouth to continue his training, the hit-and-run raids along the south coast were beginning. German fighter-bombers started sweeping over the Channel, dropping a few bombs, and then streaking back to France. The cheerful and courageous reaction of the recipients of this new and callous kind of warfare aroused Keith's immediate and growing admiration. Thus was born a respect for the English people he was never to lose, a respect which explains why he still numbers Bill Edrich, Denis Compton, and Godfrey Evans among his most treasured cricketing friends and why two of his four sons were christened Bill and Denis.

During the English spring of 1943 Keith was invited to take part in his first game of cricket on English soil. He believes his participation in it saved his life. The game was conducted on the Dulwich College Ground and Keith's future cricketing 'cobber' Keith Carmody, then doing his training at the Langham Aerodrome near Cromer in Norfolk, was also a member of the R.A.A.F. side.

Keith returned to camp near Bournemouth on the Sunday afternoon, soon after a German hit-and-run raider had struck there. Seven of Keith's friends were killed when the bar at which he and they normally lunched received a direct hit from a bomb.

For a time that Sunday and early on the following morning it was feared that Keith had also been killed during the raid. Three men were still unaccounted for and he was thought to be one of them—he had not received an official leave pass to play in the game at Dulwich College on the Saturday.

General relief followed roll call on the Monday morning when a manly voice answered 'Present and correct, Sir', to the call of 'Number 410608 Miller, K. R. Sergeant'.

I have not travelled in an aeroplane flown by Keith Miller. Ian Johnson's 'pilotage' of a DC3 during our trip from Port of Spain to Princess Margaret's favourite island, Tobago, in April of 1955 was quite enough for one lifetime. But I have endured a journey in a motor car driven by Keith.

(Indeed, once in 1948, I loaned my own car to Keith while I was away in Sydney. It was a pretty solid, British-manufactured car, fortunately—one I had bought, come to think of it, at what he called 'a bargain price' from that obdurate batsman and artful dodger Sidney George Barnes. And it survived a week of Miller's ministrations—albeit minus a radiator cap and one or two hubcaps.)

That car ride was sufficient for me to imagine just what kind of fighter-bomber pilot Keith must have been from 1943 to 1945. Most of the evidence I have been able to glean from his navigators confirms the impression I had gained in England during the latter part of the war.

Most of it, I say, because it is only fair to add what I learned when I sat next to the famous R.A.A.F. Wing-Commander Neville Reeves, D.S.O., D.F.C., during a dinner in London in 1944. Reeves had begun to make his name as a Beaufighter pilot in the Middle East. Later he became Keith's wing-commander at the Great Massingham Aerodrome in Norfolk, where the renowned Hughie Edwards, V.C., D.S.O., D.F.C., and Bill Edrich, D.F.C., had served earlier in the war. Reeves died at Great Massingham while testing the first jet aeroplane after the war.

When I asked him during that dinner in 1944 what sort of a pilot Keith was, he replied, 'He was one of my finest; perhaps the bravest and most willing I had under my command. He wouldn't be alive today but for what we all came to call "Miller's luck". He kept taking the most fantastic risks and they all came off.'

I have struggled persistently, even heroically, to persuade Keith to recount some of those exploits for publication in this biography. But in my experience the only returned servicemen who are prepared to expound upon their wartime adventures are those who seem a trifle uneasy about their contribution to the cause.

As far as I have been able to gather there were very few real heroes; men who really and genuinely loved being at war. Most of us were scared to death but, fortunately for our reputations, even more scared about showing it than about being killed or, worse still, permanently incapacitated.

Miller was one of the exceptions. The excitement of being a fighter-bomber pilot on expeditions against enemy airfields in Germany, Holland, Belgium, and Occupied France appears to have captured his imagination. Reuter's cricket correspondent and London author and biographer, Reg Hayter, in 1956 *did* manage to extract some facts from Keith and one of his navigators about his flying adventures.

Early in his career as a pilot in Britain he was dispatched on a night training exercise from Cranfield Airfield. Soon after becoming airborne he discovered that his plane's oil-pressure gauge had sunk suddenly to zero. Deciding to ignore this warning Keith continued with his mission. Another instrument on the panel soon indicated another fault. Keith had a navigator with him and he decided to turn back. Later that night another pilot flying the same Beaufighter crashed. He and his navigator were killed.

Returning from a subsequent nocturnal operation over Occupied France Keith misjudged his approach to the runway. Bouncing from the tarmac he revved both of his engines with the idea of regaining altitude and attempting a second landing. Only one of the engines responded; the plane skidded, became uncontrollable, and headed for a hangar. Keith managed to avoid crashing into this by only a matter of centimetres before bringing his plane to rest.

Transferred from a Beaufighter to a Mosquito squadron, Miller began flying fighter-bomber missions over Germany. Mosquitos at that time carried drop tanks beneath each of their wings. These were loaded with a highly inflammable compound and with Mills bombs. Pilots were instructed to swoop low upon enemy airfields and release the drop tanks from point-blank range. As he was approaching his target at about 900 feet, Keith's plane was caught in a searchlight's beam. After veering to avoid it he turned back on target and, when he was almost above this, pressed the tank release-lever.

Only one of the tanks was freed and the unbalanced plane slewed from its course, narrowly evading a hail of anti-aircraft flak. Had both tanks dropped the plane must have collided with the flak and been destroyed.

Providentially one calamity had been avoided, but the problem, an unprecedented one for Keith, of landing his aircraft with an unexploded drop tank and that Mills bomb under one of its wings, remained. He radioed his base for instructions and was told to attempt as normal a landing as possible: he was also informed that a fire-fighting crew would be awaiting his arrival in case of emergency.

Keith negotiated the landing successfully. 'Where's the other tank?' demanded a suspicious member of the ground-crew after examining the plane.

Eventually it was located near the far end of the runway: partially released over Germany it had been jolted free when the Mosquito's wheels first contacted the ground. 'Miller's luck', already growing to be a legend, had saved him again.

A month or two before Germany's unconditional surrender Keith was granted a fortnight's leave in London. All his money spent, he returned to his base near Norwich, Norfolk, several days ahead of schedule.

To take a plane into the air during a leave period was regarded as tantamount to inviting disaster, flirting with fortune, particularly at that stage of the war. Keith had already enjoyed far more than the average pilot's luck. He was bored with his inactivity, however, and decided to give both himself and the ground-crews some thrills. Some low-flying aerobatics would 'fill the bill'.

Choosing an unattended and old-fashioned trainer plane, one constructed mainly of laminated wood, he began a series of hair-raising stunts directly above the aerodrome, 'just for the hell of the thing'.

It was as he was looping-the-loop above the base cricket ground that he discovered his starboard engine was ablaze. Using his fire extinguisher he eliminated the flame only to find the engine had failed. Keith had not landed a plane on one engine before and he looked down with envy at the thirteen 'flannelled fools' below him. One of them was easily recognisable as his wing-commander, Neville Reeves, and this did not help.

On his first attempt at a landing Keith came in too high. Regaining altitude, despite the loss of one engine, he turned back across the cricket field and gazed nostalgically at it; he had recently played in a match at Lord's Cricket Ground and was anxious to do so again.

When landing a plane one of the most important things to do is to lower its tail as swiftly as possible. Or so I am informed. The tail of this old crate just refused to obey its pilot and he had no alternative but to attempt a bellylanding, though still travelling at flying speed.

Yet again his luck held: the plane was the 'write-off', not Keith. And he decided to celebrate his miraculous escape by joining in a game of soccer. At long last he had tilted too often with fate: suffering from delayed shock he was carried from the field and taken to hospital. Here intensive examination disclosed he had injured his back during that landing; had created a condition in his spinal column which was to recur throughout his cricketing life—to have intermittent effect upon both his bowling and his batting.

Between his bombing raids on enemy airfields and of the V1 and V2 rocket-launching sites across the North Sea and other vital targets, Keith and his growing coterie of R.A.A.F. friends—Keith Carmody, Stan Sismey, Ross Stanford, Mick Roper among them—took part in a series of cricket matches against English sides gathered from Royal Navy, British Army, and R.A.F. servicemen.

Among the first of these, as Denis Compton recounts in a foreword to this book, was one played at Lord's Cricket Ground in the spring of 1943. There were to be many more as Carmody and his young 'cricketing cavaliers' began to win the imagination of the English people—and not only of their cricket-loving public—in 1944, and captured it completely in 1945.

Which brings us to the astonishing coincidence which produced the title to this chapter. Keith Miller, as we have seen, was a specialist batsman for his club and Victoria during his brief, pre-war career as a cricketer. Indeed, his club captain at St Kilda, Hector Oakley, did not regard him as capable of providing even reasonable batting practice at the nets.

Keith, as Compton has indicated, became a fast bowler (one of the few truly great fast bowlers of cricket history) by accident. He developed into one of the game's greatest all-rounders by accident.

So, a quarter of a century before him at Kennington Oval, London, in 1919, had that other highly spectacular Australian all-rounder Jack Gregory—known today as the 'Keith Miller of the first World War' as Keith in 1945 became known as the 'Jack Gregory of the second World War'.

In April of 1919 Australia's military moguls, Field Marshal Sir John Monash and General Thomas Blamey, ordered each Australian army unit whose troops were still in England to send its best cricketers to Kennington Oval, the site of the 1882 'Ashes' Test, where twenty practice pitches had been prepared.

From almost 100 candidates ten of the squad of fifteen required for a series of games against English County teams and other local sides had been chosen when perhaps the most dynamic all-round cricketer Australia, even until today, has yet produced was discovered like a diamond out of the rough.

Charles Kelleway, the original captain of the First A.I.F. team and Herbert Collins, its subsequent leader, were on the point of placing the remaining names in a hat when Collins, the 'Lindsay Hassett of the first World War', was attracted by the speed and menace being revealed in one of the far nets by a young bowler of most formidable physique.

He walked across to the 'big, long feller', who was 'firing the ball down like a two-legged tornado' and striking fear into all the batsmen who faced him. Collins took stock of the broad shoulders, sturdy hips, long arms, and a pair of hands 'that would have done for buckets', of the 193-centimetre 'typhoon'. He also noticed the extraordinary amount of energy and zest he was applying to his play.

'What's your name and who have you played for?' asked Collins, who had learned his own cricket under that 'martinet' M. A. Noble and alongside Victor Trumper for Paddington and who was to score 104 against England at Sydney on his Test match debut in 1920–21.

'Jack Gregory—North Sydney Fourths, a bit,' came the answer.

On Collins' recommendation, the 23-year-old Gregory was named Number 11 for a game that Saturday in Norfolk against a team which contained that most prolific of all batsmen, Jack Hobbs, and the 'Pride of Kent', Frank Woolley.

When the Australians took the field Kelleway asked Gregory what fielding position he preferred. 'Somewhere where there's something to do,' he said. Kelleway sent him out to the boundary. Here the man, who was soon to become the most predatory and acrobatic slip fieldsman cricket has ever known, looked awkward—even incongruous.

Eventually, after the A.I.F. team's regular fast bowler Cyril Docker strained his back, Gregory tripped over one of his trouser cuffs and trod on his left hand. Collins suggested to Kelleway he give their new, young 'Jackeroo' a bowl.

The results were so devastating during the remainder of that innings and in the game against Surrey, Hobbs' county, that followed that the Australians realised they had stumbled upon a champion—upon a bowler who could humble even England's most masterful batsmen; upon a left-handed batsman whose cover-driving and square- and late-cutting were so laden with power that they gave fieldsmen little chance of interception; and upon a slips fieldsman of incredible powers of anticipation, whose arms appeared to be made of elastic.

In their eleventh-hour recruit from the North Sydney Fourths the First A.I.F. Team had found the cricketing force that inspired and paraded them towards triumph after triumph. All told in England, South Africa, and Australia during the next eight months, Jack Gregory took 197 wickets and scored 1320 runs against the finest cricketers in those three countries.

In the match between the A.I.F. Team and Australia's most powerful State team of the time, New South Wales, he hit a century in each innings and took more than half the opposing wickets. Later, in another first-class game in Australia, he took the first nine wickets of an innings and, while his bowling partner Arthur Mailey was doing his utmost *not* to take the tenth, threw the Number 11 batsman out after arresting a particularly hot, straight drive.

Gregory, like Miller, was that kind of cricketer—as spontaneous as he was unselfish.

4
Majesty at Lord's – England 1945

It is mid-May of 1945 in London; 19 May to be exact. Hitler is dead; Nazi Germany skulks and sulks defeated. Sixteen days have passed since its unconditional surrender at Luneburg Heath. The most horrible and horrifying war in history is over and newly-painted, red, double-decker buses are spurting competitively by the Dorchester and Grosvenor House, along leafy Park Lane, to swing around the Marble Arch into Oxford Street, and then northward (past what a V2 rocket has left of Selfridges) to Lord's.

Here the 'Old Jack' and the 'Southern Cross' are fluttering proudly again from their flagpoles at either end of the Members' Pavilion. Here, on the grey roof of the Grandstand, the gaunt effigy of 'Old Father Time' is bowing to inspect the bails in the ferrules of the stumps he has guarded so gallantly from the buzz bombs, the rockets, and 'The Blitz'.

Here, afore and behind the great glass windows of the famous Long Room and in the private boxes of the Grandstand galleries, sit many of England's most illustrious statesmen, many of her most richly decorated Army and Air Force commanders, and of her most distinguished pre-war cricketers, gazing out at the green field and that pitch which Australia's wartime Prime Minister John Curtin has recently declared 'Australia will always find enough soldiers to defend'.

For almost seven years have passed since England, captained by Walter Hammond, scored 903 for 7 declared at Kennington Oval to defeat Australia, captained by Don Bradman, by an innings and

579 runs in the Fourth and final Test of 1938; the Test which most Englishmen, except Winston Churchill, and most Australians, including Don Bradman, believed would be the last ever played between their countries.

Among those perched on the high stools and polished tables of the Long Room beneath the black-bearded and black-booted life-size portrait of Dr William Gilbert Grace are former England captains Sir Pelham Warner (1903–04) and Charles Fry (1912) and their guest Sir Stanley Melbourne Bruce, now the Australian High Commissioner to Britain.

Diagonally to their left beyond the rectangular field, rows upon rows of British, Canadian, and Australian soldiers and airmen help to swell the 20 000 strong crowd. Close to them the fanatical, strident, and 89-kilogram 'Yorkshire Annie' is exercising her lungs preparatory to calling upon Yorkshire-born Leonard Hutton, who scored 364 runs in 13 hours and 17 minutes in that 1938 Oval Test, to get cracking when he takes strike to that saturnine Australian Army captain Albert Cheetham, one of the 'Rats of Tobruk'.

Behind and above the rows of khaki- and blue-clad servicemen, and almost immediately below 'Old Father Time', Lord Louis Mountbatten's successor as Chief of Combined Operations, General Sir Robert Laycock, and Air Marshal Lord Tedder are regaling their guests with chicken sandwiches and champagne in their adjoining private boxes.

Sir Robert, who led the daring but unsuccessful raid on Rommel's headquarters in the Western Desert in 1941 and then tramped all the sandy way back to Cairo, had always been crazy about cricket. With him are his lovely, blue-eyed wife Angela and her sister the popular elf-like West End actress Penelope Dudley Ward, the subsequent Lady (Carol) Reed. With him, too, at this first of the 'Victory' Tests, is the friendly Lord's and Marylebone Cricket Club secretary Ronnie Aird. Those champagne corks are popping as they have not popped at Lord's since the West Indies Test of June 1939.

Up in the scoring box beside the Australian dressing-room, old Bill Ferguson, or 'Fergie' as he is affectionately known throughout what remains of the Empire, is sharpening his pencils as he prepares to produce diagrams of the stroke play of a new generation of batsmen, the kind of diagrams Douglas Jardine studied before planning his 'Bodyline' fields of the early 1930s. Alongside Fergie are his fellow scorers, former Surrey and England wicketkeeper Herbert Strudwick and former Middlesex and England batsman, Elias Henry 'Patsy' Hendren.

Fergie has just come from the Australian dressing-room where he has been renewing his acquaintanceship with the captain of the Australian Services Team, Warrant Officer II Lindsay Hassett. He hasn't seen Hassett since the disastrous 1938 Oval Test.

Hassett has introduced him to a tall, dark, and blue-eyed R.A.A.F. Pilot Officer just as the latter is enquiring of a silvery-haired dressing-room attendant why Lord's doesn't provide showers for visiting Australian cricketers.

'I wouldn't be knowin', Sir, that I wouldn't. But we ha' some pretty historic baths, Sir. I can still see the old Doctor sittin' in the one o'er there, Sir, about the turn o' the century. Can still see his great beard, Sir, hangin' over the side.'

'I'd still prefer a shower,' replies Miller with the kindliest of grins.

That smile provides a startling contrast to the facial expressions of most other members of the Australian side—they, to crib Jim Russell's favourite simile, resemble stunned mullets. All of them, like Miller, have been chosen from among Australian airmen and soldiers serving in the European theatre of war. None of them, except their captain, have played in a Test match—even an unofficial Test match as the Australian Cricket Board of Control (fearing defeat, if not annihilation) has ordained that this one and the four to follow it will be.

About to confront them on the famous green field are Test record scorer Hutton; his subsequent Test batting partner Cyril Washbrook; Middlesex and England's Jack Robertson; the great Walter Hammond; that superb wicketkeeper-batsman Leslie Ames; Bill Edrich, who scored 219 in the 'Timeless Test' at Durban in 1939; former England captain Walter Robins; Colonel J. W. A. Stephenson; Arnhem glider-pilot hero S. C. Billie Griffith; Douglas Wright; and Alf Gover. All of them either have played, or are to play, in official Tests. Indeed England's team, apart from Denis Compton, is the strongest she can field at that time. And this, of course, explains why the English authorities,

Top left: Keith Miller shaking hands with King George VI when the Australian team visited Balmoral Castle in 1948. The player nearest the camera is Colin McCool. *Top right:* Ron Saggers and Keith Miller stroll with Princess Margaret in the grounds of Balmoral Castle in 1948. *Bottom:* Miller shakes hands with Queen Elizabeth as the King shakes hands with wicketkeeper Don Tallon. Princess Margaret is at the far left (*Photos—Keith Miller*)

Top left: Everton De Courcey Weekes, the West Indies' 'Black Bradman' of the 1950s, at the finish of his famous leg-sweep (*Photo—Press Association*). *Top right:* Gary Sobers, the West Indian champion and captain whom Sir Donald Bradman described in 1968 as 'unquestionably the greatest cricketer of all time' (*Photo—United Press International*). *Bottom:* Clyde Leopold Walcott, the third of the 'Three Terrible Ws'. During the 1955 Australia–West Indies series in the Caribbean he scored five centuries (*Photo—Sport & General Press Agency*)

unlike the Australian Board of Control, have wanted this match and the other four to be branded as authentic Tests.

Apart from Hassett the only members of the Australian side who have represented their States in the Sheffield Shield competition are Cheetham (18 matches); Cecil Pepper, originator of the palm-flicked off-break (10 matches); Stan Sismey (8 matches) of New South Wales; Keith Miller (9 matches) of Victoria; Graham Williams (15 matches) and myself (32 matches) of South Australia.

The other four Australian players—batsmen Jim Workman and Ross Stanford (South Australia) and left-handed googly bowlers Charlie Price (New South Wales) and Reg Ellis (South Australia) have been club performers at best.

These four, especially, are uncomfortably aware that there are cricketers back in the South Pacific—notably Arthur Morris, Ray Lindwall, Ian Johnson, and Sid Barnes (*and* Don Bradman and Bill O'Reilly, if considered fit) far better qualified to participate in this historic match.

Indeed it would be no exaggeration to say that at least nine of the Australians are waiting with deep and haunting misgiving for proceedings to begin—with misgiving that is almost extinguishing hope, fearing they may make complete and utter fools of themselves before this huge crowd in the 'Cathedral of cricket', when either Umpire Beet or Umpire Fowler calls 'Play'.

That is why Miller's breezy, nonchalant approach to the whole business is so heartening to his colleagues. 'What the hell if destiny calls, I once bowled three curates with three bloody balls!' he could well be thinking; like that probably apocryphal character who is reputed to have taken the hat trick against, I think, the Church of England in, I think, the 'Denominational Series'.

The plan for conducting the 'Victory' Test series in England (as soon as possible after the second World War ended) originated, according to our old friend 'Plum' Warner, at Lord's during the English summer of 1944.

The idea of holding it dates back even further to the English summer of 1943. Or so Sir Pelham told me over lunch in his conservatively but comfortably furnished apartment in Morden Court, across from the South Kensington Underground station, in May of 1953.

'I first conceived the idea myself,' Sir Pelham said, 'after watching Keith Miller and Keith Carmody batting for the R.A.A.F. against a British Services Side at Lord's and watching Miller deliver a few very lively overs to Denis Compton. I knew we must do everything possible to revive the game immediately hostilities ceased. And what better way than a Test series between England and Australia?'

I assure you that Sir Pelham can be believed. Born in Trinidad, the son of the British Governor there, on 2 October 1873, 'Plum', thirty years later, was chosen in preference to that colossus of English cricket Archie Maclaren to lead the first Marylebone Cricket Club managed side to Australia in 1903–04. Of Sir Pelham in his and Jim Swanton's *A History of Cricket* (Allen and Unwin) former M.C.C. President Harry Altham has written: 'Among the figures that challenge oblivion in the long vistas of the game—W. G., with his black beard and M.C.C. cap, Ranji in fluttering sleeves of silk—few surely were more familiar, none certainly was better loved, than that of "Plum" Warner, the "Happy Warrior" in his Harlequin cap.'

The plan began to take shape during a visit to Lord's by the Australian Prime Minister, the Right Honourable John Curtin, and Australia's highest-ranking soldier, Field Marshal Sir Thomas Blamey, early in June of 1944.

Hearing they were in London, Sir Pelham invited Curtin and Blamey to Lord's to watch a match between the R.A.A.F. and a British Services XI captained by Walter Hammond. During play he stressed how the tremendous zest the Australian Air Force players had brought to their cricket, under the leadership of Sunderland and Beaufighter pilot Flying Officer Carmody, had captured the imagination of all who watched them.

The batting of Miller and Carmody, who reminded Englishmen of Stan McCabe, had created a profound impression.

During the winter of 1943–44 Walter Hammond, England's 1938 and 1939 captain, had returned to England from service as a liaison officer with the Royal Air Force in Cairo. Len Hutton, holder of that world record Test score of 364 against Australia, had recovered from a multiple fracture of his left forearm. Bill Edrich, who like Carmody and Miller was a fighter-bomber pilot, was also based in England.

All these champions and probably Denis Compton, 'Plum' stressed, would be available for matches if peace came, as was beginning to be expected, early in 1945. It would perhaps be asking too much of the R.A.A.F. players to make a match of it with an England side containing them, he suggested.

Sir Pelham knew that Sir Thomas had created a Second A.I.F. side in Egypt in 1941, a side led by Gunner Lindsay Hassett and containing such Test and other first-class cricketers as Ted White, Alec Hurwood, Ray Robinson, Jack Rymill, and Albert Cheetham. He knew Hassett's team had won all its matches in Alexandria, Maadi, and Cairo against sides drawn from the British, South African, and New Zealand forces; had even beaten a team captained by Freddie Brown and containing Bill Bowes at the world-famous Gezireh Club.

'Where are Hassett and his players now, Sir Thomas?' Warner asked.

'Dotted about the South Pacific. We do have a war on out there, too, you know?' Blamey replied.

It was at this stage of the discussions that Mr Curtin is supposed to have made that immortal remark of his: 'You Englishmen will always be able to find enough Australians to defend those twenty-two yards of yours out there. Lord's and its traditions belong to Australia just as much as to England.'

'We could do with a few more of them here next summer, Mr Curtin?'

'We could send some over, Blamey? What's to stop us?'

'Only a few million Japanese.'

But the full implications of Sir Pelham's remarks were beginning to register on the Field Marshal. He did not want the R.A.A.F. to be stealing *all* the thunder.

'I fancy we can handle the Japs without the help of Gunner Hassett and one or two other cricketers,' he said.

So it was that Gunner Lindsay Hassett, Captain Albert Cheetham, Sergeant Cecil Pepper, and several other either experienced or promising Australian cricketers found themselves members of the Second A.I.F. Reception Group which embarked under the genial command of Brigadier Eugene Gorman, M.C., K.C., on the S.S. *Bloemfontein* from Sydney to San Francisco in late-June of 1944.

Their officially specified tasks included a 5-kilometre ticker-tape march down Broadway from the Battery to New York's City Hall to say 'thank you to the United States for coming to the aid of Australia in 1942' and parachuting on to prisoner-of-war camps in Nazi Germany to help free Australian soldiers. The real intention for their dispatch at the Australian taxpayers' expense across the world was, for political and military reasons, to be kept secret.

Back in 1941, as General Officer Commanding the Second Australian Imperial Force in the Middle East, Sir Thomas had managed to over-rule General Sir Leslie Morshead of the Ninth Australian Division and secure the release of Captain Cheetham from the siege of Tobruk in order that he could participate in those cricket matches at Alexandria, Maadi, and Cairo.

'Don't you know there's a war on?' Sir Leslie had signalled in reply to the original Cairo Army Staff instruction. 'Yes, Blamey!' Sir Thomas had tersely rejoined.

But Sir Thomas was now under the command of that formidable American, General Douglas Macarthur. He doubted whether it would be advisable for him to apply to have that promising young fast bowler Ray Lindwall and equally promising young left-handed batsman Arthur Morris extracted from the ranks in Papua-New Guinea.

He was adamant, however, that Gunner Hassett should be promoted to officer rank and appointed captain of the combined Army and R.A.A.F. side for the projected Tests in England. The Army, after all, was the senior service to the Air Force. But Squadron Leader Lex Rentoul, later to become manager of Sydney's Australia Hotel but then senior R.A.A.F. liaison officer to the War Office in London, and most members of the R.A.A.F. serving in Europe, including Flying Officer Carmody, Pilot Officer Miller, Squadron Leader Stan Sismey, Pilot Officer A. W. 'Mick' Roper, Flying Officer Ross Stanford, and Australian Board of Control delegate Flying Officer Keith Johnson were none too happy about this proposed intrusion upon what they regarded as their preserves.

Carmody, Miller, and company, they argued, had broken the ground for the formation of this combined team. Additionally, Carmody was an officer; Hassett was not and the probable England captain Walter Hammond was a Squadron Leader, even if he had not led any squadrons. *And*, as he was a periodical sufferer from fibrositis and no Douglas Bader, was unlikely to do so during the dregs of the war.

To complicate matters Carmody was shot down early in 1945 while attacking four German ships off the Hook of Holland. Rescued by a German R Boat he was placed in solitary confinement at Venlo and Frankfurt then marched 240 kilometres to a concentration camp near Berlin.

Liberated by the Russians he was held by them throughout a very grim April before he escaped, crossed the Elbe and, after some particularly alarming adventures, joined the advancing American armies.

Carmody had become something more than a hero to his comrades, and his return to England was regarded as imminent. The Australian team was to be styled The Australian Services Eleven, not Australia. Australia was still at war with Japan. Strong arguments these, the Air Vice-Marshal commanding the R.A.A.F. in Europe (when he was not flirting with Eve, the beautiful barmaid of Fleet Street's companionable Codgers Hotel) contended for the appointment of a commissioned officer—for the appointment of Flying Officer Carmody—as captain of an Australian Forces' team.

Sir Thomas Blamey and members of his staff had anticipated that a situation such as this might arise and that it would count against Hassett. When Lindsay, who had begun his war as a gunner, had advanced reluctantly to the rank of Lance-Bombardier and then sergeant, arrived in September of 1944 at the Second A.I.F. Reception Group's headquarters, the Cumberland Hotel at Eastbourne, Sir Thomas instructed Brigadier Gorman to promote him to the rank of Lieutenant.

But Lindsay can be an obstinate customer, as a number of international bowlers have discovered. He refused to accept a commission based upon his prowess as a cricketer. The most he would agree to was appointment to the rank of Warrant Officer II, which his new army duties justified.

Hassett's cussedness was then, and is in retrospect, greatly to be admired. It was not expected in 1944 that Don Bradman, who, like Hammond, was suffering from the 'disease of the great', would make a comeback to international cricket.

The Australian captaincy for official Tests after the war thus seemed wide open. Hassett's appointment as his nation's captain in these unofficial Tests could help him towards the greater honour.

But even the combined efforts of Field Marshal Sir Thomas Blamey, Lieutenant-General Ken Smart, G.O.C. the Australian Army Staff in London, and Brigadier Gorman, M.C., K.C., could not budge the 'Tisket, the Tasket' as he was then known.

Hassett's integrity and altruistic attitude eventually became known to the R.A.A.F. cricketers. Though it impressed them, their loyalty to their own leader Carmody remained steadfast and some of them made no effort to conceal their disappointment and disapproval when early in May of 1945 Hassett was appointed captain for the entire series of Victory Tests. They believed he should have been appointed for the First Test on 19 May and the matter put to a team vote before the Second Test at Bramall Lane on 23 June.

In most sporting teams rivalry exists between individual players, sometimes between groups of players. The examples of Bradman and Ponsford, O'Reilly and Grimmett, Len Hutton and Denis Compton, of West Indians John Goddard and Jeff Stollmeyer, South Africans Dudley Nourse and Eric Rowan, and their respective supporters come readily to mind.

When Carmody returned to England late that May of 1945 the R.A.A.F. immediately chose him to lead their team against the R.A.F. at Bristol.

Carmody, despite his lack of match practice and the unsettling experiences he had undergone, was to be included in the Australian Services Team for the Bramall Lane Test on 23 June only because R.A.A.F. batsman Ross Stanford, who had scored 49 in his one innings in the First Test at Lord's, insisted on standing down.

But this was all in the future and feelings in the Australian dressing-room when the bells rang for commencement of play at Lord's on 19 May 1945 were a trifle mixed. I don't feel they had a detrimental effect on our team's performances, however; rather, as events were to prove, the reverse.

As Miller says almost half a lifetime later: 'There *were* members of the R.A.A.F. who resented Lindsay's appointment for the entire series before Carmody was given the chance to prove his form. But, as we all deeply realised, we had a tremendous task on our hands and Hassett had not sought the captaincy. On the contrary. And we were all Servicemen—happy just to be alive and fit and well.'

'The majority of the R.A.A.F. members of the side were disappointed but, after a sane look at the situation, we readily accepted Lindsay,' Keith added.

So back to Lord's on that May morning of 1945.

According to an old adage of the theatrical world, stars will always find their stage. Keith Miller was smartly to become something more than a star—he was to become a comet of the cricketing world. All the footlights were aglow.

Indeed, I cannot imagine a more perfect stage for Miller to begin his first-class international career upon than the one he was about to bestride.

Incentive, continuing incentive, was always his vital necessity. It was so because application, sustained application, was invariably his chief problem.

Well, the incentive was there and stayed there almost throughout that English summer of 1945. He was representing his country in first-class matches for the first time; he realised that cricket was to provide his ladder and security in life; he was a specialist batsman, not an all-rounder, when the series began and could concentrate all his energies and ability on scoring runs. He was planning to get married, to have a family, and establish a home soon after his return to Australia. His prospective bride was a member of a reasonably affluent family, used to the comforts of life. Only through success at cricket and its corollaries, he believed, could he provide them for her, himself, and their children.

These are but a few considerations, but the main ones I believe, which caused Keith to score 568 runs, including three superb centuries, at Lord's alone, at the Bradman-like average of 94·5 that summer. It was because of them that he agreed to accept the responsibility of becoming his team's fast-bowling spearhead when called upon to fill that role during the Third Victory Test in mid-July.

It was because of them that he became, and remained throughout most of that summer, such an inspirational, zestful, dedicated, and competitive figure whether batting, bowling, or fielding.

When play began in that first Victory Test on 19 May the dismissal of Hutton 1, and Hammond 29, both by former South Australian and now R.A.A.F. pace bowler Graham Williams, compensated for the contributions of Cyril Washbrook 28, Jack Robertson 53, Les Ames 57, and Bill Edrich 45. And it was Miller, brought on as the Australians' fifth bowler as Ames and Edrich were steering England ominously towards 200 with only four wickets down, who bowled Edrich to open the way through the 'tail' to an eventual by-no-means-unpassable total of 267.

On the Saturday, the second day of this three-day match, Hassett and wicketkeeper Sismey 37, had the Australians 136 for 3 when Miller joined his captain.

Though now advancing through the fifties, Hassett had failed to produce his scintillating, pre-war form. Burdened with responsibility he was unrecognisable, especially when facing Douglas Wright as the batsman who in the 1930s usually had produced his best form when confronting those even-finer wrist-spin bowlers Bill O'Reilly and Clarrie Grimmett.

And, unlike his captain, Miller had often found top-class wrist-spin bowling to be his *bête noire*. He had reached that first and only Sheffield Shield century of his against South Australia at Melbourne in the New Year's match of 1939–40 only after the dourest of duels with Grimmett.

Now he had to find the answer to Wright, whose best leg-break and wrong-un could be more dangerous deliveries than those of the slower-paced Grimmett. *And* the answer to Walter Robins, that other wrist-spinner who had twice dismissed Stan McCabe in the Adelaide Test of 1936–37.

Realising that, were he dismissed cheaply and were Hassett, as seemed highly probable, to follow him out, there could be a complete collapse, Miller steeled himself to the crisis and began to settle in. When the Australians were 171 for 3 and still 96 behind, however, Hassett swung adventurously across a good-length ball from Lieutenant-Colonel J. W. A. Stephenson and lost his middle stump. It was an uncharacteristic stroke, one that Lindsay should not have attempted at so vital a time. 171 for 4 and Ross Stanford, playing his first first-class match innings, the next batsman.

Though Keith, owing to his flying commitments over a dwindling Germany, had enjoyed little match practice that English spring, he began to pierce the cover cordon when opposed to the medium and fast-medium pace of Stephenson, Gover, and Edrich. Keeping his classically-produced drives strictly along the turf, he also appeared to be gaining the upper hand in his duel with Wright.

Yet, even when Stanford threatened to overtake him, he maintained a highly-responsible approach. By the time Stanford departed for 49 of 270 for 5 and the Australians had established a first innings lead, Miller was rising to his most resplendent and majestic form, producing easily the most handsome strokeplay of the match.

His next partner, Cecil Pepper, because of his massive physique known affectionately as 'The Ox', had represented New South Wales in ten Sheffield Shield matches. Though valued mainly as a wrist-spin bowler, Pepper had scored 81 against Queensland with the help of seven 6s and eight 4s (74 in boundaries) in Brisbane in November of 1939 and 'Oxen' are not easily overawed.

He and Keith took the Australians to 357 for 6, or 90 runs ahead, before Miller was caught by Ames for 105—a century in his first first-class match innings at Lord's.

Long before he had achieved this honour and helped his team to add 221 vital runs, the connoisseurs of the Lord's Long Room, including Charles Fry, realised Australia had produced yet another champion batsman, one fitted by temperament and technique to follow in the footsteps of such artists as Alan Kippax, Archie Jackson, and Stan McCabe.

It was obvious, as Harry Altham put it, that 'a brilliant new star had joined the cluster of the Southern Cross'.

To cap all this that 'human emu', the 193-centimetre and string-bean legged Graham Williams, whose batting average in 15 Sheffield Shield games for South Australia was 17·73 and who until a month previously had been teaching braille to blinded R.A.A.F. prisoners-of-war in Germany, contributed a swashbuckling 53. Pepper 40, and C. F. T. 'Charles Fox-terrier' Price

35, helped their team to an eventual 355.

Four of its R.A.A.F. members had contributed 244 of 455 with Miller the only century-maker. A few of its airmen found difficulty in concealing their delight.

Trailing by 188 an astonished and dismayed English side managed to compile 294 in their second knock. But their two finest and most famous batsmen, Hutton 21 and Hammond 33, again disappointed while our R.A.A.F. wicketkeeper, Squadron Leader Sismey, took his tally of victims to seven for the match.

Seventy minutes play remained when the Australian Servicemen began their chase of 107 for victory at the rate of 90 runs an hour. Hassett promoted himself to Number 2 and Miller to Number 3 on the batting list. But it was 9 for 1 and 11 for 2 when Miller was run out for a single. Hassett, stroking far more freely than in his first innings, scored 37 before being caught by his counterpart Hammond at 63 for 3. At 76 Cheetham was also run out and, with Pepper and Price together, 34 runs were needed in just under twelve minutes—about 175 runs an hour!

Pepper and Price, both Army sergeants, were close friends and always shared rooms together. Price wisely left the fireworks to 'The Ox' and in the penultimate over Cecil pulled a straight ball of excellent length from Lieutenant-Colonel Stephenson high on to the top tier of the Grandstand. Here General Sir Robert Laycock's sister-in-law, the beautiful Penelope Dudley Ward, had just been exclaiming, 'What a lovely game, Bob. How I enjoy watching the red ball gliding between the white fieldsmen over the green field.'

That mighty and unlovely smite left five runs to be scored with six balls to be bowled. Alf Gover, the fast-medium Surrey and England bowler, had been ordered to deliver them.

Price trickled the first of these towards mid-off; Doug Wright almost smothered it while a single was taken. Pepper opened his massive shoulders at the second but mistimed his stroke and the ball soared high behind Wright. Not relishing this limelight at so crucial a stage, the Kent wrist-spinner circled back tentatively, clutched at the ball with both hands, then juggled it several times before, eluding his frantic grasp, it fell to the turf. The exasperated Wright then kicked it accidentally towards mid-wicket and two were run.

Pepper blocked the third and fourth balls and Gover walked back along his curving run before delivering the fifth of this six-ball over.

The 25 000-strong crowd (there was a three-day match attendance of 67 660) maintained a tense silence until Pepper stepped back to a ball just short of a length and forced it through mid-wicket to the white boundary rope immediately in front of the seats occupied by the Australian and Canadian servicemen. Then pandemonium was let loose.

The cricket correspondent of the London *Daily Express*, South African tank commander and Springbok fast bowler Major Robert Crisp, D.S.O. and bar, D.F.C., wrote: 'A well-deserved win by a team which set the tempo of the match all the way through.'

Submitting to almost universal clamour for changes in their team England's selectors dropped Gover, Ames, and Robins for the Second Test replacing them with George Pope (Derbyshire and England swing bowler), Maurice Leyland, who scored 187 of England's 903 for 7 declared at The Oval in 1938, and Lancashire seam bowler Dick Pollard, who was to accompany Hammond's 1946–47 side to Australia. When Leyland and our 'Leo Carillo' J. W. A. Stephenson withdrew, the selectors brought in Surrey and England batsman Errol Holmes and the steady, unimaginative, Lancashire left-hand spin bowler W. B. Roberts.

The only change in the Australian side was Keith Carmody for the unselfish Stanford. The Australians now had two released prisoners-of-war in their ranks.

The venue for the second Victory Test, Sheffield's Bramall Lane, had been heavily bombed by the *Luftwaffe* during the war. Both grandstand accommodation and playing surface were severely scarred and we all wondered whether those notorious stokers in the silverware factories had lost their knack of producing clouds of black smoke from the chimney stacks when visiting batsmen were at the wickets.

Maybe it was because Saturday, the second day of the game, was a working holiday, that Hassett sent England to the wicket after winning the toss.

His move must have proved an unqualified success had not Hammond, now right on his mettle with England one-down, played what two England captains, who had seen Wally score 251 at Sydney, 200 at Melbourne, and 119 not out and 177 at Adelaide in successive Tests against Australia in 1928–29, described as his finest century.

Late that afternoon Hammond said, 'Pepper's spin bowling between lunch and tea was among the finest I have faced'. He had faced O'Reilly and Grimmett!

Washbrook 63, Pope 35, and Robertson 26, helped England to 286 and then Carmody 42, top-scored for the Australians, who replied disappointingly with 147. Miller, run out for the second time in three innings, contributed only 17 and Hassett 5. Pope, who delivered his late outswinger off the side of his bent middle finger (as the great Sydney Barnes used to do) took 5 for 58 from 21·5 overs.

The English and Australian teams were sharing the same dressing-room. As Len Hutton, who had scored 1, 21, and 11 in his three innings for the series, was carefully combing his hair, after fastening his pad straps before walking out to open England's second innings, Miller grinned and said, 'That's right, Len. If you can't *be* a batsman, at least try and look like one.'

An enigmatic and inscrutable smile was the world record Test score-holder's only response. It and 46 out of 129 for 3.

Miller delivered 13 overs in this innings to dismiss Washbrook 24 and Robertson 1, at a cost of 38. Though Hammond followed his exact 100 with 38, England were all out 190 and the Australians needed 330 to win. Though 108 without loss at one stage and 171 for 2 at another, they failed by 41 runs to go to a two-nil lead in the series.

Late on this tense and highly exciting day Lieutenant-Colonel Errol Holmes, while fielding on the boundary in an immaculately tied cream cravat, allowed a stroke from Pepper to trickle through his fingers for four.

Called a Yorkshire patriot 'Whaat's thaat tha haast abaat neck, Guvner—a cravaat?'

Holmes, who was standing immediately in front of his wife and their friend Bob Wyatt, sadly nodded his handsome head.

'Well toighten it, Guvner, toighten it.'

One Test all and three to play. George Pope, greatly to the Australians delight, declined selection for the Third 'Test' due to begin back at Lord's on 14 July. Pope, like his great prototype

Sydney Barnes was a temperamental and touchy character. Aggravated by some 'treatment' he alleged he had received at Bramall Lane, he pleaded a coincidental Lancashire League engagement. It had been the late swing and seam bowling of Pope and Pollard under northern England conditions which had confined Australia's two finest batsmen, Miller and Hassett, to a joint contribution of 60 runs at an average of 15 just when success for them could have had Australia leading two-nil with three to go. At that stage of his career Miller was a total stranger to this kind of bowling on a responsive pitch. And back in 1930 Bill Bowes had had even Don Bradman laughing at his own helplessness on a damp Yorkshire pitch.

Despite England's victory at Bramall Lane several of her critics kept demanding that young players be brought in to replace some of the veterans in her side. In response the selectors went from one extreme to the other. They omitted Robertson and Holmes and brought in Repton School captain Donald Carr, Portsmouth Naval Cadet John Dewes, and Cambridge 'fresher' the Honourable Luke White to replace them and Pope.

Though Miller had delivered 26 overs to take 2 for 47 at Sheffield, he had bowled from an exceptionally short run for a bowler of his pace. The London *Daily Express* writer, former Springbok fast bowler Bob Crisp, renewed his campaign for Hassett to give Miller the new ball. 'What better time than now, against this cavalcade of youth?' he demanded.

The Australians made only one change in their side, introducing the slow-medium right-hand leg spin and googly bowler Bob Cristofani in place of Price, who had damaged a finger on his bowling hand.

When Hammond won the toss and sent Hutton and Washbrook to the wicket Hassett showed his disregard for even so knowledgable and obviously pro-Australian a critic as Crisp by giving Graham Williams and Albert Cheetham the new ball and using Pepper and Ellis before calling upon Miller.

Williams dismissed Washbrook (8) at 11 for 1 and Pepper had the fibrositic Hammond stumped for 13 at 76 for 2. It was during a stubborn stand by Hutton and the left-handed Dewes, who was to tour Australia under Freddie Brown in 1950–51, that Hassett threw the ball to Keith.

Miller had been reading Crisp's comments. He measured a far longer run than he had been using and began firing the ball down at a pace which aged denizens of the Long Room agreed was 'The fastest and most hostile they had seen since they last watched Harold Larwood'. Down went Dewes off stump for 27 at 107 for 3 and, just after tea, down went Carr's for 4 at 162 for 4 and Len Hutton's for 104 at 169 for 5.

Despite Bill Edrich's valiant 38 and Billy Griffith's equally courageous 36, England were all out 254. Miller's analysis of 18 3 44 3 was excelled only by Cristofani's 13 1 43 4. New-ball bowlers Williams and Cheetham had 1 for 92 between them.

Naturally that subsequent author of *Brazen Chariots*, Bob Crisp, D.S.O. and Bar, D.F.C., drove in some even heavier tanks on the question of Miller and the new ball.

The Australians were 50 for 3 when Keith joined Hassett. Dick Pollard bowled Miller for 7 with a semi-shooter at 71 for 4 and had Pepper lbw with another such for 0 at 72 for 5. Then Hassett, playing his best innings of the series for 68, Carmody (now known as 'Bendy' by both R.A.A.F. and Army team-mates) 32, and Cristofani, also 32, took the total towards 194.

When England batted a second time Dewes replaced Washbrook, who had damaged his thumb. Miller had bowled Dewes in the first innings with an old ball and Hassett flung him the new one. A superlative late out-swinger laid the Naval Cadet's middle stump low before he had scored: 1 for 1—Hammond 'absent ill' made it virtually 2 for 1. But Hutton and Edrich defied what they afterwards called the 'Dambuster' and at stumps on the second day England were 110 for 3 with Hutton 48 not out and they were 170 in front. Early on the Monday, however, Miller bowled Edrich for 58 and, later, Pollard for 9 to finish with 16 2 42 3, or 34 5 86 6 for the match.

England 254 and 164, was 224 ahead with 300 minutes remaining.

This time the Australians were 104 for 3 (Sismey 51) when Miller joined his captain. Keith's second innings after his failures at Bramall Lane and in the first knock at Lord's, was elegance itself. Charles Fry described it as: 'a showpiece in which superbly-stroked and directed cover-driving of the pace bowling formed the most telling and majestic feature.'

At tea the Australians were 136 for 3. Ninety more runs in two hours against tiring bowlers was no difficult contract and Miller, 71 out of 225 for 6, was there at the end. The Australians led by two Tests to one with two to be played in this series in which their Board of Control feared they would be annihilated.

And there was no dissension among players or Press as to who had been the 'Man of the Series'. So far Miller had scored 209 runs at 41·8 and taken 9 wickets at 18·5. And his best, as a batsman, was yet to come.

In the Fourth Test, again at Lord's, he improved upon his form of the previous game while scoring a chanceless 118 with ten, again mostly cover-driven and cover-hit, boundaries. His two centuries and 327 runs at 54·4 placed him above that Test record score holder Hutton, 252 runs at 42·00, and that greatest of English batsmen of the late 1920s and the 1930s Walter Hammond, 213 at 42·6. His brilliant batting and hostile fast bowling already were causing England's most distinguished cricket writers to call him 'The Jack Gregory of the second World War'.

England were on their mettle now, however. Laurie Fishlock 69, Hutton 35, Robertson 25, Hammond 83, Washbrook 112, and Edrich 73 not out, outscored Australia's 388 by 80 runs and though Jack Pettiford 39, Miller 35 not out, and Stanford 33 not out, had the Australians 60 in front with six wickets standing at stumps on the third day honours were fairly even at the end.

Though Miller failed to take a wicket as the opening bowler in England's innings his 23 overs cost only 49 runs and he greatly impressed most members of a total attendance of 93 000 for the three days.

Well though he had batted at Lord's, Miller reserved his finest innings of this 'Victory' series for the 'green top' pitch provided for the final match at Old Trafford. Entering at 66 for 4, he contributed 77 of the 107 runs that took the Australians on to 173 and was undefeated at the end. Once again he stood out above his comrades—competent, confident, and commanding. His 77 occupied only 135 minutes in an atmosphere and on a surface that gave considerable movement and erratic lift to those fine fast-medium bowlers Eddie Phillipson, Pollard, and Pope. 'Cloisterish' was the word Charles Fry used to describe Keith's innings. Certainly it owned an exclusive dignity.

Again given first over with the new ball, Miller dismissed Fishlock lbw for 9, at 14 for 1, but Hutton 64, Hammond 57, Washbrook 38, and Edrich 23, helped England to 243 and a lead of 70.

Losing five wickets for 46, including those of Hassett 1, and Miller 4, the Australians recovered to 210 all out thanks almost entirely to a sensational display of batting bravado by their leg-spin and googly bowler Bob Cristofani who disdained even to take block, then struck a century out of 126 and remained undefeated on 110 compiled at above 60 runs an hour.

Needing 140 to win, England's most powerful and redoubtable batting ranks of the series saw her home by six wickets to level perhaps the most delightful Test series ever played between England and Australia—a series during which the England captain Hammond acted as frequent host to his adversaries after play in London and during which the two teams either shared or were in and out of each other's dressing-rooms match after match.

Miller emerged from the rubber with the highest aggregate, 443, and highest batting average, 62·8, for either side; and he also took 10 wickets at 27·7 each. As a batsman he had outshone and outscored England's two greatest players Hutton and Hammond, whose figures were 369 at 46·1 and 380 at 42·2, respectively. As a bowler he was second only, among the Australians, to Cristofani, who, in the last three Tests, had taken 14 wickets at 15·2.

The demands of playing a double role did not worry Keith in 1945. 'I just loved playing cricket. It was fun to be in the game all the time. If you missed out, say, with the bat, you tried harder to contribute with the ball,' he said in 1979.

'But looking back now,' he added, 'I really believe fast bowling does sap not only one's energy but also one's powers of concentration when batting. Later in my career if I had done well with the ball I sometimes—batting after Bradman and Hassett, remember—relaxed with the bat.'

Sir Donald Bradman and Johnnie Moyes never saw those 1945 performances of Keith's, of course. And they seem to have lacked the imagination to understand what militated against their repetition season after season in the years to follow.

Certainly had Bradman been at Lord's on the Saturday and

Monday of the match which Sir Pelham Warner organised between a Dominions XI and England in August of 1945 he could never have classed Keith as 'a great fast bowler, but apt to be over-rated as a batsman'.

In the Dominions XI's first innings of 307 that talented and stylish New Zealand left-hander Martin Donnelly played a glorious 133 which included two 6s and eighteen 4s. Replying for England, Walter Hammond scored a truly delightful 121 in 160 minutes, which included two straight drives into the Members' Pavilion. His seventh wicket stand of 177 with Bill Edrich, 77, placed England on terms with the eight Australians, one West Indian, one New Zealander, and one South African.

Batting again in mid-afternoon of the Saturday (the second day, mind you) the Dominions lost their first two wickets rather cheaply. But by stumps they had recovered to 145 for 3 with Miller, 61, and Donnelly the not-out batsmen.

On the Monday Miller played what England's 'Cricketers' Bible' *Wisden*, and Johnnie Moyes in his *Australian Cricket. A History*, (Angus and Robertson) described as 'one of the most masterly innings seen for a generation'.

'Miller,' said *Wisden*, 'outshone even Hammond and, though travelling at the rate of 185 runs in 165 minutes—for the latter part of his innings at the rate of 124 runs in 90 minutes—played absolutely faultless cricket. In all he struck thirteen 4s and seven 6s. One of the 6s landed on the roof of the broadcasting box above the English dressing-room, carrying even higher than the famous hit with which Albert Trott cleared the Pavilion of his day.'

Trott's stroke, the only known instance of a batsman hitting a ball over the Pavilion at Lord's, occurred when, appearing for the Marylebone Cricket Club against his former countrymen on 31 July 1899, he drove Australian fast-medium swing bowler M. A. Noble 'so far and so high that the ball struck a chimney pot and fell behind the building'.

The broadcasting box and its 1945 occupant, the internationally famous Howard Marshall, were not, of course, present on that earlier occasion.

Miller's other six 6s all cannonaded into the seats below or adjoining the Long Room windows, causing several elderly gentlemen who had experienced some of the severest German artillery bombardments of the Kaiser War, to desert their favourite positions and seek sanctuary in the Members' Bar.

In the outcome, despite another century from the immaculate Hammond, the Dominions, helped by seven wickets from Pepper, won by 45 runs with eight minutes to spare on the Tuesday.

In the match against 'Shrimp' Leveson-Gower's English side at Scarborough Miller scored 71 with three 6s of the Australians' first innings 506. But this time it was Pepper who stole the limelight by striking six 6s, one of which cleared the roofs of neighbouring houses, during his 'wonderfully powerful' 168, and taking another six wickets.

The Australians had defeated a virtual England side by an innings and 108 runs to put the final bloom on their achievements of a truly memorable and valuable summer.

You may imagine the feelings of Hassett and his men when, following their return to their own country, only Hassett, denied the national captaincy and vice-captaincy, and Miller were selected for the autumn 1946 tour of New Zealand, when Pepper was 'administered' out of Australia to join a Lancashire League club and when no South Australian member (there were five) of the Australian Services combination was even chosen in his State's 15-man practice squad.

5
Champion or comet? – India 1945

Earlier in this book I began to explain why Keith Miller's contribution to the Australian Services Team's tour of a still-British India from mid-October to early December of 1945 came as such an anti-climax to his phenomenal performances in England earlier that year.

His own explanation, one given in 1979, is: 'The long war in Europe, the packed 1945 English cricket programme, the Indian climate, tummy troubles caused by Indian food and cooking, and the surprisingly high standard of the Indian opposition.'

Other factors which temporarily upset the Miller momentum in September, October, and November of 1945 included Indian captain Vijay Merchant's indefensibly negative tactics in the Bombay Test, the highly questionable umpiring at Lahore in the Calcutta Test, and the disappointing approach to their cricket of one or two of Keith's R.A.A.F. colleagues in the Services Team.

Others still were the psychological effect of initial contact with the appalling conditions under which the great majority of Indians lived. Keith has always held sympathetic regard for the underdogs of this world and there were enough underdogs in India in 1945 to fill the kennels of England, Scotland, Wales, and Ireland—*and* of Alsace-Lorraine, where, I understand, those huge Alsatians hail from.

There were more than 400 million Indians—Hindus, Muslims, Sikhs, Parsees, Buddhists, and Christians—then. There are about

600 million Indians and Pakistanis now. Keith was, and is, appalled at the plight of the great majority of them.

Four hundred million; six hundred million. The words roll easily from the typrewriter but do they really register upon the Australian or English mind? Even 400 million is 100 times the population of modern Sydney and there are only three or four cities (I fancy three—New York, Chicago, and Los Angeles) in the United States with larger populations than Sydney.

I do not exaggerate when I say that of those 400 million (now 600 million) human beings at most 10 per cent have enjoyed, even following independence, a way of life and means of livelihood equivalent to that of most Australians. For the remainder each hour, each day, each week, each month, and each year, has been a desperate struggle for survival—for physical survival, let alone mental acceptance; for resignation. And for the essential maintenance of some form of spiritual faith.

The shock for all of us, the fifteen players, our manager Keith Johnson, and our treasurer John Mallyon, was profound when we first saw the crowded confines of Bombay; when we strolled and taxied through its cluttered streets; when we came upon thousands upon thousands of men, women, and children of an evening lying like so many human bananas side by side along the centres of the cluttered thoroughfares because they could find no other beds for the night.

For Keith Miller, Keith Carmody, Stan Sismey, and Ross Stanford, who had spent three or four years risking their lives over the English Channel, the Bay of Biscay, and enemy-occupied Europe in the hope they were helping to produce a better world for *all* mankind, that shock was even more distressing and distracting. Cricket, even international cricket, began to seem comparatively unimportant.

On our long voyage from Liverpool to Bombay in the S.S. *Samaria* Miller, Stanford, and I were privileged to spend many hours with a young Canadian missionary and his wife. They were returning to a leper colony on India's eastern, Coramandel Coast after two months' leave in Toronto.

'You must be horrified at the prospect of going back?' I recall Keith asking the attractive young woman.

'On the contrary,' she replied with an excited smile, 'we are eagerly looking forward to it. Our work in India has provided the most rewarding years of our lives. You have to experience the goodwill and the gratitude we have received from our lepers to understand what I mean. I doubt if we will ever take long leave again. There is far too much to be done.'

During the afternoons we spent with that brave and unselfish young man and woman on our long voyage through the Mediterranean, down the Red Sea, and across the Arabian and Persian gulfs, Keith, Ross, and I learnt a lot about India and the Indians. But we still had a deal more to learn when we steamed past the mysterious and sinister-looking Elephant Island, arrived at Bombay's Ballard Pier, and gained our first sight of the massive stone arch that is the Gateway to India and of that imposing hotel known as the Taj Mahal.

What better encyclopedia could one consult than the man who had volunteered to be our host while we were in India—the handsome, genial, Indian-born England-educated Test batsman Kumar Shri Duleepsinhji, nephew of the great Ranjitsinhji, the former Maharajah of the Princely State of Nawanagar, and, himself, later to become independent India's High Commissioner to Canada and Australia?

'Duleep' told us that only the United States of America could solve India's most serious problem (the starvation and near starvation of its millions) by helping to finance the construction of giant dams at the base of the snow-clad Himalayas and thus making possible the effective irrigation of the wheat and corn basins along the banks of the Jumna and Ganges rivers. Maybe he should have told John Kennedy.

Most everyone who visited Bombay in the 1930s and 1940s, including hosts of Australian soldiers, were taken or directed to its notorious Fort Road to see the brothels—those 'human zoos' of that depressing and revolting district.

One night during our first week in India's then secondmost populous city Keith, his currently most frequent companion Mick Roper, and I called a taxi and directed its driver to take us to the Wellington Sports Club. Like many Bombay taxi-drivers he got his targets amusingly mixed and we suddenly found ourselves in the middle of Fort Road at a different kind of sports club, indeed.

Here in filthy, barred cages; here behind tawdry, tattered, and transparent green, gold, and crimson screens, crouched women. Women who once had been human beings and now were worse than animals; black, brown, yellow, even white Eurasian women with painted bodies and faces—available for the asking, taking, and regretting at the price of our taxi fare and God knows at what other cost.

Disgusted and depressed we ordered our driver to get us the hell out of there and back to the Cricket Club of India. Here we ordered three double Scotches and soda (you were warned not to drink water in India) but the memory of that 'human zoo' still lingers today.

All the way back to the palatial C.C.I. the taxi traversed crowded streets where the Indian chauffeurs of gleaming American-manufactured limousines kept incessantly and arrogantly tooting those 'untouchables', the hordes of grey-white robed pedestrians, out of their apparent intention to commit suicide and their desperate efforts to cadge even half-smoked cigarettes.

Yes, it was all very depressing. And Bombay in 1945 was paradise compared to Calcutta and Madras.

Keith kept his feelings about all this very much to himself and his most intimate friends, but he was profoundly affected.

As the Services Team boarded the Frontier Mail from Bombay to make the 2000-kilometre journey to its first match at Lahore, Duleep, who came just after dawn to bid them farewell, said the countryside would remind everyone of the Kalgoorlie–Port Augusta stretch of Australia's now Indian–Pacific railway. It was, to quote him, 'Thousands of miles of damn-all'.

On its winding way out of Bombay, the train passed through the worst of the city's slums. Here naked boys and girls with grey, emaciated bodies abounded in every street and lane. Despite their scragginess they looked so blissfully innocent that the only wonder was that young children have ever been clothed. But this was late October and the weather was sunny and warm. We did not dare imagine the situation which would exist when the wet, monsoonal season came.

And better things lay ahead?

Duleep had been unduly modest about his native land. Soon we were to come to the hills and deep river valleys, green almost as England in springtime. White temples with minareted towers stood deep in the shady re-entrants or perched on the hilltops. Glistening, black, water buffaloes bathed their great hulks in the reedy swamps while graceful white and blue cranes glided overhead and colourful kingfishers swooped by. Slim, stately, Indian women in their saris and with earthen pitchers and baskets or bunches of fruit balanced impregnably upon their heads, walked to and from the mud-hut villages across the green fields.

The Indian peasants were, or seemed to be, better off than city dwellers. It was only when the train swept through or past the hundreds of villages that the congestion and the squalor re-appeared. Here thousands of youngsters in tattered rags and wielding rough, uncarpentered sticks kept careering about in chase of wooden balls—preparing, we gathered, to maintain India's high standing in the hockey world. Their spirit was irrepressible and, rightly or wrongly, this saddened some of us even more. What a waste of talent through lack of opportunity. It could not be measured.

As we steamed laboriously northward past Agra and Shah Jehan's real Taj Mahal towards the North-West Frontier, white-robed and turbaned farmers marched like biblical prophets down the dusty trails behind their oxen and elephants. Following them came their womenfolk bearing water pitchers from the wells. Mysterious and mystical India at its best.

The Indian peasant may not have learnt to read or write or even turn a TV dial, but he had learnt contentment: how to till the fields of his world; to worship his god, be he Allah, Buddha, Krishna, Siva, Vishnu, or Christ; how to appreciate the peace obtainable from puffing at a pipe towards the sunset hour alongside a village well.

The carriages of that Frontier Mail, British India's nearest approach to Agatha Christie's Orient Express, had no corridors. Keith, Reg Ellis, and I shared a compartment next to the engine. Throughout the first night of the journey the Hindu enginedriver kept sounding his ear-splitting whistle. In the morning, when we alighted at a station to stretch our legs and adjourn to the dining car, Keith asked the happy little driver if he could reduce the whistling on the second night of the 44-hour odyssey.

'Must whistle, Sahib,' he replied. 'If not, might kill sacred cow.'

On the third morning the Frontier Mail arrived two-and-a-half hours behind schedule at the holy Sikh city of Amritsar. Most of the delays had occurred at stations. Here, whenever the engine-driver was inclined to get on with the job, he first had to blow that whistle to scatter the myriads of peddlers, peanut vendors, beggars, and thieves who crowded the platforms, if any, and swarmed over the tracks.

At Modhopur monkeys and baboons kept running wild along the roofs of carriages and then leaping through windows to sneak bananas and mandarins. One of the monkeys, an old male with a very domineering expression and an extremely roseate rear-disappearance, kept close and constant watch upon his harem of females—all with babies clinging fearfully about their waists and sagging bosoms.

According to the enginedriver, who saw him twice each week on his 4000-kilometre round-trip, the old fellow tolerated no 'monkeying' with his lordship of the brood. Indeed, as soon as any of the young males reached a susceptible age he murdered them callously and then restored all the unpregnant females to what then was known as 'an interesting condition'.

Yes, we all grew very fond of that old enginedriver; and many of the Indians we met along the way from Bombay towards Peshawar and the Khyber Pass grew more and more concerned that Providence, or 'Uncle Sam', should eventually improve their lot.

And that partly is why, thirty-one years later, when Keith Miller, at the age of 57, learned that Dennis Lillee, Jeff Thomson, and Ian and Greg Chappell had either ignored or declined invitations to participate in the series of matches being planned to commemorate the centenary of the birth of the founder of Pakistan, Mohammed Ali Jinnah, he contacted Alan Barnes, secretary of the Australian Cricket Board of Control, to inquire if the Board was 'doing anything about the matter'.

Learning to his consternation that Australia would be the only cricketing country not represented at this important celebration, Keith then contacted his old Pakistani opponent and friend A. H. Kardar, assistant-manager of the 1972–73 Pakistani team to Australia, and offered his services free of charge. 'I could just stand in slips to show that Australians care,' he suggested.

The Pakistanis, including their ill-fated Prime Minister Mr Bhutto, were so delighted that they immediately booked Keith on to a Pakistani Airlines flight to Karachi. And back in the old Punjab he did more than just stand in slips. He performed quite respectably with the bat. How respectably he would not say. Amazing, is it not, how great batsmen will boast about their bowling (e.g. Hassett); how great bowlers will boast about their batting (e.g. Bill O'Reilly, Ernie McCormick, and Arthur Mailey) but never about their achievements at what they do best? However this may be, the 57-year-old Miller did his stint in Pakistan.

The 'Grand Old Man' of English cricket, Dr W. G. Grace, scored 74 on his fifty-eighth birthday for The Gentlemen of England against The Players at The Oval in July of 1906.

Thirty minutes after leaving Amritsar in October of 1945 the Frontier Mail crossed the border into the Punjab and completed its 2000-kilometre journey after 44 hours of almost continuous whistling. That evening Hassett and his team struggled from their beds to become guests of honour at a dance at the Lahore Gymkhana Club's Montgomery Hall. Here they were plied with chota pegs about the cocktail bar while an affable but bumptious female named Bumpstead, the proprietress of a Srinagar (pronounced Ser-rin-nargar) Hotel showed them colour photographs of the fountained gardens of the Shalimar, the snow and cloud-capped peaks of the Himalayas, and the dreamy lakes and ancient caravan routes, remembered nowadays (when they are remembered at all) because of the lovely 'Kashmiri Love Song' and 'Less Than the Dust Beneath Thy Chariot Wheels'.

Yes, India and its Punjab (now the northern part of Pakistan) was a land of extreme contrasts in 1945; it probably remains so today.

One of the Australian cricketers, airman Bob Cristofani, who recently had compiled that astonishing, even-time century and taken 5 for 55 in England's first innings at Old Trafford, was now to contribute an anachronism all of his own.

After Miller and Roper, both suffering from what now is called 'Delhi belly' had delivered two unrewarded overs at the Northern Zone's opening batsmen on our second day in Lahore Hassett tossed the ball to Cecil Pepper and Cristofani. Cristofani took four cheap wickets before what dew there is up there of a morning left the grass.

Then wicketkeeper-batsman Imtiaz Ahmed probed forward at a leg-break and edged it knee-high across first slip to second slip. The fieldsmen waited for Imtiaz to 'walk'. He didn't. A unanimous appeal to the umpire was refused, and at the end of that over it was Cristofani, 4 for 30 odd, who walked—all the way back to the red-gabled pavilion.

Cristofani, Australia's future Trade Commissioner to Ceylon, South Africa, and Britain, was still there in that pavilion when the Northern Zone 400 for 4 (Imtiaz Ahmed about 170) were batting in the evening light. Maybe Cristofani then sensed that the dew had returned to the pitch? Suddenly we saw him leaning with his back to the pavilion gate. Then we saw him prance out on to the field and gaze at Hassett, seeking a direction as to where he should field.

The twelfth man, too aghast to react, held his ground. Hassett gradually recovered control of himself and, when Cristofani had zig-zagged about twenty metres towards mid-off, Lindsay, enigmatic as ever, raised his right arm to arrest his progress.

A series of hand signals, which put our one wicket-taker into reverse zig-zag, followed. Eventually to his own embarrassment and the astonishment of about 30 000 Punjabis, Bob again found himself standing with his back to the pavilion gate. Like some cricketing Toscanini Hassett then gave the final dismissal signal and Cristofani vanished.

During that first day's play at Lahore Keith Miller was attacked by a swarm of wasps in the outfield. During the third day there our batting order was dictated by the state of our stomachs—our individual estimates of just how long each of us could be expected to avoid visiting the 'loo'.

Finally, quite a number of chota pegs and countless wasp bites later, the Australians struggled to a draw at Lahore and re-boarded the Frontier Mail for the return journey to Bombay.

Australia's 1935–36 Test captain, Victor York Richardson, then serving as Welfare Officer for the R.A.A.F. in India and gilded by sunshine and atebrin tablets, was at the New Delhi station to greet his compatriots. Welfare was exactly what they needed.

Vic said the young new Maharajah of Patiala would be captaining 'a truly formidable' batting side against us at India's capital city. Our host 'Duleep' already had taught us quite a deal about the young Maharajah's more memorable father, who had died in 1938 leaving 94 sons and an uncounted number of daughters behind him. One day when 'Duleep' and his Princess Jay Raj were strolling through the Patiala Palace gardens they came by a building simply crowded with children.

'Is that a school, darling?' Jay Raj had asked.

'Tush, darling, no. They're the Maharajah's *younger* offspring,' 'Duleep' had whispered.

This senior of the male children, Vic Richardson said, stood 200 centimetres tall—before he donned his blue or pink Sikh turbans. Imagine Joel Garner in a turban. We began eagerly awaiting the spectacle of Patiala and our captain, the 170-centimetre Hassett, tossing for choice of innings.

Another tale 'Duleep' had told us about the old Maharajah was less amusing—following the brand of umpiring encountered at Lahore. The former Maharajah had made a practice of inviting teams of Indian or overseas cricketers to play his own side at Patiala and to enjoy his renowned hospitality during the matches. In these games he invariably opened his team's innings.

One eager young visiting bowler managed to get an early ball through the portly Maharajah's defences and struck His Highness just below the right knee. 'How's that?' the bowler screamed, only to be greeted by an embarrassing silence and an astonished frown from his host.

At the end of the over the umpire had a chat with the young bowler. 'His Highness decides when he wants to get out,' he said. 'If you want to share your weekend with one of the more beautiful hostesses I suggest you remember this.'

At New Delhi in November 1945 we were denied any chance of watching the younger Maharajah at the wicket; but we were intrigued by the spectacle of him stationed at cover in a sky-blue turban, while his aide-de-camp, in a salmon-pink turban, danced attendance upon him whenever the ball arrived below knee height.

After the Maharajah had won the toss, the mercurial Mushtaq Ali, the dynamic Lala Amarnath and the elegant Vijay Hazare, all scored centuries—all three of them on the one blistering day.

Miller, still suffering from 'Delhi belly', again failed to trouble the scorers but, thanks mainly to Hassett's scintillating 187 and dutiful 112 not out, the Australians managed another draw.

On their last evening in New Delhi they were the guests of Field Marshal Lord Wavell, who preceded Lord Louis Mountbatten as Viceroy of India. When Hassett introduced Keith to Lord Wavell the Viceroy adjusted his monocle, smiled, and said, 'I have already met Mr Miller, Mr Hassett. He trod on my toes as he was leaving the field this afternoon. Accidentally, of course.' High-ranking officers have excellent memories for faces.

Keith had just recovered from another embarrassing incident, involving an R.A.A.F. spin bowler and Lord Wavell's blond and handsome aide-de-camp, in the palace cloakroom. The aide-de-camp, we were told, was then a highly-fancied suitor for Princess Elizabeth's hand.

As he gave his blue Air Force issue greatcoat to the aide-de-camp the spin bowler had asked, 'Do you think it will be safe to leave it here?'

It was at this stage that Miller had trodden on his second set of toes for the day—this time deliberately.

After cocktails with the Viceroy we taxied to the famous Maidens Hotel to dine with General Sir Iven Mackay, who commanded the Sixth Australian Division in the Western Desert in 1941, and his aide-de-camp, Colin Troup Moodie, subsequently to become Australian High Commissioner to New Zealand and Ambassador to the Netherlands, South Africa, Lesotho, Swaziland, and Botswana. More importantly, in our eyes, Colin had a secret and, it seemed, inexhaustible source of South Australia's famous Cooper's Ale, even in New Delhi.

Maybe it was the form shown by Keith Carmody 115, Jack Pettiford 124, Lindsay Hassett 53, and Cecil Pepper 95, from a total of 531 that dissuaded Miller from exerting himself with the bat in the Bombay Test.

Forced to follow on, India set the Australians 104 for victory in just above half an hour. India's captain Vijay Merchant was not only a great batsman and a many-times rupee millionaire, he was also as fanatical about cricket—about winning or not losing at cricket—as the late Douglas Jardine.

Though we had been called upon to score that 104 at over

three runs a minute, he set nine of his fieldsmen on the offside of the wicket, five of them along the boundary in an arc extending from behind mid-off to third man. Yet Hassett and Miller, who had decided to 'have a crack' at this cricketing miracle, walked determinedly out to face Vijay Hazare and the new ball.

Almost all of the eight balls of out-swinger Hazare's opening over were pitched at least 60 centimetres wide of the off stump, but Hassett managed to stroke three of them through that timidly-placed offside cordon. Trying to repeat the performance in Hazare's next over, however, he dragged a half-volley from the edge of the pitch on to his off stump. Cecil Pepper, who two months previously had crash-driven some thirteen 6s against 'Shrimp' Leveson-Gower's team at the Scarborough Festival, joined Miller to continue this crazy chase.

Pepper, like Roper, was a somewhat insubordinate character and was known as 'The Ox'. He had his own ideas about Merchant's tactics. He took block meticulously a metre outside the off stump from an astonished umpire before facing Hazare. At the end of that over he and Miller had a conference and 'shut up shop'.

As Merchant led his team back into the members' sanctum of the Cricket Club of India with our score 1 for 31, our host Duleepsinhji called across several rows of seats, 'Merchant, you have brought eternal shame upon the name of Indian cricket by the timing of your declaration and the placing of your field.'

'Duleep's' remark was not lost upon Keith Miller. If this was the way *unofficial* Test cricket was to be conducted after six years of total war, just what would *official* Test cricket between England and Australia be like when the battles for the Ashes were resumed in twelve months' time in Brisbane?

From Bombay we took an electric train up into the beautiful jade-green hills about Deolali and Poona and its world-famous British Officers' Club. Here a young University of India side amassed a total of 600 for the loss of four wickets against us. A tall, slim, and affluent Parsee named Rusi Modi and Imtiaz Ahmed, he who had refused to 'walk' and been given not out when 4 of 186 at Lahore—given not out after being caught a metre from the ground at *second* slip—added over 300 for that fourth wicket. Roper, to put it mildly, was ropable.

Mick organised a meeting of some of the Air Force members of our team at our Poona hotel and suggested that we either abandon the tour or alternatively replace Hassett with Miller or Carmody as captain; this, unless Lindsay agreed to insist that henceforth we travel by air. Ten of the fifteen members of our side and also its manager Keith Johnson were from the R.A.A.F. Things were beginning to look black—either for the remainder of the tour in Calcutta, Madras, and Colombo, or for Hassett.

But Johnson was a member of the Australian Cricket Board which had organised the tour and that made it nine to six. As team treasurer, Army Captain John Mallyon also had a vote, it was nine to seven, provided all members of the A.I.F. stayed loyal to their skipper.

I do not know what transpired at that meeting of the R.A.A.F. players in Poona but after it Stan Sismey, a teetotaller, joined the A.I.F. players at the hotel bar and informed them that a crisis was imminent. Would we all vote for continuation of the tour under the present leadership? he asked. Yes, we replied. 'Then I'll support you,' Sismey said. That made it eight against at most eight.

Bradman, at that time, was thought to have retired from first-class cricket. The future leadership of Australia could have hung upon that vote. If Hassett was to be replaced as our leader Miller, not Carmody, probably would have gained the captaincy on a vote of the entire team.

Eventually it was Sismey, a subsequent New South Wales selector, who produced the solution. He was a squadron leader and had been stationed at a Sunderland flying boat base in Britain. He arranged for the Australian Air Force unit in India to provide a plane to take us on to the distant Calcutta and from there to Madras and Colombo.

The tour went on with Hassett as our captain.

Yet more trouble lay immediately ahead in Calcutta—India's most populous and, as it was to prove, currently most putrid city. Here we were greeted by a five-day-old garbage strike and news that the Australian Board of Control had organised a tour of Australia for us—one which was to include matches against all six States, these on top of the five months' tour of England and the three months' tour of India and Ceylon. The R.A.A.F. and

Australian Army authorities had supported the Board's plan. Only Bradman, now considering a return to the game, Sid Barnes, Ray Lindwall, said to be almost Larwood's pace, Bill O'Reilly, and 'Big' Bill Johnston, claimed to be of Bill Voce's 1932–33 velocity, stood between us and our homes.

Roper urged another protest in our dressing-room at Calcutta's Eden Gardens Ground during the preliminary to the Second Test, a match against the Eastern Zone, whose side contained Denis Compton.

This time Roper received almost universal support until deeper consideration of the consequences and cooler heads prevailed.

Despite a superb innings by Compton and an invasion of the ground by thousands of irate Indians, during which anything except peace prevailed o'er Eden Gardens, we managed to hold off the Eastern Zone.

This time it was Hassett who saved the day. After the ground had been invaded by two long snakes of demonstrators, their leader advanced upon Compton who was 88 not out. 'You play very fine innings for us Mr Compton, but you must go,' he said. 'Five of our friends have been shot by the British police.'

'You'd better speak to Mr Hassett. He's in charge around here,' said Denis pointing to Lindsay at the far end of the wicket.

As the leader of the rioters advanced threateningly towards him, Lindsay gave one of those disarming smiles of his and asked, 'Have any of you fellers got a cigarette?'

There ended the riot and, after about an hour was occupied in clearing the ground, on went Compton's innings and the match. I have often wondered how Keith Miller, had *he* been our captain, would have reacted that day. Though he often featured in newspaper advertisements promoting Black and White cigarettes, he was a strict non-smoker.

In the Test that followed, we began with 472 and India replied with 350 for 4. Of these Merchant scored an undefeated century. During his innings we believed that at a conservative estimate he had been either leg before wicket or caught at the wicket at least seven times.

When Merchant was 99 not out, Roper was the bowler.

By this time he was down to Greg Chappell's pace and about to be replaced. There was a deep hole level with the bowling crease and he was delivering the ball about 30 centimetres behind it.

Before he released the crucial delivery to Merchant the umpire no-balled him. Fielding at first slip I noticed that Merchant's back foot was already outside the off-stump—ready for the hook.

The boundary took the Indian captain to 103. At the end of his over Roper turned to the umpire and said, 'I always thought you were a bloody cheat and now I'm certain.'

'You send Mr Roper off the field, Mr Hassett,' the umpire demanded. Again Lindsay used his initiative. Roper could hardly hobble up to the wicket at this stage. 'I'll tell you what I'll do. I won't bowl him any more,' Lindsay said and peace breathed again o'er Eden Gardens.

Because the wickets were unsuited to fast bowlers Miller had had a relatively restful tour. We were beginning to understand why whereas England, in Tom Richardson, C. J. Kortright, W. H. Lockwood, Harold Larwood, Ken Farnes, Fred Trueman, Brian Statham, and Frank Tyson, has produced at least eight great fast bowlers, and Australia, in Frederick Spofforth, Ernie Jones, 'Tibby' Cotter, Jack Gregory, Ted McDonald, Tim Wall, Ray Lindwall, Keith Miller, Dennis Lillee, and Jeff Thomson has produced at least ten, India as yet has produced only Kapil Dev and Pakistan only Imran Khan.

On one of the few occasions that Hassett did bowl Miller for any length of time on that tour—during the game against the Southern Zone at Madras—a most remarkable, indeed perhaps unique, event occurred. Lindsay had brought Keith on to try and dispose of that plucky little left-handed Muslim Gul Mohammed. When Gul Mohammed was in his 40s, the 95- to 114-kilogram and immobile Mick Roper was stationed alone at slip. As Miller ran into bowl that other Muslim, the fiery batsman Mushtaq Ali, who was sitting in the players' enclosure, exclaimed utterly spontaneously, 'He's out, caught at slip.'

Sure enough, Gul Mohammed edged an attempted cover-drive. It flew fast, low, and at least a metre-and-a-half to the left of Roper. The ungainly Michael sprawled towards its path, clutched it with one hand, and held it high above his head. A miracle, indeed, and one of the few wickets Miller took on that tour. We almost abandoned Christianity and became Muslims then and there.

As a batsman Miller had played only one knock really worthy of his ability during the seven weeks' tour of India. This was his 82 in Australia's first innings of the Calcutta Test. Batting first we were more than 250 for 2 when Miller came out brandishing a new bat, a bat belonging to the batsman he was about to join.

'I asked you not to use my bats,' this player complained as Miller reached the wicket. 'Why don't you find one of your own?'

'I'll take great care of it. There won't be a mark on it when I've finished. You'll see.'

Keith had to face the left-handed Vinoo Mankad, a bowler who eventually was to take 162 wickets at an average of 32·31 in 44 Tests.

Beyond the high, tarpaulined temporary stand behind Mankad's arm and just outside the ground was a water-lily pond. Four of the five remaining balls of Vinoo's over landed among the lilies.

'I thought you said you'd be careful with my bat?' Keith's partner exclaimed.

'I *am* being. Every one of those hits went off the middle. Here, take a look at your bloody bat.'

It was, indeed, unmarked.

Unfortunately, Miller aggravated a back injury during his knock of 82 and was unable to bowl when Hassett badly needed him during India's innings. This Test, like the first, was drawn.

After the decisive Third Test which India won by six wickets, the Australians were wined and dined at the Connemarra Hotel as guests of the Governor of Madras.

Next morning in the local newspaper we read, 'His Excellency presided at a farewell dinner to the Indian and Australian Test teams last night at the Connemarra Hotel, but had to leave early as he was not *doing* (sic) so well.'

6
Home to another kind of war

Between Bombay and Calcutta, while flying through forked lightning above thunderheads that reared their black tors from sinister seas of leaden cloud, nine of the ten R.A.A.F. members of the Australian Services Team had made no secret of their anxiety.

They knew of the risks inseparable from long flights in the 1940s; were aware of the fallibility of ageing and over-taxed planes. They kept listening for irregularities in the engines, glancing at those ominous black sentinels protruding from the clouds that concealed the jungle.

A conspicuously philosophical exception had been Miller, who seemed blessed with inexhaustible, even fountaining, faith in his luck.

Following a relaxing match under a pastel artists' sky in Colombo we were driven to the airport to embark upon our 4800-kilometre flight southward over the Indian Ocean to Perth. A weather- and war-scarred, twin-engine Liberator stood in isolation by the runway.

Liberators have short, fin-like wings and incongruously bulky bodies. On first sight of them one doubts whether they will even leave the ground. We had learned of their uniquely high casualty rate over the mountains of Papua and New Guinea. We had been told that our one sight of land and calling place on the journey ahead would come some 2400 kilometres out from Colombo at lonely Cocos Island, a speck in thousands of kilometres of shark-infested sea—first tigers and now sharks.

The Liberator's pilot was an Australian. Fourteen of his wartime friends, their alternative was another six months in India, had hitched a ride home. The pilot explained that they could cram themselves into the corridor between our seats.

Besides our personal luggage we had twenty bags of cricket equipment on board. It seemed certain the Liberator would be carrying far more than its authorised load. Uneasiness, bordering upon alarm, prevailed.

Shortly before we were due to weigh our luggage Miller arrived with a carry-all bag, a Sinhalese bearer, and several large, black, elephant-hide trunks.

One of his colleagues informed him of the situation. 'You can't bring all those trunks, Keith,' he insisted.

'Weigh your own bag,' Keith said, pointing to the scales.

The protestor obeyed and found it exceeded 22 kilograms. Miller instructed his bearer to stack the elephant-hide trunks on the scale; they totalled less than 18 kilograms.

'There's nothing in them; they're Christmas presents for my pals,' he grinned.

Most of us had forgotten it was 12 December. Keith had not.

When we were some 1600 kilometres out over the ocean, most of them flown above unbroken cloud, R.A.A.F. members of the side (especially our between 95 and 114 kilogram 'fast' bowler, Roper) began to detect, or imagine they were detecting, disturbing noises in the starboard engine. Hours later the plane headed towards a towering white mountain of cloud. The E.T.A. at Cocos had passed. All of us now believed we had overshot the island and began trying to reconcile ourselves to a watery grave with sharks for undertakers.

As the Liberator nosed into the clouds Keith left his seat and joined the pilot and navigator in the cockpit.

Keith's passion for gambling had taught him how to present what is known as a poker-face. His countenance was expressionless when he returned and handed a sheet of paper to the occupant of one of the front seats. He began to smile, however, as the paper was passed from hand to hand along the crowded plane.

It read: 'In a few minutes we will descend through the clouds. You will see an island below. Don't become impatient. You won't be looking at Cocos Island but North Keeling Island, where the

Australian cruiser H.M.A.S. *Sydney* sank the German raider *Emden* in 1915. In another few minutes you will see another island, Cocos Island, where we will spend the night.'

Keith had signed a great number of autographs for English and Indian kids. We all recognised the writing on that sheet of paper and were surprised at his knowledge of history. Keith *had* become a box of surprises, however, we again were thinking, as our pilot landed very smoothly and swept along the runway past a sign that read 'Cocos 5 Feet'.

Lining the palm-fringed shores of this island later that evening stood a score or so of eighty years and older men. Among them stood their womenfolk—equally stately, richly-attired, and sharing their silence and introspection.

They were not Cocos Islanders but white men and women and they were staring out across the sea towards the sunset. They did not appear to be studying the sunset but rather to be dwelling upon what, for them, lay beyond it.

What were these old people, these still proud but obviously anxious people, doing here on this out-of-the-way island, I wondered and inquired.

'They are Dutch exiles, former owners and executives of the oil wells of Java and Sumatra,' a bystander said. 'They are on their way to Holland. They have lost their work, their wealth, and most of their possessions.'

I turned to see Keith Miller standing behind me, looking at the old men and women and at the sea. Tall, strong, and youthful he formed a striking and refreshing contrast to the line of refugees.

'Your life still lies ahead of you, brilliant with opportunity. You have the world at your feet,' I thought. 'Are you going to grasp that opportunity or allow it to elude you and, in *your* old age, be tormented with regret?' I wondered.

Keith and I later were to share a remarkable flair for mental telepathy as we travelled the cricketing world together. It helped us many times when cricketing fanatics approached with the words, 'You don't remember me, of course, do you?'

When mental telepathy failed, we would resort to a pre-arranged system of signals. Our sign language we called it and more often than not it worked.

Looking back over almost thirty-five years now, I still wonder whether Keith read my thoughts that evening on faraway Cocos Island. All he said was, 'For Christ's sake let's find the bar.'

Soon after our arrival in Perth Roy Paxton, part-owner of the picturesque and popular Esplanade Hotel by the Swan River, invited key members of the Services side for drinks in the cocktail bar that formed part of his bedroom suite.

Roy had served with Brigadier Eugene Gorman in the Middle East during the early stages of the war and had helped him to maintain and manage the Hotel Fast for the Australian Comforts Fund near the Jaffa Gate of Old Jerusalem.

On his way back from London to Melbourne, Brigadier Gorman, who had played a prominent part in the formation of the Second A.I.F. Team at Eastbourne in 1944, called on Paxton and left a message for him to deliver to us.

The message read: 'You fellows have built a fine reputation in England. You have great reason to be proud of your record there. I know you are all anxious to rejoin your families but I trust you will put that wish second to your cricket, will give of your best in Australia, as the First A.I.F. Team did in 1919. Good luck.'

We were all silent after we received that message, conscious of our lapses of form in India. Then Keith looked at each of us, turned to Roy and said, 'I shall for one'.

W. A. (Bert) Oldfield, the former Australian Test wicketkeeper and at that time a very dapper major in Army Amenities, had been entrusted with the organisation of our Australian tour. He greeted us thus: 'Bill O'Reilly's back to form, Don Bradman will lead South Australia against you next week in Adelaide. They are saying Ray Lindwall's the fastest bowler since Larwood. You'll meet him in Sydney. Sid Barnes has been scoring thousands in club and charity games there. You'll also meet a character named Bill Johnston in Melbourne and he bowls like Bill Voce.'

Thanks partly to Miller who, obviously, was battling to recover his English form, we managed to keep Western Australia and her most hostile bowler Charlie Puckett at bay.

We had been told that Bradman's cricketing future would depend upon his performance against us in Adelaide. Stricken by fibrositis, he had been transferred from the R.A.A.F. to the Australian Army and then discharged from military duty in 1942. He had not played serious cricket since early January of

1941 when he scored 0 and 12 for his own side against Stan McCabe's team in Melbourne.

Our captain Hassett had been given leave to rejoin his family in Melbourne during the weekend of the late December match against South Australia in Adelaide. It had been decided before our return to Australia that Cheetham and Graham Williams, both stationed in Adelaide, would be included in our side. Both of them were new ball bowlers and maybe this was why Miller was omitted.

Looking back now I wonder what would have been the outcome had Keith been the spearhead of our attack during that drawn game against South Australia—had he bowled at 'the Don' with the speed and hostility he had shown against Hutton and Hammond at Lord's and was soon to show against Sid Barnes in Sydney.

Had he done so against a man who claimed to be still less than fully fit and was short of match practice, the history of post-war Anglo-Australian cricket could have taken an entirely different course. Bradman's return to the Australian captaincy and his triumphs against England in 1946–47, against India in 1947–48, and against England in 1948 may never have eventuated.

As it was, Don, after a tentative start, produced technically the finest innings we had watched since we had previously seen him; an innings of 112. His return to Test cricket seemed assured despite his refusal to indulge in speculation on this already momentous question.

During that tentative start of 'The Don's' Cecil Pepper beat him with a top-spinner that struck him low on the left pad. Over to Keith Miller and his chapter on Bradman in his book *Cricket Crossfire*:

'Most of the players on the field believed that Don was plumb leg before. Stan Sismey, the wicketkeeper and as fair a man as you could wish to meet, said there was no doubt that Bradman was out. There was a terrific appeal, but Umpire Jack Scott did not grant it. In the heat of the moment Pepper turned to Scott and said something. I was not on the field so I did not hear.

'Scott reported him. I saw the report and it finished Pepper's career. He should have been a cast-iron certainty but was not picked for the tour of New Zealand, which took place immediately afterwards . . . He quit Australia and took up professional cricket in England. I hold no brief for Pepper making the remark he is supposed to have made, but it would be a poor look-out for all of us if our careers were held forfeit for one remark said in temper. I think Bradman should have realised that and intervened on Pepper's behalf. He could have done so very easily. Surely he had the power to save Pepper. As it was, a potentially great Test player was lost to Australia.'

I *was* on the field at the time of this incident and I *did* hear Pepper's remark. I was fielding at first slip. In those days we did not appeal for leg before decisions when fielding at slip, even at first slip, unless the batsman was right back on his stumps. Bradman had stepped forward. I do not know whether he should have been given out. I *do* know that when Scott refused the appeal, Pepper threw his arms in the air, clasped his huge hands to his forehead, and called, 'What do you have to do?' to Scott.

At the end of the over I also heard Bradman, who had just scored a single, ask Scott, 'Do we have to put up with this sort of thing?' I also know that Scott, because he told me so much later himself, eventually decided he must lodge a report to the South Australian Cricket Association, that he did so, and that it was forwarded to the Australian Cricket Board of Control.

Though he does not say so in *Cricket Crossfire* Miller was also aware of the consequences of this incident, and it affected his opinion of Bradman more deeply than he admitted in print.

Pepper was a superb all-round cricketer, an inveterate trier whose duel with Wally Hammond in the Victory Test at Bramall Lane caused Sir Pelham Warner to describe Hammond's century there as 'one of the best innings he has ever played'; caused Hammond himself to say, 'Pepper's was some of the finest spin bowling I have ever faced'.

As a leg-break and 'flipped', zipping, front-of-the-hand, off-break bowler Pepper maintained an impeccable line and length. As a batsman he had a sound defence and was one of the most powerful strikers of a ball of any era. Don't forget that at Scarborough in 1945 against Leveson-Gower's XI he scored 168 with six 6s, one of which cleared a row of high-gabled houses behind and beyond the sightboard, and took 6 for 121.

As a cover, slip, and close-to-the-wicket fieldsman he was of the highest class.

Some who have watched Pepper and Richie Benaud at their best class Pepper as the more gifted and formidable all-rounder. He turned his leg-break further and more sharply than Benaud. His 'flipped' wrong-un was better disguised and came more swiftly from the pitch. His batting technique was far more correct and there was little to choose between the two players in the field.

Pepper was exactly the kind of player whom Hassett needed in England in 1953, whom Ian Johnson would have welcomed in 1956. And, come to think of it, whom Greg Chappell so desperately required in 1977.

His loss to Australia was immeasurable and the manner of his virtual banishment was thoughtlessly and ruthlessly executed. Naturally Miller was deeply disappointed by it.

Having drawn with South Australia and, despite Miller's 37 of 118 and 59 of 182, been soundly thrashed by Victoria, the team flew on to Sydney to face O'Reilly, Lindwall, and Barnes.

Members of the First A.I.F. Cricket Team contend it was in 1919 against New South Wales that their champion Jack Gregory played his greatest match. A number of the New South Wales side had not served overseas during the 1914–18 War and Gregory and his comrades were deeply conscious of this.

History is apt to repeat itself and on our plane journey from Melbourne to Sydney we formed a plan, the main target of which was the man whom Ray Robinson has dubbed 'The Artful Dodger'—Sidney George Barnes.

Barnes had spent his war in Sydney, had made a heap of money for himself by purchasing equipment, including a motor launch, from the quartermasters of American Army and Air Force bases there and re-selling it at considerable profit. Barnes would be opening the innings for New South Wales. We were determined to cause him some shocks—to give him all the curry we could.

After Hassett had lost the toss, Barnes swaggered jauntily to the wicket; Miller measured out and then added two metres to his run.

Keith had read his papers that morning, including an article which said: 'This Australian Services Team is a write-off. There is no player in it to compare with Jack Gregory. English cricket must be weak, that is the only explanation for the results of the Victory Tests!'

Hassett had also read this comment. He stationed himself at gully and set himself for the catch he believed would come before Barnes had accustomed himself to Miller's pace.

Lindsay did not have long to wait. Miller reared in like an untamed thoroughbred, his black mane of hair jerking back and forth with each gathering stride. Barnes cut the fifth ball straight to our captain. It came fast and cosily to him at about knee height, slipped from his hands, and fell to the turf.

We looked askance at the usually reliable Lindsay. He was standing there like some Twentieth Century Guy Fawkes whose bomb had failed to go off.

Miller measured a further two metres on to his run and began bumping the ball at Barnes at frightening pace, varying his bouncers with late out- and in-swinging deliveries of immaculate length.

But Barnes, the batsman, had his own special brand of courage, and great ability. He went to his century without offering a semblance of another chance. New South Wales had 551 runs on the grey Hill scoreboard when we began our battle with Lindwall and Ernie Toshack, whom Australia's 1924–25 and 1926 captain Herbie Collins that day was to class as the finest pair of new ball bowlers New South Wales had fielded since Gregory and Kelleway in the 1920s.

After we had lost Carmody (14), Stanford (4), and Hassett (1) for 25 Miller strode in to face Lindwall and O'Reilly under a sea-blue Sydney sky. Roused to his greatest by the unknowledgable and uninformed criticism, his side's plight, and the unflattering welcome home we had received from cricketing authority, Keith began to bat as he had batted in England in the Victory Tests—keeping the ball always along the turf and finding the gaps with drives that would have done for the watching and admiring Kippax and McCabe.

When our tenth wicket fell he was 93 not out. Filled with admiration of Miller's display and believing he deserved a century, the New South Wales captain (that fine sportsman O'Reilly) suggested our twelfth man Jim Workman be allowed to bat while he went to it. Keith finished with 105 not out of 204.

This time the Press could not claim he had faced 'weak' opposition. 'Johnnie' Moyes in his *Australian Cricket. A History* wrote 'O'Reilly bowled with the life and fire of his greatest days'.

Trailing by 347 we followed on to New South Wales' 551 for 7 declared. Pepper 63, and Miller 46, were the highest scorers this time, but four other batsmen contributed another 150 runs during some defiant resistance to this superb attack.

On the evening of the day on which Keith scored his undefeated century against O'Reilly and Lindwall I came across that 'artist batsman of the 1920s and 1930s' and former captain of New South Wales, Alan Kippax, outside our dressing-room.

Of Miller he said: 'He's a great cricketer, probably a greater one even than Jack Gregory. Very few batsmen I have watched had his rare ability to blend beauty with power.

'There's one vital thing, however, and Herbie Collins agrees with me about this—he must always be allowed a free hand so he can be himself.'

I have never forgotten those words of Alan's.

After an evenly-drawn contest against Queensland (Miller 2 for 74 and 4 for 49) and a lone victory in Tasmania the Marco Polos of the Australian Services Team went to their homes and then, in some cases, in search of work.

They had defeated England in two of the 'Victory' Tests by margins of six wickets, beaten a representative English side at Scarborough by an innings and 108 runs. They had been within 70 runs of victory with nine wickets standing in the first Test against India, had held the upper hand for much of the Second Test at Calcutta, and lost only to powerful Victorian and New South Wales sides in Australia.

Miller, following his performance in Sydney, was again the hero. Moyes said of him, 'Australians had seen Miller bowling for the first time in big cricket and they liked what they saw. It was perfectly obvious that another Test player had been developed by a Services' Team, a batsman of high quality and a fast bowler with real speed and clever skill as well.'

But, as we have seen, only two members of the team were chosen to tour New Zealand with the Australian side in March 1946. And Hassett was given neither the captaincy nor the vice-captaincy.

It is small wonder that the returned cricketers drew the conclusions which they unanimously held at the time.

7
Cricket under Bradman

Hassett and Miller sensed that the prevailing antagonism to some members of the Services Team, the prejudice against the team as a whole, extended beyond Australian officialdom to a number of the nation's leading cricketers (by no means all of them).

They attributed this attitude partly to envy of the experiences the team had undergone during its eight months' tour of England and India.

There was probably more to it than this. An uncomfortable, often embarrassing, rubicon existed at that time, dividing Australians who had, and Australians who had not, enlisted for service abroad. The Returned Servicemen's League did more to encourage than discourage it.

Following their matches against Australian State sides, Lindsay and Keith were well aware of the wealth of cricketing talent which had developed during their absence. It included Charlie Puckett in Perth; Bruce Dooland and Geff Noblet in Adelaide; Bill Johnston, Ken Meuleman, and Ian Johnson in Melbourne; Ray Lindwall, Ernie Toshack, and Sid Barnes in Sydney; and Colin McCool in Brisbane.

The two undiscarded members of the Services Team were determined to win selection for the approaching Test series against England and steeled their concentration so as to give of their best when they disembarked in New Zealand in late February of 1946.

Against Auckland in the opening game Miller 139, and Hassett

121, top-scored in a total of 579; but Barnes 107, Bill Brown 68, and Ken Meuleman 53 also performed well with the bat—and Toshack 7 for 91 rivalled O'Reilly's 9 for 103 with the ball. Against Wellington Hassett with 114 was the most successful batsman and in the Test there Brown 67, Barnes 54, and Miller 30, did best as batsmen and O'Reilly 8 for 33 and Toshack 6 for 18 as bowlers.

On an uncertain wicket in that only Test of the tour only 295 runs were scored. O'Reilly 5 for 14, and Toshack 4 for 14, dismissed New Zealand for 42. Australia closed on 199 for 4. O'Reilly 3 for 19 and Miller and Toshack, each 2 for 6, were the destroyers in New Zealand's second innings' 54.

Miller had now been away from home for more than four years. The burgeoning specialist batsman and easy-going youngster of the early 1940s had matured, had toughened, had learned a great deal about life and his fellow men. He was recognised as something of a war hero and outside Australia as the most colourful, probably the outstanding, all-round cricketer in the world. He was nonchalantly conscious of the name he had made for himself. Now 26, he was alert to the realities of the post-war world; realised that the pound of 1939 and a lot of other things, including gratitude and sincerity, had halved in value.

He was engaged to be married, confronted with responsibility. He had mixed with the establishment, sporting and otherwise, both in England and India, and had sampled their way of life. He was determined to provide a comfortable home among pleasant surroundings for himself and his wife—the kind of home and environment she had shared in Massachusetts.

Before joining the R.A.A.F. in 1941 Keith was employed by the Vacuum Oil Company in Melbourne in a junior and lowly-paid job. While waiting for an interview with the company manager in May of 1946 he saw a lot of young men who had remained in Australia throughout the war, saw them sitting in what he has described as 'cushy' positions. During his interview he was told that the only employment open to him was a dead-end position at a branch office in Yarraville, one of Melbourne's less-attractive suburbs.

He declined the offer. Then, after a fortnight without pay, changed his mind.

The humdrum and monotonous work he was given and the claustrophobic environment of Yarraville, however, came as a discouraging and dispiriting anticlimax. Receiving word that a passage on a ship to San Francisco was available he applied for two months' leave without pay to go to America and marry Peg Wagner.

'You have been away long enough. It's time you settled down and did some work,' his boss told him. Keith still had a good proportion of his deferred Air Force pay and, greatly incensed, he resigned on the spot.

Before leaving for America he called on an official of the Victorian Government and received a letter of introduction to an influential American. On arrival in California an immigration officer refused to allow him to disembark. The officer asked if he intended returning to Australia and was not satisfied with Keith's verbal assurance that he did.

Keith had not opened the letter from the Victorian official, believing it might be confidential. Feeling about as desperate as the boy David Copperfield on the London–Dover Road, he took the letter from his pocket and read: 'Please do what you can to see the bearer secures an early passage home to Australia. We need him for the cricket Tests against England this summer.'

Crossing the United States Keith married Peg Wagner in some style at Milton, Massachusetts. After a honeymoon, which included more visits to Boston Symphony Orchestra concerts beside the Charles River, he began planning his return to Australia.

Passenger planes were now spanning the Pacific. Keith landed at Essendon Airport in mid-November just in time to represent Victoria in its first Sheffield Shield game since 1940.

Short of practice, married, and unemployed, he had a deal on his mind when he took post at cover point against South Australia, led by Don Bradman, on the Melbourne Cricket Ground on 15 November. South Australia's opening batsman R. T. Craig drove the first ball of the match straight to Keith. It went through his fingers and legs to the boundary. 'Yer not on yer 'oneymoon now, Miller,' bawled a barracker from the Richmond end.

Keith silenced him by first taking 2 for 32 and then scoring 188 run out of Victoria's first innings 548, and 33 of its second innings 79 for 1.

According to *Sun-Pictorial* columnist and author Keith Dunstan's *The Paddock That Grew*: 'the next glimpse Melbourne had of the new Miller at full throttle was in the Victoria–New South Wales match. Miller came in when Victoria was 31 for 1. He had made just three runs when Toshack came on at the Richmond End.

'Miller, with a mighty hook, sent the third ball over the fine-leg fence, the sixth he lifted to a great height over square-leg and it carried the distance for another six. The seventh ball he drove with appalling force straight into Toshack's hands and it bounced out again. The crowd by now was roaring and, to celebrate his escape, Miller lifted the last ball high over the long-on fence—three sixes in one over.'

'That day,' continued Dunstan, 'the M.C.G. seemed to shrink in size. It was reported that every time Keith shaped to Toshack the crowd in the boundary seats ducked. He reached his 50 in 41 minutes and he had made 153 when he was run out.'

Hammond's M.C.C. team had arrived in Perth in October. During that season in Sheffield Shield games, before and between Tests, Miller scored 667 with a highest score of 206 not out for Victoria at an average of 133·40. As a bowler he took 11 for 231 at 21·00. The first Test Australians were to see for almost ten years began in Brisbane on 29 November.

Keith had been looking forward to meeting his old friends and foes Compton, Edrich, Hutton, and Hammond again, this time in an official Test, but a letter arrived for him, a letter from Lancashire, a few days after his return from the U.S.A. It offered him £1000 a season for the following three seasons with the Rawtenstall League Cricket Club.

Though he was regarded as a certainty for selection for Australia following that 188 against South Australia, he was still unemployed and he decided to accept what in those times was a highly tempting offer.

Learning he had done so his wife Peg said, 'You'd better post off another letter. Don't sell yourself short. And, besides, I don't fancy moving again.' Luckily, Keith had to pay only £50 to escape from that contract.

Keith's performances for Victoria and Australia that summer obviously were vital to his future. Upon his success or failure depended his chance of securing attractive employment at the end of the season.

After a deal of uncertainty Don Bradman had decided he was fit to return to Test cricket and resume the national captaincy. His performance, and Australia's, at Woolloongabba were also tremendously important to him. Winning the toss, he joined Sid Barnes with the total 9 for 1. After proceeding gingerly to 28 of 46 for 2, Don chopped with a diagonal bat at an offside half-volley from Voce. The ball travelled slowly and waist high to Ikin in the gully. Ikin grasped it and the Englishmen waited for Don to depart, believing no appeal was necessary.

But Don stood his ground and Umpire George Borwick decided in his favour. Hassett, who was at the bowler's end, has since supported Borwick's judgment, contending that the catch came from what is known as a bump ball. Hammond, fielding at first slip, had other ideas. At the end of the over he muttered to Bradman, 'This is a bloody fine way to begin a Test series.'

Bradman was not to forget that remark. He believed the ball had not flown direct from his bat to Ikin, that he had struck it while it was in contact with the pitch. The slow flight of the ball supported this explanation.

Overall in my experience of him Bradman deserved great credit for the manner in which he accepted his dismissals. I have never known him to show displeasure or dissent when umpires ruled against him, rarely even to question their decisions in the privacy of a dressing-room.

On that important day at Brisbane in November of 1946, however, Miller disagreed with Hassett and agreed with Hammond and the English team. He believed Bradman had been clearly and fairly caught, that he should have 'walked'. And, as he waited with his pads on for his turn to bat, he was reminded of another occasion at Melbourne in 1939 when *he* had been the batsman and Bradman the fieldsman.

At the M.C.G. over New Year in 1939–40 Keith had just passed that first century of his in big cricket, was 108 not out, when he played forward to a ball from Garth Burton and it went into Bradman's hands.

'I thought it was a bump ball,' he says in *Cricket Crossfire*. 'I stayed put at the crease but, as Bradman took the ball, he shouted,

"Oh, well bowled". I said inwardly, "Oh no, you aren't catching me napping like that". The umpire thought about it for some time and finally up went his finger.'

In Brisbane in 1946 as he watched Bradman 187, and Hassett 128, complete that decisive partnership of 276 of theirs Keith also thought of the Pepper incident at Adelaide and of Bradman's ruthless reaction to it. Big-match cricket played the Bradman way, he decided, was not going to be the friendly game he had grown to enjoy so much in England. On this very first day of this first post-war series between England and Australia it had threatened to develop into a substitute for war. Bradman clearly had not forgotten Jardine and 1932–33 or Hammond and that Fourth Test of 1938. 'In everything he undertook,' Keith was later to say, 'Don just *had* to win.'

Lindsay Hassett, who took 344 minutes to make his 128, appeared to have reached the same conclusion and he decided to conform to the pattern his captain was so obviously determined to set.

Following Don's dismissal at 322 for 3, Keith contributed what Johnnie Moyes described as 'an attractive and stately' 79 (actually he passed 50 in 80 minutes) towards an eventual total of 645, Australia's then highest total in Australia.

Bradman chose Lindwall and Miller not Lindwall and Toshack to open the attack. Soon after England's innings began, fierce, tropical storms brought torrential rain. Hot sun next morning burnt a crust on the wicket and converted it into one of those dreaded old-time Australian 'stickies' upon which the bounce and turn of a ball was unpredictable.

Though Lindwall failed to take advantage of the conditions Miller bowled Hutton for 7, dismissed Washbrook for 6, a gallant Edrich and Compton for 17 apiece, and then Ikin for nought to have England 5 for 56. Bradman had quickly replaced Lindwall with Toshack but the left-hander, operating under ideal conditions —similar conditions to those in which 'Dainty' Ironmonger at Melbourne in 1930–31 had taken 11 South African wickets for 24 runs inside 23 overs—had so far failed to take a wicket. The adaptable Miller had all five.

'Talent does what it can; genius what it must.' Though he had not bowled on a pitch like this one before, Miller had immediately

Top: Keith Miller and his wife Peg at Romano's, Sydney, soon after their marriage in 1946 (*Photo—John Fairfax & Sons*). *Bottom:* Keith Miller completes his famous straight drive during his first official Test innings—against England at Brisbane in 1946. Len Hutton is at slip (*Photo—News Ltd*)

The end of Miller's undefeated 141 in Australia's first innings against England in the Adelaide Test of 1947 (*Photo—News Ltd*)

and accurately assessed what was required of him. He kept the ball well up to the bat at well-controlled pace in line with the stumps and allowed the wicket to do the rest.

Only Hammond, with a brave and classic display of straight driving, delayed Keith's progress to an innings analysis of 22/4/60/7. From the other 60·5 overs bowled England lost 3 for 81.

While waiting for Hutton and Washbrook to come out to open England's second innings, facing a deficit of 504, Bradman led Toshack along the pitch and showed him exactly where he wanted him to pitch the ball. He had no need to instruct Miller. This time Don dispensed with Lindwall's services and gave the new ball to Keith and Toshack.

Rested after 11 overs, during which he had dismissed Hutton nought, and Washbrook 13, Miller emerged from his first official Test against England with an analysis of 33/7/77/9/8·55. Add to this his score of 79 and you will find few, if any, comparable all-round performances from a debut in the annals of Test cricket.

Australia won the Test by an innings and 322 runs. If that Vacuum Oil Company executive in Yarraville was at all patriotic and had studied the detailed scores in the Melbourne *Sun-Pictorial* he must have been at odds both with his conscience and his judgment.

Bradman, who had reinstated himself in Test cricket and led his country to its most colossal victory over England, seemed reasonably satisfied. But, for him, this was to be just the start of what can only be described as systematic slaughter.

Don has an encyclopaedic memory. That remark of Hammond's had found its pigeon-hole. His first Test match had been played in Brisbane in 1928. He scored 18 and 1. In it England defeated Australia by 675 runs. After it he was dropped from the Australian side, the most ludicrous piece of selection, surely, of all time.

Following his second dismissal, Maurice Tate called to the bowler J. C. 'Farmer' White, of Somersetshire, 'What do you mean by getting my rabbit?' Bradman overheard that remark and has never forgotten it—or 1932–33, or 1938.

History was vividly in his mind during the nine days that separated the first and second Tests of 1946–47 and he had never held any great liking for Hammond. For Don, England was far more than a cricketing opponent, she was Australia's, and his, traditional cricketing enemy.

Keith Miller had found Hammond a charming and sportsmanlike captain during the Victory Tests of 1945. He remembered that generous gesture of his during the Fourth Victory Test, that invitation for Hassett to use our twelfth man, Carmody, as wicketkeeper following the injury to Sismey. Hammond, as we have seen, had several times played host to the Services Team at dinners in London after play at Lord's.

On his way to Australia on the *Stirling Castle* in September 1946 I showed Hammond a cable from my editor which stated that Bradman would be returning to Test cricket and probably captaining Australia.

'That's grand. It will be a fine thing for cricket,' Wally immediately replied and his reaction was published in the Sydney *Sun*. Miller was told of it.

For him Hammond was a great and gallant opponent. During the Second Victory Test at Bramall Lane, as we have also seen, the Australian and English teams shared the same dressing-room. On the field competition between them was keen but never unfriendly. The members of both sides had experienced more than their fill of war.

England's annihilation at Brisbane had resulted mainly from the impossible state of the wicket on which she was twice forced to bat. Several of her batsmen, outstanding among them Hammond, Edrich, and Compton, had shown great physical courage on that diabolical and dangerous pitch—the kind of courage England's airmen had shown during the Battle of Britain. Faced with the same conditions Australia's batsmen, as Keith knew, probably would have performed far less admirably. He was hoping conditions would be fair to both sides when the tussle was resumed in Sydney.

As we were soon to see, Bradman had other ideas. Don, who had not experienced the horrors of total war, who had not been privileged to witness the average Englishman's stoic reaction to them, was determined to grind his old cricketing enemy into the dust if he could—to do so at the game England had invented, at the game she had adopted as a formative part of her way of life. England, if Bradman had his way, was not merely to be defeated but annihilated and humiliated. Keith found himself less than happy, as did the majority of sports-loving Australians (including two of their former Test cricket captains, Warwick Armstrong and Herbert Collins), with what now was to follow. And he lost a deal of regard for Bradman as a man, if never as a cricketer.

In that book of his, *Cricket Crossfire*, he says: 'Perhaps it was inevitable that Bradman's tough start, his tough break into first-class cricket, should contribute towards making him a ruthless opponent on the field.'

Rarely has even Don been more ruthless than he was in that Sydney Test of December 1946—and I stress this solely because I believe his conduct and control of it deeply affected Keith's approach to the remainder of the series; because it partly explains why only in Adelaide when Australia was in difficulty did he produce the batting form he showed consistently in Sheffield Shield games that summer for Victoria while amassing 667 from six innings at 133·40. Playing under a captain one not only admires but likes, under one whose policies one agrees with, can be an inspiring experience. Miller was not to have that good fortune. Not in 1946–47, 1947–48, or in 1948; anyway.

Of the Bradman and Hammond of 1946–47 he has written: 'The rivalry between these two was unmistakable from the start of the tour. In my opinion, the two great players were jealous of one another. There were times in the series when I felt it was not so much a battle between England and Australia as a battle between Bradman and Hammond.'

Of himself and Bradman he has written: 'Looking back I suppose it was inevitable that The Don and I should have clashed. Our temperaments [Keith could have added "our outlooks"] are so different.'

We shall come to examples of the clashes later. Now for that Sydney Test.

Hammond won the toss and England batted first. Lindwall, suffering from chickenpox, was unavailable and Fred Freer, a steady, Victorian, fast-medium bowler, became Keith's third new-ball partner in three Test innings.

A private, personal crisis in England and South Africa was preying upon Hammond's mind; it had begun to do so in Adelaide in late October and was to continue doing so for the remainder of the tour. It affected his usually sound judgment both as a batsman and captain and caused him to become defensive—at times almost paranoiacal. Hammond, despite the persistent barbs of the Press and the bewilderment and deep disappointment of his team, kept this problem a secret from all but his friend and team manager Rupert Howard.

Australia's attack this time was based mainly on the high-trajectory spin of George Tribe, Colin McCool, and Ian Johnson. Before England batted Hammond instructed his batsmen, and I have Bill Edrich's and Denis Compton's word for this, to refrain from dancing to the pitch of the ball and tackle it from the crease. Now 43 years of age, and less agile than he had been, Hammond adopted the same policy and it proved disastrous.

Hutton 39, Compton 5, and Hammond 1, were all caught at the wicket by Tallon from defensive strokes. Though Edrich scored 71 he fell lbw to McCool, also when playing back.

In the outcome Johnson took 6 for 42 from 30·1 overs and McCool 3 for 73. England, on a batsman's pitch, was dismissed for 255.

Johnson had been permitted to bowl without an outfield.

Sid Barnes and Arthur Morris had hardly opened Australia's innings when a heavy downpour interrupted play for more than three hours.

On resumption Edrich bowled Morris for 5 at 24 for 1 and Bradman, reported to be suffering from muscular strain, sent in his normally Number 7 batsman Ian Johnson as nightwatchman.

Australia was 27 for 1 over the weekend. On the Monday the pitch was perfect but Bradman, still handicapped by a strain in his leg, promoted Hassett and Miller above himself. Though Hassett scored 34 and Miller 40, Australia was 159 for 4 when 'The Don' joined Barnes.

They were separated only after adding 405 runs, still a record Test stand for any country for the fifth wicket. Bradman compiled his 234 in 394 minutes with twenty-four 4s—a very reasonable rate of progress when you compare it with Hutton's 364 in 797 minutes at Kennington Oval in 1938 and (even when allowance is made for the far slower over rates of 1977) with Geoff Boycott's marathons at Trent Bridge and Headingley.

Bradman had scored his 309 not out at Leeds in 1930 in less

than six hours, however, his 254 at Lord's that same year in 330 minutes, his 304 at Leeds in 1934 in 415 minutes at rates of 52, 46, and 44 runs an hour, respectively. This time he had progressed at under 36 runs an hour. News of his injury had been kept secret and his innings was classed as implacable.

Barnes' eventual 234 occupied 640 minutes and included only seventeen boundaries. He had travelled at 22 runs an hour without demur from his captain and the general impression gained as Australia, with six wickets standing, advanced to a lead of more than 300 runs, was that nails were being driven callously into England's coffin.

This impression was accentuated on the fifth morning of the match.

While the Englishmen waited for Bradman to inform them whether he intended to bat on beyond 600 or declare, Don spent some twenty minutes examining first the pitch and then the state of the sightboard at the Paddington end. Receiving no such notification, they trailed back on to the field and were kept there until 34 minutes before the luncheon interval.

By this time an undismissed Freer 28 and Tribe 25 had added 42 for the ninth wicket and Australia, 659 for 8, had broken the innings' record total all so recently established in Brisbane.

England would have to make two starts to their innings, one before lunch and another afterwards. They needed 404 runs to avoid a second, consecutive, innings defeat.

I visited the England dressing-room during the ten-minute interval and have never seen so angry a Test team. There was no obligation upon Bradman to notify his opponents of his intentions that morning, but the Englishmen, quite understandably in my opinion, regarded his failure to do so as an act of extreme discourtesy; as just another attempt to humiliate them.

Hammond instructed Hutton to demonstrate his team's displeasure immediately he took strike. Hutton, as a batsman, remains for many Englishmen as much of an enigma as does Miller, as an all-rounder, for many of the Australians who watched him.

During dinner one evening of 1960 in the Hastings–London train a friend of Denis Compton's asked him for his opinion as to whether he or Sir Leonard had been the greater batsman: 'I am looking for an honest answer or none at all, Denis. I won't divulge it to anyone. There's no occasion for you to be modest,' he said.

Denis replied unhesitatingly: 'Len was infinitely superior to me. The one thing about him I've never understood, however, is why in view of his great talent as a strokeplayer he allowed so many mediocre attacks to dominate him.'

In Hutton's case the answer probably lies in heredity, *and* upbringing. Sir Leonard, like Herbert Sutcliffe and Geoffrey Boycott, was born and bred in Yorkshire. He was groomed as a youngster in Pudsey by Sutcliffe, captained by Brian Sellars. He learned all the tricks of the cricketing trade in a Yorkshire classroom. That, I believe, is why he so often batted with the monastic discipline that Sutcliffe imposed upon himself in the 1920s and in the way Boycott did at Trent Bridge and Headingley in 1977.

Hutton's make-up was such that his nature was rarely at war with his technical brilliance. I have seen several examples of the degree of that brilliance and believe it is no exaggeration to say that had Len been born and reared in Kent, Sussex, Surrey, or Middlesex he would have developed into England's nearest approach to Victor Trumper.

Only when some extraordinary situation demanded it, or when he was ordered to do so by his captain, did Hutton take his foot from the pedal.

Hammond knew his Hutton, knew what he was doing when he chose Len to launch the onslaught upon Bradman's attack that December afternoon of 1946.

During the 24 minutes play before lunch he scored 37 against Miller and Freer; savaged their bowling with a display of strokes—hooking, driving, cutting, and glancing—that sent the memories of most of the octogenarians in the Sydney pavilion racing excitedly and happily back to the most electrifying exhibitions their idol Trumper had paraded before them.

Fate can be cruel, however. Attempting to hook Miller yet again to the leg boundary off the last ball before lunch, Hutton, still not completely recovered from the wartime fracture of his left forearm, lost control of his bat and it fell from his left shoulder on to his stumps.

There was no immediate cheer from the great crowd—only an awesome hush of sympathy and disappointment. It was as Hutton came towards the pavilion that the crowd rose and cheered him from the field. To a man, the tens of thousands present were saddened by his departure. They will remember that 37 when Bradman's 234 and Barnes' 234 are forgotten.

Though Washbrook 41, Edrich 119, Compton 54, Hammond 37, and Yardley 35 also expressed their disgust, and England reached an admirable 371, she failed to force Australia back to the creases.

Following victories by the colossal margins of an innings and 322 and an innings and 33, Australia led two-up with three Tests to play.

To the second massacre Miller contributed 40 runs and a match bowling analysis of 20/5/61/1, that wicket of Hutton's in the second innings.

England's destruction due to the weather in Brisbane and to Bradman's tactics in Sydney had fanned Keith's natural sympathy for the underdog. He did not enjoy the humiliation of men who had proved themselves champions before the war and who, during and after it, had grown to be his honoured and affectionate friends.

It is certain that Keith's feelings were shared by the majority of the Australian public and their Press. Australia's 1920–21 series captain Warwick Armstrong in his comments made no secret of his disapproval of what was transpiring, and Armstrong had led Australia to eight successive victories over England following an earlier World War.

Bradman, the batsman, was still Australia's hero. His courageous return to Test cricket with scores of 187 and 234 ensured that this should be so. It was his ruthless and implacable attitude as the nation's captain that caused him to lose popularity and, in some quarters, respect.

In these circumstances, enveloped as he was by so unpleasant, abrasive, and contentious an atmosphere, it was difficult for a person of Miller's nature and temperament to concentrate wholeheartedly and happily upon his cricket. For him a lot of the joy had gone from the game. It was no longer 'great fun'.

8
The reason for that mane of hair

Additional clues to the mystery of the change in Keith Miller's attitude to Test cricket came to me in Melbourne between the second and third Test matches of 1946–47.

They came from what most Australian cricketers and cricket writers of the 1930s, 1940s, and early-1950s—Jack Fingleton, Ray Robinson, Percy Beames, Arthur Mailey, Tom Goodman, and Jim Mathers—would have classed as a highly eccentric source.

The source was that truly Dickensian character, that 'Mr Dick' or 'Mr Winkle' of his time and circle, Percy John Millard, the senior cricket correspondent of the Melbourne *Herald and Weekly Times*.

I find it easy to appreciate why Jack Fingleton and company regarded Percy as more than something of a fool, as a character deserving rather of ridicule than of respect; why they believed he knew little of the finer points of cricket; why it was a constant cause of amazement for them that he had managed to hold down the most prized cricket-writing job in Australia since 1936.

They never took the trouble to seek below the surface of this naturally genial, occasionally (to his underlings and competitors) irritable, invariably flustered medley of a man. And Percy never invited such an inspection—for he had more than an average share of personal pride, was thin-skinned, and easily hurt.

Physically he was tallish, rather flabby. Facially he was demandingly caricaturable. He dressed conservatively, even drably, as a rule, but would astonish everyone on occasion by appearing like some downtown dandy (sporty bow tie, Edwardian waistcoat, and all) at important social functions.

Yes, I can well understand why, for Fingleton and Ray Robinson, Percy was a species of involuntary Falstaff or Touchstone at the Court of King Bradman. But I am surprised that these bookworms did not pause to reflect that neither of those jesters of William Shakespeare's were clots.

Both Falstaff and Touchstone were shrewd judges of character as well as jesters, and it is partly with judgment of character that this biography of Keith Miller is concerned.

Percy, who served as a foot-slogger and trench-dweller in France during the 1914–18 War, may well have fitted comfortably into that popular television series of the 1960s and 1970s *Dad's Army*; but for anyone who really took the care to know him he was nobody's fool.

What's more, as I came to discover soon after I met him, he knew a great deal about Keith Miller, had followed his career as a schoolboy cricketer, as a club cricketer, and during his first season in Sheffield Shield cricket.

Percy, as I have said, gained his job as the senior cricket correspondent of the Melbourne *Herald and Weekly Times* in 1936.

It was during the First Test between Gubby Allen and Don Bradman's teams in Brisbane, in December of that year, that his opportunity came.

The regular cricket writer of the *Herald* became unwell and Percy, his understudy, was flown north to cover the final day's play.

Before it had ended Allen 5 for 36, and Voce 4 for 16, had dismissed Australia—Bradman, Fingleton, and Badcock each nought—for 58. Australia, the strong favourites, had lost by the monumental margin of 322 runs.

'This isn't cricket. It's massacre,' Percy cabled his editor—at urgent rates. And, on the strength of those five graphic words, he was instructed to cover the remainder of the M.C.C. tour. Thus began a career that, admittedly, was to have many most peculiar, at times hilarious, moments.

Irrespective of the state of a match or the quality of the play during the 1946–47 Hammond team tour, with which we are involved, Percy always left the Press box well before stumps. Once his last deadline had been met he would replace the battered cover of his old, black typewriter, gather his copy paper and carbons together, pack them, his *Wisden*, and his notebooks into his dilapidated briefcase, don an ancient pair of gloves, and make tracks for his home or hotel.

The cricket, at least for an hour in the eastern States and (owing to the time lag) for three hours in Perth, went on without him. It is really no wonder that the mechanics of this ritual of his were watched with both amusement and amazement by Fingleton, Robinson, and Arthur Mailey. And by Beames with disgust.

Once during the Melbourne Test of 1946 Percy aroused the curiosity of his colleagues by returning rather furtively to his seat some minutes after he had vacated it. Removing his gloves, opening his typewriter, and strewing some papers about his desk he began staring at the play as if his life depended upon it.

'What's happened Percy? Why are you back?' Arthur Mailey inquired.

'Saw our managing-director Sir Keith Murdoch coming through the Members' turnstile,' Percy explained. 'Damn nuisance. Won't get a taxi now.'

During England's first innings of that Test Cyril Washbrook was caught at the wicket by Don Tallon off Bruce Dooland and Percy had not been paying attention.

'How was he out?' he demanded.

'Caught behind,' he was told.

'Who caught him?' he asked, before he had gathered his thoughts.

I am afraid Percy, who has long departed this earth, will always be remembered for that bloomer of his on that early January day of now more than thirty years ago—for it and for the occasion at Headingley, Leeds, when this flustered and frantic dispatcher of urgent cables, this man who seemed to work through fear, found a carrier pigeon alighting alongside that trusty, old, black typewriter of his.

On that second occasion the pigeon behaved less than well, missing the typewriter by a very small margin. Seemingly unmoved by the unique intrusion, and the laughter it occasioned, Percy did the necessary mopping up and returned feverishly to his task.

Before we get to the crux of this chapter, the reason for its inclusion in this book, I find myself unable to resist reporting yet another peculiarity of Percy's.

This senior correspondent of the Melbourne *Herald* was deeply conscious of his limitations as a writer, knew he was no Neville Cardus. To compensate as best he could, he carried a pocket dictionary and an old, black-covered notebook about with him.

In the notebook in alphabetical order, he maintained a list of adjectives which he used with impeccably impartial frequency—heedless of their relevance or irrelevance at the time.

In Percy's opinion a cover-drive by Bradman, Hammond, Hutton, or Compton could be 'copybook', 'crashing', 'dazzling', 'devastating', 'elegant', 'graceful', or 'handsome'.

Each time he used one of these words he inserted a tick in the column alongside it in that notebook; kept a running score of its usage from hour to hour. Seven cover-drives later he would use it again. There was no televised coverage of cricket in the 1930s, 1940s, and early-1950s. What the hell if some of Hutton's or Hammond's most elegant cover-drives were described as 'crashing' or 'devastating' when they merely glided through the gap to the boundary?

For Percy, as senior cricket correspondent of Melbourne's most prestigious newspaper, his prose was the most important thing. I suppose it was because I had befriended him, helped him with many of his problems (as he had helped me, a rookie cricket writer, with mine) along the trail from Perth to Brisbane and back that summer, that during the Second Test in Sydney Percy suggested I stay with him and his wife during the few days preceding the New Year's Test.

'You must be sick of hotels and hotel food,' he said. 'Besides I have told my wife about your kindness to me and she very much wants to meet you.'

It had never occurred to me that Percy should have a wife. Not because he was a philanderer. On the contrary, he had never in my experience of him shown the slightest inclination for the company of the opposite sex—was far too busy, I gathered, keeping those records and that notebook of his up to date, dogwatching for snippets of news.

Just what sort of woman, I wondered, would accept Percy for her partner in life? What would he be like in his own home? Would this frantic news-gatherer and dispatcher ever be able to sit still, to relax for more than a few seconds? It would be interesting to discover these things. Additionally, I wanted to have a long talk with him, if this were at all possible, on the subject of Keith Miller.

For these reasons I decided to accept his invitation.

I'll never forget our arrival at his home from the airport that night. After opening his front gate he crossed the lawn to what appeared to be a garage, opened the door and glanced up at the rafters under the galvanised roof.

On one of them rested a newish car battery which Percy, I correctly deduced, had removed from the gleaming, also newish, family model car beneath it.

There was a delighted, almost boyish, gleam behind my host's thick and metal-rimmed bifocals.

'She hasn't found it,' he exclaimed.

'Who hasn't found what?' I asked.

'My wife hasn't found the car battery. The last time I was away she disobeyed me, drove the car, and had a minor collision. She's a terrible driver, even for a woman.'

My anxiety to meet Mrs Millard increased. My curiosity mounted.

'Don't say we've been to the garage,' Percy said as we re-crossed the lawn to the lighted main door, lugging our luggage.

When the door opened I received another surprise. Mrs Millard proved to be tall, slim, shapely, and strikingly handsome for a woman whom I judged to be in her early forties—handsome yet severe, elegantly dressed. There was an air of Daphne Du Maurier's Mrs Danvers about her.

Despite the trick Percy had played upon her—the trick she, no doubt, had discovered—she greeted him affectionately. Her regard for him was clearly considerable.

Only later, as she listened to and watched him in the living-room, did she bestow in my direction a conspiratorial wink.

It was after we had supped very well, shared a bottle of excellent French wine, and were sipping some fine, old, French brandy from most expensive-looking goblets that the conversation turned to Keith, for whom Mrs Millard, like most women who have known him, held an extremely soft spot.

'What happened to Keith in India?' she asked.

I did my best, without delving into idle gossip, to elucidate.

'Keith will always be Keith,' Percy said.

'And what exactly do you mean by that?' I asked, grasping my opportunity.

'I've known and watched him since he was a boy. Watched him play cricket and football for Melbourne High School and for South Melbourne and St Kilda. He was an outstanding footballer, could have represented Victoria regularly at football had he wished. So could have Lindsay Hassett for that matter. Keith was a full back, Lindsay a rover.'

I did not want the conversation to turn to Lindsay.

'I'm more interested in Keith at the moment, in what you think, what both of you think, explains his attitude to his sport, why he's so unpredictable, so contradictory, so different in so many ways from other champions,' I said.

'For one thing, he was very self-conscious as a youngster; still is,' Percy replied.

'Not Keith,' I said, wondering what self-consciousness had to do with the matter, how it explained what I was trying to elicit.

'Yes, Keith,' Percy replied and I saw Mrs Millard nodding her head in agreement.

'What's he got, what's he had, to be self-conscious about?' I asked.

'As a youngster it was his height—or lack of it, rather. He hated having to look up at other boys of his age—and at girls of his age. He was deeply embarrassed about it. He didn't begin to grow at all normally, you know, until he was sixteen.'

'Well, he doesn't have to worry about his height now. He's inches over six feet.'

'No, now it's his head.'

'His *head*?' I exclaimed, thinking Fingleton, Robinson, and Beames were right, that Percy was 'bats', or at best batty.

'Yes his head. Why do you think he's grown that mane of hair?'

I hadn't thought deeply at all about that; about Keith's reasons for sprouting locks that would be normal, even conservative, nowadays; that would hardly have satisfied Max Walker, Ian

Chappell, or Dennis Lillee—let alone Bob Willis.

'I don't know. I haven't a clue,' I said.

'It's because he has such a small head, one quite out of proportion for a man of his size. He's very self-conscious about it—even now he's grown that mane. Haven't you noticed how he's always running his fingers through his hair and rubbing his face?'

'Yes, now you've mentioned it.'

Mrs Millard had left the room. She returned a few moments later with two framed photographs of Keith, one of them taken when he was in his teens and had short-cropped hair, the other of more recent vintage.

'Percy is right, you know,' she said. 'Look at these.'

'Haven't you noticed that his hands are never still?' Percy continued after I'd studied the photographs. 'If you tied them behind his back he'd be inarticulate.'

This was the pot calling the kettle black if ever there had been an example of it. I decided to let it pass, however, and Mrs Millard contributed another of her winks.

'How does all this affect his cricket, though?' I asked.

'It affects his greatest problem, his concentration. He's never completely relaxed, involved. He can't ever forget when he's on the field, most of all when he's batting, that he's being watched by thousands of people. He just has to do something about it. That's why he's always playing to the gallery, though it's quite out of character for him to do so. He's a very modest and self-effacing person, really.'

'There *are* times when he's completely involved,' I insisted.

'I know; those times when he achieves his greatest performances. I'm speaking generally.'

I had begun to understand what Percy was getting at, to appreciate the significance of his disclosures.

Had Bradman suffered from, been distracted by, self-consciousness, he must have made a lot less runs, even *his* concentration must have wandered.

'Keith enjoys bowling now far more than batting, you know,' Percy went on. 'When he's bowling he doesn't have to stand still. There's a lot more to it than what I've told you, of course. Keith's a very temperamental person, a very moody one and his moods affect his play. He needs to feel he is liked, though he's embarrassed by applause. I've often seen him go out of his way, even take risks, to make sure the crowd are on his side.'

So had I, I recalled; had done so many times; had seen Keith lose his wicket in consequence.

'He's always had a chip on his shoulder, too,' Percy went on.

'Why, do you think?'

'Partly because he was such a midget as a kid, partly because of the setbacks he met when he was trying to break into club and big cricket. That's partly why he's so often at odds with authority; so often on the side of the underdog.'

'He certainly has been this summer—in the Sydney Test, anyway. I hardly think he approves of what Bradman seems bent on doing to the "Poms".'

'Was there trouble between Lindsay and Keith during the Services tour?' Percy asked.

'Why do you ask that?'

'We heard there was. The two of them have never been very close. They're totally different people. Keith always likes to call a spade a spade. Lindsay keeps his thoughts to himself.'

'There was never any *open* trouble between them,' I said.

'There will be between Keith and Don Bradman,' Mrs Millard interjected. 'It's a certainty if Don keeps on the way he is.'

I attributed her remarks to women's intuition at the time; but all too soon they were to prove all too right.

It was just before we all went to bed that Mrs Millard said, 'We're very fond of Keith, you know, Percy and I. We worry about him, always have. I hope he has friends in the Australian side. He's going to need them.'

'He has friends in both the Australian and English teams,' I said. 'Ray Lindwall, Don Tallon, and Colin McCool are his best Australian friends, I think, and Denis Compton, Bill Edrich, and Godfrey Evans his best English ones. He gets on quite well with Arthur Morris.'

'And what about Wally Hammond?'

'Why Hammond?'

'Because there's going to be an open blow-up between Hammond and Bradman before very long and if Keith's loyalties are confused Bradman will soon know and it won't help Keith, could harm his whole career. Don's always been a dictator, expects his team to be 100 per cent his way.'

'You seem to know a lot about cricket and cricketers, Mrs Millard?' I said. 'For a woman, I mean.'

'Percy confides in me a great deal.'

'Keith had a great liking for Wally in England. He admires him tremendously, of course, as a player. I think Wally's got him a bit puzzled at the moment. And not only Keith, his own team as well—especially Denis Compton. Wally's a changed man on this tour, has been since they reached Adelaide. He's allowed things to get him down.'

'Probably developed Bradman-phobia, and so will Keith unless he controls himself.'

Strange that Mrs Millard should be so bad a driver, I thought. She seemed to have heaps of commonsense. Thanks to her and her husband the jigsaw puzzle that for me had been Keith Miller was beginning to take shape.

Top: MCC manager Rupert Howard, Australian captain Don Bradman, and England captain Walter Hammond dining together during the torrid 1946–47 series. According to Miller this was more of a feud between Bradman and Hammond than a fight between Australia and England (*Photo — Sydney* Sun). *Bottom:* Miller clean bowled by Johnny Wardle on the first day of the Second Test at Lord's in 1953. The 'keeper is Godfrey Evans, Denis Compton is at slip, and Alec Bedser is at top left of the picture (*Photo — Associated Press*)

Top: Keith Miller with his famous bowling partner Ray Lindwall (*left*) and Australia's magnificent left-handed opening batsman Arthur Morris (*centre*) (*Photo—John Fairfax & Sons*). *Bottom:* Miller after being hit on the thumb by a ball during the Australians' game against Yorkshire in May 1953. He was 109 n.o. at the time (*Photo—Central Press Photos*)

9
There's wisdom in women

The people of Keith's home city Melbourne, including Mrs Millard, had not seen him perform in a Test match. They had read of his exploits in England, however. His exhilarating innings of 188 against South Australia and his century of the previous week against the traditional enemy New South Wales (that 153 in almost-even time, those 6s he had struck off Toshack) were fresh in their memory.

They were hoping to see him at his greatest, both as batsman and bowler, when they flocked to the Jolimont Ground, that 'Paddock That Grew', during the first week of 1947.

In the event he scored 33 out of 365 and 34 out of 536 and took 2 for 75 from the 21 overs that Bradman gave him of the 206·5 bowled by Australia.

Australia's batting stars on this occasion were Colin McCool, 104 in the first innings; and Arthur Morris 155, and Ray Lindwall 100, in the second. Eight scores of over 40 were compiled by Australia's batsmen. Even its wicketkeeper Don 'Deafy' Tallon dashed up 92 in 88 minutes during an eighth-wicket stand of 154 with Lindwall.

Bruce Dooland, 4 for 69 in the first innings, was Australia's outstanding bowler. Miller's two victims were Ikin and Alec Bedser towards the close of the drawn, six-day match.

Throughout most of its 1800 minutes Keith seemed oddly uninterested in proceedings; in helping to hammer the third and decisive nail in England's cricketing sarcophagus.

Maybe the manner in which his two best English cricketing friends Bill Edrich and Denis Compton were dismissed in their first innings contributed to this—those two highly controversial dismissals which toppled England from 167 for 2 to 179 for 4 in chase of 365?

Though he claimed to have snicked the ball, Edrich was adjudged lbw to Lindwall on 89—when 11 runs from his second lost-cause century in successive Tests. Though Compton's pad seemed between 15 and 30 centimetres outside his leg stump, he was ruled lbw to Toshack when 11 and showing positive signs of a return to top form.

Some ten years later Jack Scott, the umpire concerned, confessed tearfully to me at the Adelaide Oval that he had taken twelve aspirin before officiating that day to deaden the pain in his hip.

'I know I shouldn't have gone on to the field. I was half-drugged and couldn't concentrate properly,' he said. 'I realised I had made two vital mistakes and spent much of that Wednesday night wandering about the streets of Melbourne.'

Keith, as we have seen, is intolerant of injustice. Probably he had no wish to take advantage of it while England struggled to 351. Or when Australia batted again.

I know that he spent the early part of that second night of the Test with me in my room at the Australia Hotel in Collins Street during which time the last thing he wanted to discuss was cricket.

'I couldn't care less about it just now,' he said.

We helped to brighten that second very hot night of the new year, I remember, by taking schooners of iced ale to the bewitching blonde and brunette lift attendants, Maggie Nolan and Biddy Jeans, by handing them to them every quarter of an hour or so as they paused at the eighth floor.

Fortunately lifts can't collide.

Eventually some cricketing fanatic rang and invited us to a barbecue at Warrandyte along the Yarra. Though it was after 10 p.m. Keith suggested we accept. This total stranger had a chauffeur and chose Miller as his companion in the rear seat of his big, black car.

As we were reboarding the car for the 20-kilometre return journey to the city, Keith said, '*You* can share the back seat with him this time,' and dived in alongside the chauffeur.

We hadn't travelled far before I understood why Keith was laughing his head off up front. Fortunately I managed to hail a taxi in Toorak Road.

This character had certainly misjudged his Miller; as so many before and since have done.

England were two Tests down with two to play when the series was resumed on 31 January in Adelaide. Compton, two centuries, and Joe Hardstaff, 188, had at last found their true form in Tasmania. Wally Hammond had been enjoying a fortnight's rest in Glenelg, that Adelaide beach suburb which is spellable back to front.

Don Bradman has insisted that he contacted Wally during that fortnight and invited him to dine at his home in Kensington Park, and that the reaction of England's captain was an immediate and unsociable 'No'.

The Ashes battle between Australia and England, between Bradman and Hammond, was to continue in the same acrimonious atmosphere. England for the first time won the toss and totalled 460—Compton 147, Hutton 94, Washbrook 65, and Hardstaff 67.

At one stage of his innings Denis Compton walked down the wicket to dispose of a stray piece of grass. Bradman's reaction was, 'Keep off that wicket, we've got to bat on it next.'

Referring to this incident in *Cricket Crossfire* Keith has written: 'Anyone who knew Denis knew he just would not damage a wicket deliberately . . . What a narrow attitude.'

When Australia batted, Bedser made a swift, double breakthrough. Pitching the ball on what some highly imaginative journalist alleged was a 7·5-centimetre diameter dent, he bowled Bradman for a duck to make it 18 for 2.

In *Cricket Crossfire* Keith wrote: 'When he came back to the dressing-room Don was at great pains to tell everybody he considered this was one of the best balls ever bowled to him . . . Bradman tried to infer that this was an unplayable ball . . . He would have done better to keep the opinion to himself. He did no service to those who still had to face Alec.'

Fair comment, one suggests, considering Australia, with Mervyn Harvey and Bradman gone, was trailing by 442.

Fortunately Arthur Morris 122, and Lindsay Hassett 78, encountered no 'unplayable' balls and by 4.40 p.m. of a hot and humid Monday Australia was 207 for 3. Despite Morris and Hassett's stand of 189, however, it still was 253 behind when Miller came in.

Something, possibly Bradman's brush with Compton or his reaction to his own dismissal—more probably Australia's still serious situation—had restored Keith's competitiveness. He was raring to succeed.

At stumps on that third day the total was 293 for 4. On the Tuesday, to complete what 'Johnnie' Moyes described as 'a grand innings', Keith hit a 6 from the first ball he faced and continued brilliantly for an additional 61 in 71 minutes to be 141 not out of 487. He had scored those 141 out of 260 while seven wickets fell.

Nobody except that imaginative archaeologist in the Press box had discovered any signs of a dent in the pitch. Keith had chosen the right time to compile his first century in an official Test, had played a magnificent knock for one who, in his captain's opinion, 'was apt to be over-rated as a batsman'.

It was that night in my old home town that I hit upon what I still believe to be the skeleton key to the make-up of the hero of this biography.

Keith needed some unusual situation, some exceptional occasion, some extraordinary incident, some irritating conduct by colleague or adversary to incite him to his superlative best, to ignite his somnolent ambition, to help him discipline his wayward concentration.

Release from the perils of war, his team's need, his own need to prove himself, and the rivalry between its R.A.A.F. and A.I.F. players had sharpened incentive during the Victory Tests. So had his debut as a fast bowler. His determination to show he could outbat even Hammond and Hutton had done so during that great innings of his for the Dominions at Lord's.

His anxiety to dismiss Sid Barnes cheaply and outshine everyone as a batsman had been the spurs during the Services Team's contest with New South Wales. He had been riled by the contemptuous comments of the Sydney Press.

That opportunity to exploit a sticky wicket had provided the challenge in his first official Test match at Brisbane.

Why had only his partner's complaint about the burglary of

that bat at Calcutta done so throughout the three months' tour of India? I have done what I can to explain.

As we follow Keith's career onward from that great innings of his at Adelaide to his retirement in 1956 we shall find much to confirm and little to refute these contentions.

They, when added to Mrs Percy Millard's diagnoses, surely account for Keith's overall inconsistency; what might be called his fickle flirtation with fame. They explain why one naturally imbued with the 'killer instinct', and equipped with the instruments for indulging it, should have disdained so many opportunities for slaughter and neglected so many chances of displaying his greatness.

Keith lacked the consistent urge to conquer, to excel, to annihilate that was so conspicuous in Bradman and O'Reilly, in Larwood and Trueman and, as a captain, in Douglas Jardine.

Unlike so many of history's greatest batsmen, W. G. Grace, Sir Jack Hobbs, his boyhood idol Bill Ponsford, Herbert Sutcliffe, Bradman, Walter Hammond, Hutton, and now Boycott, he had no interest in his average or in the breaking of records. Bowling, for him, was just an avenue for adventure, a favourite way of releasing and expending his exceptional physical resources, of indulging his appetite for experiment.

Maybe, had he never become a great fast bowler, he would have been far more consistent as a batsman. No cricketer in history, not even Gary Sobers, has established a position among the leading few, statistically, in both departments of the game.

Back to our war of 1946–47 and the fortunes of our wayward warrior.

When England batted again at Adelaide Hutton and Washbrook hooked the frequent bumpers of Lindwall and Miller so heartily they scored the first 87 of their eventual 100 stand in 57 minutes.

Those sitting at right angles to the pitch were in no doubt that the snick which brought Washbrook's dismissal for 39 by Lindwall bounced well short of wicketkeeper Tallon. But the umpire, both umpires, disagreed with them. England had been unfairly treated yet again.

At the end of that tiring day Miller, to quote his own words, 'was sitting in the dressing-room as near to exhaustion as I can remember and replacing lost energy with a glass of beer.

'Bill Jeanes, the secretary of the Australian Board of Control walked in and said, "Come on, hurry up, Keith. We've got to get off. The taxis will be ready soon."

'I said, "I'm pretty tired. We've been in the field all day and it was damned hot out there."

'Jeanes was the manager of the team and he replied, "The taxi bill is getting hot, too." He again ordered me to hurry. That made me mad. "You fellows have been sitting all day doing nothing," I snapped back and a row quickly developed.

'Jeanes promptly reported me to Bradman. Soon afterwards I got a message from "The Don" asking me to go and see him next morning at his office. Bradman explained that Jeanes had been recently ill. He conceded that Jeanes probably was hasty and asked me to forget the incident. That was OK as far as it went, but Bradman's peremptory "summons" irritated me. I had to walk from my hotel to his office and as I walked my thoughts ran: "Here I am just back from the war, a war which has been dangerous for me in parts, and I am sent for like an erring schoolboy called to the Head's study. He could have come to my room or spoken to me at the ground, but—oh no, that wasn't good enough for 'The Don'."'

Lindwall and Miller had disposed of Yardley and Bedser, respectively, late on that Wednesday evening, Compton and Godfrey Evans were the not-out batsmen, and England at 274 for 8 were 247 ahead with 330 minutes' play remaining.

Evans, who took 95 minutes to score his first run, and Compton 103, who made his second century of the match, survived the morning session on the Thursday. England 340 for 8 now led by 314 with 210 minutes play remaining.

Hammond, probably because he remembered Bradman's dilatory declaration at Sydney, sent Compton and Evans back to the wicket after lunch. After one ball had been delivered he closed the innings. Australia now had 195 minutes to get those 314 runs and had only to draw the match to decide the series. England needed to win to keep it and the destination of the Ashes open.

It was an extraordinary policy of Hammond's and attributed by some to spite.

Commenting on Australia's reaction to it, her 1924–25 and 1926 captain Herbert Collins said: 'Morris gave Australia a great start on a still-perfect wicket but, after the first wicket fell, Bradman monopolised the strike and played copybook but not victory-seeking cricket. With so many wickets in hand and two Test matches up her sleeve Australia should have kept a few solid batsmen in reserve and sent her big hitters, Lindwall, Miller and company, in to give it a go. Australia forgot that day that cricket is only a game and I told Bradman so to his face. "You're a little strong, aren't you?" he replied.

'But I know the crowds that flocked down to the Adelaide Oval that afternoon and paid to see a fight for a win will never forget or forgive. The attendances at cricket matches at Adelaide Oval have not recovered from that blow.'

I have quoted Collins simply because Miller, despite that summons to Don's sharebroking office earlier that day, proved himself a big enough person to disagree with him.

This is what he has to say in *Cricket Crossfire* and it shows that his opinions are based neither on idolatry nor enmity.

'I thought Hammond batted on after lunch more to annoy Bradman than to give Australia ten minutes less to get the runs. Our task was hopeless at lunch. Bradman was criticised for not sending me in after our first wicket fell (at 100). I had made 141 not out in the first innings and in some quarters it was suggested that, if I had gone in at first wicket down and not Bradman, I would have scored faster and Australia might have won. They were wrong . . . Actually I admired Bradman for not sending me in first wicket down. Had he done so he might have made certain of avoiding the risk of getting the first pair (of ducks) of his career. Instead, he faced up to it and made 56 not out.'

Arthur Morris, 122 in his first innings, was 124 not out in his second. He and Compton had both scored dual centuries in the same Test which finished with Australia 215 for 1, 99 short of its target.

There ended the war between Bradman and Hammond, indeed Hammond's great Test career. Alleged to be suffering from fibrositis, he withdrew into history from a Test career begun nineteen summers before in Johannesburg.

From 140 Test innings Hammond scored 22 centuries, eight of them (including four double-centuries) against Australia, made 24 other scores of 50 or more. His Test aggregate is 7249 and his average 58·45. From 7967 deliveries he captured 83 wickets at 37·83. At first slip, where probably only Bobby Simpson was his peer, he held 110 catches.

It is tragic that he should have left the cricket stage as he did, more tragic that he should have died as he did, nineteen years later.

Fate is no respecter of cricket champions. As Wally was driving home up the Durban–Pietermaritzburg Road one evening the nearside tyre of an oncoming truck blew out. The vehicle veered directly towards Hammond's car. Left with no alternative except a head-on collision or a desperate swerve down a steep embankment, Wally chose the latter. As his car overturned three times his foot was jammed between the clutch pedal and the floor and he received fatal injuries to his head.

So, inside three years the world lost in tragic circumstances two of its most memorable batsmen, Hammond and McCabe. Within four months in 1915 it had lost W. G. Grace and Victor Trumper.

The old Italian saying, 'Non rammentare che le ore felici' (Remember only the happy hours) seems especially appropriate before we proceed towards Keith Miller's part in the final Test of 1946–47.

In this anti-climax to so torrid a series he contributed 23 and 34 not out and took the wickets of tailenders Wright and Evans at a cost of 42 runs.

The Test, which Australia won by five wickets, was played in Sydney and it was Sydney's Ray Lindwall, 7 for 63 in England's first innings, who was the Australian destroyer and star.

In the five Tests, however, Keith had scored 384 runs at 64·00 and taken 16 wickets at 20·87. An impressive debut; worthy of a champion if one forgets that 141 of the runs had been scored in one innings at Adelaide and seven of the wickets taken in another at Brisbane.

If one also forgets that in four Sheffield Shield games for Victoria that season he scored 667 runs with a highest score of 206 not out at an average of 133·40 against such bowlers as Geff Noblet, Bruce Dooland, Ray Lindwall, Ernie Toshack, and Colin McCool.

10
An earthquake in Adelaide

Ask any octogenarian who watched it and he will proclaim what is still known as 'Ivor Nicolle's kick' to be the most dramatic ever seen at the Adelaide Oval.

This was the penalty kick, one booted through goal from outside the western boundary after the final bell, with which the bald-headed Nicolle won the South Australian Football League premiership for Sturt way back in 1919—turned a one-point deficit into victory by five.

The suspense while that final kick of the winter, that acute-angle miracle was in flight, was certainly tremendous. The reaction as the ball bisected the goal posts was deafening. But, having been present on both occasions, I believe another kick, one that came not from the black boot of an ageing Australian Rules Football ruckman but the white boot of an Australian fast bowler, is equally memorable.

This kick of January 1948 was made spontaneously but deliberately in mid-afternoon of a cricket Test between Australia and India. It travelled no more than twenty metres without leaving the turf, trickled from the bowling crease at the Torrens River end to cover-point. But it stunned the 20 000-strong crowd.

As it progressed like a time bomb from the boot of Keith Miller to the feet of his captain Don Bradman everyone—even the sophisticated society women present—held their breath, wondering just what 'The Don' would do.

This time it was not the clamour but the silence that was

deafening. The crowd rightly sensed that this kick was a declaration of independence.

Don was then at the pyramid of his fame and authority. He occupied a pedestal, had attained a stature in Australian sport that is still unique and which may never be paralleled. Less than two months previously he had become the first (still the only) Australian to compile a century of hundreds in first-class cricket. In this very match he had made 201, his third Test century in successive innings, his fourteenth Test double- or triple-century. He held just about every record cricket exposes to an Australian batsman and as a captain he had wielded tremendous power behind what was regarded as his throne.

No Australian captain, let alone Bradman, had been treated so impudently in public by a member of his team, by a player eleven years his junior, or had been placed in so embarrassing a predicament.

Bradman had just fielded the ball and thrown it to Miller. Fieldsmen are expected to return balls to bowlers, especially to fast bowlers on hot afternoons, on the full—preferably about waist-high. Captains are expected to set an example in this respect.

Don, almost invariably, had done so during a career extending over twenty years. For once, however, he had lapsed, had unintentionally lobbed the ball on the half-volley at Miller's toes. Keith had stopped the ball with his ankle, had stood, hands on hips, staring down at it and then across at Bradman.

Eventually he took careful aim and kicked the ball directly towards his captain. Don would have to bend down and pick it up for a second time, would have to return it again to the bowler before those 20 000 spectators who looked upon him as the Caesar of cricket.

To find a parallel for Keith's action one would have to imagine some ragamuffin casting a coin at the feet of that other Caesar, Julius, on the steps of the Capitol in Ancient Rome; or one of his marshals hurling his baton at the boots of Napoleon.

The world stopped and waited. And, for a short while, 'The Don' was clearly at a loss to decide just what to do. All his inclinations must have been to kick that ball back from whence it had come.

But nobly he restrained himself and stooped—not to conquer

but to pick up the ball. Having done so, he saved (possibly gained) face by throwing it to his vice-captain Hassett, who was fielding closer to Miller at mid-off. Even the poker-faced Lindsay had difficulty in concealing his feelings as he relayed the ball waist-high to the rebel.

That gesture of Miller's signified and released feelings which had been coming to the boil for quite some time. It told his captain in the presence of those 20 000 people that, unlike some of his teammates, he was nobody's slave, that he had a mind of his own, that disagreement is a different thing from disobedience.

Earlier that afternoon Keith had asked Don to station a fieldsman between square- and fine-leg when he was bowling to Vijay Hazare. Hazare, who was well on his way to the first of his two centuries in that Test, had been repeatedly steering the ball through this inviting gap to the short Adelaide Oval boundary.

'Bradman,' Keith has written 'refused even to consider my request. I had been bowling flat out, giving it everything I had, and Bradman's action riled me. I finished one over with two slow off-spinners and he took me off.'

Keith had been warned by several of Don's contemporaries of the 1930s that he was a complete authoritarian, a law unto himself, that if you wanted to get on under his command you had to be, at least appear to be, 100 per cent *for* him.

Keith knew what had happened to Clarrie Grimmett, who had always reserved the right to speak his mind to, and about, Bradman. He knew what had happened to another of Don's critics, Victor Richardson; what had happened to Cecil Pepper on this very same cricket field only two years before. But he was determined to show he was nobody's sycophant. To hell with the price he might have to pay.

That kick on 26 January of 1948 *was* intended to be his personal declaration of independence and Bradman could react to it as he pleased. It was unconcealed evidence of the existence of a difference in outlook, an incompatibility between him and his skipper that was to continue and grow during the remainder of Don's career, and to survive his retirement.

It led to recurring repercussions in England later that year and, as I have sound reason to believe, it helps to account for Keith's original omission from the 1949–50 tour of South Africa; from the team which Don helped to choose.

It informed Bradman, as others had tried to inform him (usually to their disadvantage), that champions are nobody's bell-boys and that they have the right to disagree, if not to disobey.

Yes, that was a momentous kick and, like Ivor Nicolle's, it found and penetrated its mark.

We are ahead of ourselves, however.

At the conclusion of the Hammond Team tour of Australia, in early March of 1947, Keith faced enough personal problems to have tried the wisdom of King Solomon.

He had very little money, no prospect of reasonably remunerative or congenial employment in Melbourne, and no home of his own. His young wife, who had been reared in luxury in an idyllic part of Massachusetts, was due to join him shortly.

Even when a liquor sales company offered him a job in Sydney it presented him with another dilemma. Keith's old club, South Melbourne, for which Lindsay Hassett and Ian Johnson also played, had its best chance for some thirty years of winning the Melbourne first-grade premiership. It was favourite to take the pennant with two rounds of games to be played, two games which would be conducted over the following four Saturday afternoons.

South Melbourne is a very proud and famous club, the only Australian cricket club which has given its nation six cricket captains—Blackham, Harry Trott, Warwick Armstrong, Woodfull, Hassett, and Ian Johnson. The club had given Keith his first chance as a cricketer and had helped him considerably since then.

Without realising how deeply he would disappoint its members, he took the *Spirit of Progress* to Sydney to begin his new job and look for a home. South Melbourne failed to win that premiership and, when Keith visited it a year later, his reception was 'unmistakably cold'.

His employment in Sydney proved most unsuitable. He did not consider tramping the metropolis in an attempt to swell the sales of spirits and liqueurs would benefit either his health or his cricket. It involved the drinking of quite a deal of hard liquor and his weakness had always been for beer.

Learning of his predicament Eric Kennedy, chief-executive of Australian Associated Newspapers Limited (Don Bradman's employer of the early 1930s), offered Keith work as a sportswriter under the supervision of former Australian cricketer A. G. 'Johnnie' Moyes, at that time the editor of the new magazine *Sporting Life*.

Though Moyes was an idolater of Bradman's and had chosen him as the godfather of one of his sons, he and Keith developed a deep liking and respect for one another.

This was cemented quite accidentally when Keith made a surprising discovery one day while 'Johnnie' was absent from his desk.

Moyes' brother, the Right Reverend John Stoward Moyes, C.M.G., M.A., had been Archdeacon of Adelaide and was then Bishop of Armidale. He was also quite a 'character' for a man of his calling and high position in the church. So much of a 'character', indeed, that people who knew both of them well contended that 'Johnnie', who was apt to parade himself as a pillar of propriety, should have been the archdeacon and bishop and his brother the sportsman and sports journalist.

Soon after he began work on *Sporting Life* Keith found mysterious messages among the copy invading the office. The messages appeared to be in code and he kept passing them without comment to his editor.

Eventually his curiosity overcame him. The coded messages, he had noticed, arrived only on race days, on important race days in Sydney, Melbourne, Brisbane, and Adelaide. Pressed diplomatically upon the matter, Moyes admitted with embarrassment that they contained tips of rare reliability and had for quite some time provided him with a very welcome additional source of income. He bound his young assistant to silence, discovered he was a keen punter himself, and thenceforward they did their gambling as a syndicate.

By this time Keith had found a home near that famous surfing resort Manly, joined the Manly Cricket Club, and before long become its captain.

A year earlier, after watching and studying Keith at the Sydney Cricket Ground, that graceful Australian batsman and former New South Wales captain Alan Kippax had said, 'Miller is the most talented all-round cricketer I have seen, a greater one even than Jack Gregory, but for him to give of his best it is vital he be allowed a free hand.'

Keith had been longing to be given his chance to captain a side. Now he had it—and with it, if only in club cricket, that freedom.

His delight was increased when he learnt that his old wartime comrade and R.A.A.F. Team captain Keith Carmody had been appointed to lead Western Australia in its first summer of Sheffield Shield cricket. He was thrilled when Carmody began his new role with a score of 198 against South Australia.

What was to prove more important to Keith, and to his new State and national bowling partner Ray Lindwall, was Carmody's invention of what is still known as the 'umbrella field'.

By stationing a strong cordon of slips fieldsmen on either side of the wicketkeeper for his pace bowlers, Carmody managed to win the Sheffield Shield for Western Australia in its first season in the competition. 'Johnnie' Moyes classed him as 'one of the ablest leaders seen in post-war Australian cricket' and by so doing may have stirred Miller's ambition to one day gain the captaincy of *his* adopted State.

Under Arthur Morris's leadership Miller began well for New South Wales. From the six matches for which he was available (one against India and five Sheffield Shield) he scored 464 runs at 51·55. His innings, perhaps significantly, included an impressive 170 against Western Australia. In those six matches Keith delivered 167·5 overs to take 19 wickets at 32·1.

Keith's performances for Australia that summer under Bradman's captaincy were far less imposing.

Ironically, the Services Team's 1945 tour of India had obliged the Australian Cricket Board to issue the invitation to an Indian team in 1947–48.

Though Vijay Merchant, Mushtaq Ali, and Rusi Modi were unavailable and India well below full strength, its visit under the leadership of Lala Amarnath and the guidance of Duleepsinhji inaugurated a series of contests which continue to this day.

Keith's highest score in five innings in the 1947–48 series—which Australia won by four Tests to nil with large margins of an innings and 226; 233 runs; an innings and 16 runs; and an innings and 177 runs—was 67 and he aggregated only 185 at an average of 37·00.

Bradman, then in his fortieth year and approaching his retirement, still possessed enough incentive to amass 715 at

178·75. Hassett, six years older than Keith, compiled 332 at 110·66. Neil Harvey averaged 83, Arthur Morris 52, and Sid Barnes 43.

Miller captured only 9 wickets in the five Tests. Lindwall took 18, Bill Johnston and Ian Johnson each took 16.

During the November match at Sydney Cricket Ground between An Australian XI and India Keith came in to partner Bradman. Don was batting for that hundredth century in first-class cricket. He was playing as cautiously as Len Hutton had done when he was offered £1000 for a second century in the Third Victory Test at Lord's.

Keith rapidly began to overtake 'The Don', threatened to pass him, to reach his own hundred before him. Glancing at the scoreboard he put a brake on his strokeplay. When he was 86 he threw his wicket away.

Next morning his barber asked him why he had done this. 'I realised it was Don's day; that I was stealing the show,' Keith said.

Don moved on inexorably and inevitably to his hundredth hundred. After reaching it he raced with much of his old brilliance to 172 before deliberately skying a catch to the deep field.

Sitting in the Press box in the M. A. Noble Stand, that 'glass menagerie' which 'Johnnie' Moyes had designed, Duleepsinhji began to chuckle to himself as Don strode out.

'What are you chuckling about, Duleep?' we asked.

'I'm wondering whether I should walk down and reprimand Don. You see, when I scored 173 at Lord's in my first Test match I threw *my* wicket away. Don caught me that day off Clarrie Grimmett and, as I passed him on my way to the pavilion, he said, "You should never throw your wicket away, Duleep."'

11
David and Jonathan – England 1948

Until the 1960s Australian cricket teams, all twenty-two of them from 1878 to 1956, travelled to England by sea. Voyaging either via North America or the Suez Canal they took as long as eight weeks, never less than four, to reach their destination.

This helped greatly to create team spirit and to foster friendships between individual players, and some of these lasted long beyond their retirement from the game. More often than not the voyage tended to dampen interstate rivalry and ill-feeling—even between New South Welshmen and Victorians.

I say 'more often than not' and 'tended' because of an episode in the Tasman Sea in 1877. The vessel carrying Dave Gregory's 1878 side to some preliminary, fund-raising matches before their departure for Britain was caught in a violent storm off the coast of New Zealand. That first of all Test century-makers Charles Bannerman, though born in England, had become a New South Welshman and played for Sydney's then powerful and famous Albert Club. So did his national captain and teammates—his brother Alec 'Barndoor' Bannerman, the 'Demon' fast bowler Frederick Spofforth, and that greatest of Australian nineteenth-century batsmen William Lloyd Murdoch.

Charles Bannerman was an excellent swimmer.

'Suppose we're wrecked in this storm, what will you do Charlie?' Gregory asked him.

'Firstly I'll save Alec, then Murdoch, then "Spoff", then you,' Bannerman replied.

'What about the Victorians?'

'We'll let 'em drown.'

Some of the most memorable friendships developed on board ships among Australian cricketers have been those of Victor Trumper and Clem Hill in 1899, Bill Woodfull and Bill Ponsford ('Mutt and Jeff') in 1926, Vic Richardson and Alan Kippax in 1930, Bill O'Reilly and Stan McCabe in 1934. And Keith Miller and Ray Lindwall and Neil Harvey and Sam Loxton in 1948.

It was only natural that Keith and Ray should have become the 'David and Jonathan' of post second World War cricket following Keith's transfer from Melbourne to Sydney in 1947. They opened the bowling both for New South Wales and Australia and shared a zest for a remarkable number of other activities, notably golf, which fitted admirably into what was to become their nomadic way of life.

From 1947 to 1956 they played cricket together in a hundred or more cities in Australia, England, South Africa, India, Pakistan, and the West Indies and almost invariably shared quarters.

During the last morning of the Australia–South Africa Test in Brisbane in 1952 Keith and Ray were sharing a suite at Lennons Hotel. When I called to bid them goodday and good luck Keith was packing his bag. Ray was lying in his pyjamas on his bed.

'You two had a divorce?' I asked.

'This is no joking matter,' Ray replied. 'Keith's just been ordered to hospital and I've got gastric flu. They only need 187 to win and have eight wickets standing, including McGlew, Funston, and Roy McLean.'

At this stage Ray departed hurriedly for the bathroom.

On his return he began writhing in pain on his bed. Miller had vanished without a word.

'You can't possibly bowl today, Ray,' I said.

'*Somebody* has to get them out. The "old firm" can't let Australia down.'

Somehow Ray mustered the determination to struggle off that bed, dress, call a taxi, and make for Woolloongabba.

Bowling McLean with the last ball before lunch Lindwall took the vital wicket and went on to finish with 5 for 60 from 30 overs in the Springboks' second innings 240. Australia had won by 96 runs.

Passengers on board the S.S. *Strathaird* which carried Don Bradman's team from Fremantle to Southampton in 1948 used to say that if Neil Harvey stepped out of a lift Sam Loxton was sure to follow and it was much the same with Keith and Ray. They, too, were almost inseparable and, according to Miller, spent a deal of their time recounting their wartime experiences as an airman over Europe and as a soldier in Papua-New Guinea respectively.

A remarkable number of the coloured American troops who served along the Kokoda Track and in the Markham Valley in the early 1940s, it seems, bore the surname of Jackson.

By the time the *Strathaird* reached Southampton Keith and Ray found themselves addressing one another as 'Jackson' and have done so ever since. This has puzzled a great number of cricketing followers during the past thirty years but it has given Keith and Ray an unfailing source of amusement, created a secret bond between them that their geographical separation, caused firstly by Lindwall's move to Brisbane in 1954 and then Miller's to London for six months of each year in 1957, has not weakened.

Though Keith and Ray have enjoyed so much in common they were, during their playing days, and remain in retirement, quite different characters. Though batsmen who faced him came to call him 'The Killer', Ray was by far the more placid, the more tolerant individual—imperturbable in the extreme. Often during his cricketing career Keith could be a very impatient character, one who developed strong antipathies towards certain types of people, included among them colleagues and adversaries, captains, officials, and umpires.

Both he and Ray have a keen sense of humour but Lindwall generally laughs *with* you; Keith, like Sir Donald Bradman, is more prone to laugh *at* you.

Maybe Ray's sunny disposition reflects the blue skies and seas of his boyhood environment, Hurstville, Sydney. Maybe Keith's mirrors the more sombre shades of Elsternwick, St Kilda, and South Melbourne.

When Ray, considerably overweight, was finding difficulty in adapting to the slow South African wickets of Johannesburg and Cape Town in late December of 1949 an Australian journalist described him in the Johannesburg *Sunday Times* as 'the rather portly ghost of a once-great fast bowler'.

On New Year's Eve the journalist was dancing with a particularly beautiful Durban girl in the Cape Town Rotunda. Suddenly he felt a friendly tap on his shoulder. Stepping back from his partner he saw Lindwall grasping her in his arms and whisking her off about the floor. 'Don't worry, old chap,' called Ray over her shoulder, 'I'm only a ghost you know.'

Both before and since that incident Ray has been that writer's favourite cricketer. He had called him 'a rather portly ghost' only because he liked and admired him tremendously and believed a little needling would restore him to his best form. Four days later in the Second Test at Newlands Lindwall delivered 15 overs to take 5 for 32. A fortnight later in the Third Test at Old Kingsmead, Durban, he took 4 for 54.

Ray had sensed the real motive behind that on-the-face-of-it unfriendly criticism and he reacted as the writer had hoped he would. 'Jonathan', as I have dubbed him, was far more apt to let the world ride, than was 'David'; to accept fate rather than to become irritated by it. He was also far more amenable to leadership, even when he considered it unwise or tactless, than was Keith.

Ray managed to get on reasonably well with the Australian captains—Bradman, Hassett, and Ian Johnson—under whom he played and it is surprising, in view of their closeness, that he was never able to convince Keith of the advantages that might have accrued from following his example, from restraining the rebellious streak in his make-up.

Maybe Ray *did* try to do so in 1948 during that four-and-a-half-weeks' voyage via Colombo, Port Said, and Gibraltar to England. Certainly Miller seemed a much happier cricketer during what for him was the merriest of Mays than he had been during the 1947–48 Indian summer in Australia.

Miller began that 1948 tour much as he had left off in England in 1945. In the second game against Leicestershire he struck up 202 in 330 minutes, sharing a stand of 159 with Bradman and remaining undismissed. In the following game, a closely-fought, low-scoring one against Yorkshire, he took 9 for 91 and scored more runs than any other batsman of either side.

Back at his favourite English ground, Lord's, he made 163 in 250 minutes with three 6s and twenty-one 4s against the

Marylebone Cricket Club and his display was described as 'dazzlingly brilliant'.

All his 1945 brand of interest and delight in batting appeared to have returned and, as usual when fit, he was enjoying his bowling. In the match against Hampshire when the Australians were in danger of defeat preceding the First Test he took 5 for 25.

On arrival in London in 1948, however, Bradman had declared his intention to create a record by leading his team through Britain undefeated from late April to early September. Even Warwick Armstrong's great 1921 side had lost two unimportant matches.

Sir Pelham Warner's immediate response to Don's declaration was: 'Give us Keith Miller and we'll beat Australia.'

Don's own reactions can well be imagined, especially by those who know him. 'Give us Keith Miller', not 'Give us Don Bradman'. This was heresy.

Don grew even more determined to win every match he could and avoid defeat at all costs. It so happened that on two occasions when he was either resting or conducting business affairs in London, and Hassett was acting as his deputy, the Australians were on the brink of defeat. The first occasion was during that low-scoring game against Yorkshire at Bradford, the second was during the game against Hampshire at Southampton just prior to the Nottingham Test.

Before the final day of the Hants' match Hassett received the following cable, 'Bradford was bad enough but this is unbearable stop heads up and chins down Don.'

In *Cricket Crossfire* Keith Miller wrote: 'Bradman never forgot the way England remorselessly piled up 903 for 7 wickets during The Oval Test in 1938 when he and Jack Fingleton were injured. During the 1948 tour of England he drilled it into us, "When you get in front, nail 'em into the ground. When you get 'em down, never let up."

'Even in County matches when we were piling on the runs and some of the boys said, "Haven't we got enough now?" Bradman would give a crooked little smile and say, "I remember when England made 900 against us and kept us in the field for three days."'

Both Don and Neil Harvey have said the 1948 side was the

greatest Australia ever sent to England. Though Johnnie Moyes believed it arguable that the 1902 Joe Darling and 1921 Warwick Armstrong teams were better equipped and Armstrong himself, who played in both, declared that the 1902 side would have beaten his own by an innings, Bradman's team was a truly powerful combination. English cricket was still suffering from the effects of the second World War.

Was 'Plum' Warner's claim, therefore, an exaggeration, a flight into fantasy? The transfer of Miller from Australia to England could hardly have turned the balance of a series which produced a four-nil result in Australia's favour.

Australia won the First Test by eight wickets, the Second Test by 409 runs, drew the Third Test very unfavourably (England 363 and 174 for 3 declared, Australia 221 and 92 for 1), won the Fourth Test by seven wickets, and the Fifth by an innings and 149.

That claim of Sir Pelham's certainly was some compliment to Keith, however, and before it is ruled out as ridiculous, it is worth considering just how many Australia would have scored had Miller and Bedser instead of Edrich and Bedser, Coxon and Bedser, Pollard and Bedser, and Watkins and Bedser, been opening the England bowling. It is also worth considering just how many the rising 40-year-old Bradman would have scored had Miller been firing bumpers at him innings after innings and match after match. As things stood, Don scored 138, 0, 38, 89, 7, 30 not out, 33, 173 not out, and 0—508 at 72·57.

Batting for the strong Australian team, Miller aggregated only 184 runs in the five Tests at an average of 28·26. Had he been representing the underdog I feel he would have performed far more effectively. It is interesting to note that Miller dismissed Hutton thrice and Compton twice during the series and both of them might well have scored many more runs had he been batting with them instead of bowling at them.

The crunch, or rather crunches, between Bradman and Miller on that 1948 tour did not come during the First Test at Nottingham. Though Miller failed to score in his only innings there, he delivered 63 overs for the match to take 7 wickets (including Hutton's and Compton's each twice and Washbrook's once) for 163.

The first crunch came late in May, a fortnight or so before that Test, during the game against Essex at that citadel of the jellied eel, Southend-On-Sea. The second crunch came late in June during the Lord's Test.

Bradman's and Miller's accounts of the Saturday's play at Southend-On-Sea differ in most illuminating fashion.

In his *Farewell to Cricket*, Hodder and Stoughton 1950, Don has this to say: 'A picnic atmosphere pervaded the crowd and must also have affected our batsmen, for in one day's batting Australia put together by superlative play a total of 721 runs. This is, I believe, a world's record for one day in first-class cricket. It was simply fantastic.

'Man after man scored at breath-taking speed by beautiful strokes which left the fieldsmen helpless. Strange to say right in the middle of it all, the one man who might have really created a riot of runs, Keith Miller, was bowled first ball for 0 . . .

'Here, it seemed to me, was the first really tangible sign that we possessed a team of exceptional batting strength, one which would scourge any but the very best bowling. It was a meritorious achievement and all credit must go to the Australians who maintained throughout the opening day of the match a scoring rate of over two runs a minute.

'On the Monday just for full measure and as evidence that the pitch was not altogether a batsman's paradise, our bowlers dismissed the Essex team twice in one day and thus gave us a colossal victory.'

Sir Donald, who has invariably been modest about his own batting performances, omitted to mention that he contributed 187 of those 721 runs on the Saturday.

In his *Cricket Crossfire*, Oldbourne Press 1956, Keith has written: 'I got sick of all the slaughter when, at Southend, we scored 721 in a day against Essex. Surely Bradman could have used such games to give batsmen like Ron Hamence and Bill Brown a chance to build up their form and confidence? Hamence was one of the most promising bats we had in Australia at the time, but it was no earthly use sending him in when the score was around 600 for 4.

'During this game at Southend I walked in to bat, did not take guard, made a sleep-walking stroke, and was bowled. I turned to the wicketkeeper, said "Thank God that's over", and walked away.'

Bradman, as might be expected, was not amused—especially when Keith's action and its obvious implication, not that 721 in one day, gained the Sunday headlines in Fleet Street.

In *Cricket Crossfire* Miller continues: 'Though Bradman would not change his batting order to give batsmen like Hamence and Brown a chance, he handled his bowling very differently. Ian Johnson took 92 wickets on that tour, but he would not have done so if Bradman, who wanted him to do well, had not given him chance after chance to bowl at nine-ten-jack. There was a remarkably high percentage of tail-enders among Johnson's haul of victims.

'Colin McCool used to get bitter about this and it was understandable. Ray Lindwall, Bill Johnston, Ernie Toshack, Colin, and I would have worked hard to get the first six batsmen out and then have to make way time after time so that Ian could have a go at the "rabbits". It was all very galling.'

Ironically it was Don's insistence upon using Keith primarily as a bowler in the Test matches of 1948, a policy that patently affected his performances with the bat, that became the chief bone of contention between them and led eventually (as Mrs Percy Millard had forecast it would) to open disobedience.

In Bradman's favour it must be remembered that the 1948 team had tremendous batting strength. Examine the batting order of Arthur Morris, Sid Barnes, Bill Brown, Bradman himself, Hassett, Miller, Harvey, Loxton, Lindwall, Tallon, and Ian Johnson and compare it with the one Greg Chappell had on deck in England in 1977, and you should get the picture.

On that 1948 tour Morris scored 1922 at 71·18, Barnes 1354 at 56·41, Brown 1448 at 57·92, Bradman 2428 at 89·92, Hassett 1563 at 72·42, Miller 1088 at 47·30, Harvey 1129 at 53·76, and Loxton 973 at 57·23. On the 1977 tour McCosker scored 703 at 24·31, Davis 608 at 30·40, Serjeant 642 at 35·66, Chappell 1143 at 60·15, Hookes 685 at 29·73, Walters 630 at 27·39, Robinson 715 at 37·63, and Marsh 398 at 19·90.

In 1948 in England Bradman hit eleven centuries, Morris and Hassett seven centuries each, Harvey four, Barnes and Loxton three each, and Miller two. This adds up to 37 so I shall spare the

1977 side—possibly the weakest Australia has sent to England since that dusky one of 1868 containing those émigrés from Lake Wallace in western Victoria Jack Mullagh, Dick-aDick, Two-penny, Red Cap, Mosquito, King Cole, Jim Crow, Sundown, and company—their blushes.

As bowlers Bradman had Lindwall, Miller, Bill Johnston, Toshack, Ian Johnson, Colin McCool, Loxton, and Doug Ring. But, under the new experiment which allowed a new ball after every 40 eight-ball and 55 six-ball overs, he wanted to concentrate mainly on pace.

And it was this desire of his that caused the second crunch on the second morning of the Lord's Test.

Miller's ire had been mounting. Now it was to explode on the field, as it had at Adelaide earlier that year.

Australia (Morris 105, Don Tallon 53, and Don Bradman 47) had scored 350 in the first innings of that Lord's Test. In its second innings at Nottingham England (Compton 184 and Hutton 74) had scored 441.

Bradman was worried. Miller's chronic back injury had been worrying him—the legacy of that belly-landing in Norfolk early in 1945. On the eve of the Lord's Test Miller had told Bradman he might not be fit to bowl. Unfortunately Don was one of the people who never seemed satisfied as to the genuineness of Keith's injury. In the dressing-room before England was due to bat on the second day of the Test Bradman asked Keith, 'How's your back today?'

'I don't think I'd better bowl,' Miller replied.

Lindwall bowled the first over to Hutton and Washbrook. Miller fielded in slips. At the end of the over Bradman tossed the ball to Miller. 'Have a bowl,' he said.

Over to Miller again: 'Now there had been times before when I had a bad back and bowled, and maybe Don thought this was another of those times. Then again he might have been applying a little psychology thinking I would not have the temerity to refuse because of the huge crowd. Anyway I simply could not bowl and I told him so and walked away.'

Most reports of the incident say Keith threw the ball (one said 'brusquely') back to his captain and some of the journalists who wrote them condemned Keith for doing so. They were unaware, of course, of what had transpired between Keith and Don in the Australian dressing-room between innings and at their hotel on the eve of the Test. They were unmindful, too, of Keith's great contribution as a bowler—63 overs for 7 for 163—in the previous Test.

Under Bradman's instructions at Nottingham Miller and Lindwall had employed the fast bumper as one of their chief weapons against Hutton and Compton and had them dodging and ducking from the path of the ball. Nonetheless Compton had scored that 184 before falling on his wicket while attempting to dodge another bouncer of Keith's. And Hutton had got that 74 before Keith bowled him.

Despite Compton's heroic resistance on the final day at Trent Bridge, England had lost by eight wickets and the Nottingham crowd, still sensitive regarding Australia's reaction to their home-town hero Harold Larwood's 'Bodyline' in 1932–33, formed what can best be described as a guard of dishonour as the Australians were leaving the field at the conclusion of England's second innings.

One spectator advanced upon Keith, flung insult upon insult at him, and even threatened bodily assault.

Keith grabbed the man by the shoulders, lifted him from the ground, and carried him, struggling, to the door of the Australian dressing-room. By the time they arrived there the demonstrator was white about the gills, fearful of what would happen to him behind that door.

Keith just grinned at him and released him. But he himself had not enjoyed becoming the target for the crowd's displeasure through obeying his captain's orders, or liked directing those persistent bumpers at the batsman who had become one of his closest cricketing friends—the batsman after whom he was later to christen one of his sons: Denis Charles Scott Compton.

When all these considerations are taken into account that gesture of Keith's to Australia's captain in the 'Cathedral of Cricket' becomes far more excusable.

A number of people had facetiously described Keith's muscular problems as 'shagger's back'. More often than not he took it all in good part. But chronic and recurring pain, for the man who is enduring it, is no laughing matter. And the truth is that during that 1948 tour of England and subsequently, even in warmer climates, a disc near the base of the Miller spine often used to slip out of position when he was delivering the ball.

On his way back to his mark he would press the disc back into place with his thumb before continuing his over. He was willing to do this and suffer the pain when his team was in trouble, but he believed it unreasonable to expect him to do so when those fine new-ball bowlers Lindwall, Bill Johnston, and Ernie Toshack were available to tackle the opposition.

In *Cricket Crossfire* Miller has written: 'I thought that neither Bradman nor Hassett completely realised that after a long spell of bowling a fast bowler is physically and mentally spent for a while. There is no chance to relax when you have to go straight in or prepare for your innings after you have been bowling. Often you get out through playing a tired stroke. I have heard people say, "This Miller is a bit of a prima donna, you know. He's made a lot of runs so he won't bowl." Or vice versa. But it has never been a case of that. I know where and when my back plays me up. It is as simple as that.'

Which brings us back to examination of those statements of Bradman's and Johnnie Moyes'.

'Miller was a great fast bowler, but is apt to be over-rated as a batsman,' Bradman wrote in 1948.

'It is as a bowler rather than as a batsman that Miller will be chiefly remembered,' Moyes wrote in 1959.

If these comments have validity then Bradman must take much of the responsibility. For it was he who, while seeking revenge for his experiences in the 1932–33 and 1938 Anglo–Australian Test series, used Miller's bowling to an extent that can only have handicapped him as a batsman.

Miller's next major confrontation during that Lord's Test of 1948 was with a hat-trick in Australia's second innings after Lindwall 5 for 70, Bill Johnston 2 for 43, and Ian Johnson 3 for 72 had dismissed England for 215.

Lindsay Hassett had been watching John Bromwich playing in the Wimbledon tennis championships on the dressing-room TV set during the opening stand of 122 between Morris 62, and Barnes and the second-wicket stand of 168 between Barnes 141 and Bradman 89. When Barnes was dismissed Hassett walked to the wicket and was bowled first ball. Then he walked back to the pavilion and asked, 'What's the score? Did Brom win that game?'

Miller prevented the normally innocuous Norman Yardley from joining the seven bowlers who have achieved hat-tricks in more than 100 years of Anglo–Australian Test cricket. He then proved his point about bowler-batsmen by batting 'beautifully' and driving 'gloriously' for 74, thus enabling his captain to declare on 460 for 7 (or 595 ahead) at 3.15 p.m. of the fourth and penultimate day.

This time Toshack 5 for 40 and Lindwall 3 for 61 (8 for 131 for the match) gave Australia a resounding victory by 409 runs.

Australia now led two Tests to nil and though Compton, after retiring hurt when England were 52 for 2 at Old Trafford, returned fortified with two stitches and an 'unspecified amount of brandy' to be 145 not out of 363 in England's first innings, Bradman did not call upon Miller to bowl.

Hutton had been dropped for this Test but, even without Hutton, England 363 and 174 for 3 declared, were 224 ahead of Australia 221 and 92 for 1, at the end of the last two rain-beleaguered days.

Miller's contribution this time was a modest 31 with the bat and an economical 0 for 15 from 14 overs, seven of them maidens, in England's second innings with the ball.

In the Fourth Test at Bradman's favourite Test stamping-ground, Headingley, Leeds (Don had scored 334 there in 1930, 304 there in 1934, and 103 there in 1938), England's selectors reinstated a quietly irate and determined Hutton. Len 81, Washbrook 143, Edrich 111, and nightwatchman Alec Bedser 79 led England to 496 and Australia were 65 for 2 in reply when a promoted Miller joined his captain only to lose him at 68 for 3.

Keith's next partner was the nineteen-year-old Neil Harvey who had begun his Test career with 13 against India at Adelaide in January and followed it with 153 against India at Melbourne in February that year.

Keith welcomed Neil to his first Test match in England by sweeping and driving Jim Laker for 6s and playing a stream of strokes which set fire to the youngster's keen imagination and prodigious ability. So inspired was Harvey that he was first to his 50 and the two of them added 121 in 95 minutes to convert 68 for 3 into 189 for 4. After Miller's dismissal for 58 Harvey, partnered by his room- and cabin-mate 'Political Sam' Loxton, went to a century in his first Test innings in England. Loxton striving for his sixth 6, was bowled by Yardley for 93, and Lindwall, 77, battled Australia to 458, a deficit of 38.

Realising she needed a victory to retain any chance of regaining the Ashes, England scored at above a run a minute and Yardley delayed his declaration until after five minutes of the final day so he could use the heavy roller before play in the hope it would hasten the disintegration of the wicket.

Missed chances, many of them by that usually reliable wicket-keeper Godfrey Evans, helped Australia to 121 for 1 in the 105 minutes remaining before lunch.

Then Morris 182 and Bradman 173 not out created history by causing Australia to be the first country to win a Test match after being set 400 or more to get in the fourth innings. Morris hit twenty 4s while proceeding to his century and Bradman twenty-nine in all. 'The Don's' Test record at Headingley was thus: 334, 304, 103 and 16, and 33 and 173 not out, or the phenomenal 963 from six innings at an average of 192·6, and Australia had won by seven wickets with 12 minutes to spare to lead three-nil with two Tests to play.

Miller's contribution of 58 and 12 was comparatively minimal statistically, but again he had demonstrated that quality at the crucial moment—and not only quantity—counts.

In the game against Glamorgan Miller hit five 6s and seven 4s (58 in boundaries) while scoring 84, but failed with the bat and took 4 for 27 from 23 overs in the final Test at The Oval, which Australia won by an innings and 149.

After his brilliant beginnings both as batsman and bowler—that 202 at Leicester and 163 at Lord's, those 9 wickets for 91 at Bradford and 5 for 25 at Southampton—Miller emerged from his first official tour of Britain with 1088 runs at 47·30 and 57 wickets at 19·98.

Seven batsmen—Bradman 92·07, Hassett 71·18, Morris 70·48, Brown 58·50, Loxton 54·88, Barnes 54·36, and Harvey 49·34—had higher averages; Lindwall 86 at 16·12, Bill Johnston 110 at 16·04, Ian Johnson 92 at 17·64, and even those 'ground-staff bowlers', as they called themselves, Doug Ring 69 at 21·08 and Colin McCool 63 at 17·84, took more wickets.

It would be ridiculous to suggest that Miller's overall performance on that tour worthily reflected his ability. A great deal of iron clearly had entered his soul and nobody in the Australian camp doubted that the 'Blacksmith' had been Don Bradman.

12
Two bumpers too many?

Keith's cricketing performances in England in 1948, especially when assessed statistically, had proved disappointing not only to him but also to his large, loyal, and growing band of supporters.

I say growing because Keith's pleasant and manly appearance, his attractive and forthright personality, his gift for camaraderie, his acute sense of humour, and his zest for most facets of life had helped to expand his already considerable and diversified circle of English associates.

That circle had come to include even the then Princesses Elizabeth and Margaret Rose, Prince Philip, Lord Louis Mountbatten, Lord Gowrie, the Lieutenant-Governor of Windsor Castle, Air Marshal Lord Tedder, and the Duke of Norfolk.

It had come to embrace characters from such differing walks of life as Sir John Barbirolli, the celebrated leader of Manchester's Hallé Orchestra; Sir Norman Birkett, Q.C., England's outstanding criminal lawyer and most popular after-dinner speaker; champion jockey Sir Gordon Richards; its soccering wizard Sir Stanley Matthews; Marshal Lord Montgomery of Alamein; cartoonist Tom Webster; and writer Neville Cardus.

Always an excellent mixer Keith found himself equally at home and at ease with all of them as he was with the dressing-room attendants at Lord's, the barmen at the Park Lane Hotel, and those stimulating and affable Cockney taxi drivers of London.

Once his cricket was over for the day he liked, as did Walter Hammond, to forget it, to seek distraction from it, and in England the avenues for this were unlimited.

Cricket, for him, was becoming far more than a game—a path to an expanding way of life which helped to put cricket itself into a more balanced perspective.

His first meeting with Princess Elizabeth came during an informal visit to Balmoral Castle. The now Queen of England was surrounded by a number of her favourite Corgi dogs and Keith asked her if she had a special pet among them.

'That one, I think, but he's a bit of a devil,' Her Majesty replied. 'The other day I had a piece of cake in my hand and I wanted to do something or other. I put the cake on the edge of a table and as soon as my back was turned he jumped up and pinched it.'

The Princess's use of the word 'pinched' immediately set Keith at ease for he had believed it was a peculiarly Australian expression like 'bonzer', 'snorter', and 'bobby-dazzler'.

Keith's first contact with Princess Margaret occurred at Broadlands, the Hampshire home of Earl Mountbatten. The former Chief of Combined Operations and Viceroy of India had invited him to a small but distinguished dinner party, stating the Princess and her lady-in-waiting would be present.

After dinner a film was shown and Lord Louis said, 'Oh, Mr Miller, will you please sit next to the Princess.'

The film, a mystery thriller, starred Edward G. Robinson and Princess Margaret was deeply concerned about detecting the killer.

'Who do you think did it?' she kept asking and again Keith began to feel completely at ease.

Of her he has written: 'She has the bluest eyes I have ever seen and is a most attractive person in every way . . . She was as quick as a flash in conversation with a delightful sense of humour. Most of all I was impressed with her naturalness. Everything she did and said seemed so unaffected.'

Keith's first contact with the Duke of Edinburgh came at the East Molesley ground the night after he (Keith) had bumped into a lamp post.

'I seem to have seen your face somewhere before,' the Duke said. 'What have you done to it?'

'You should see the other fellow, Sir,' Keith replied.

Keith was to meet Prince Philip on many other occasions. On

one of them he was invited, together with a couple of Australian pressmen, for a drink in his hotel suite. It was a particularly hot afternoon. The Duke's guests noticed that the door leading to the adjoining suite was half open.

'Would you mind going to the loo and flushing it until I ask you to stop?' Prince Philip asked one of the pressmen.

Naturally, though puzzled, he obeyed without question.

On his return he saw the Prince Consort Philip had opened two bottles of French champagne.

'Her Majesty is not too keen about me drinking so early in the afternoon and these corks can be noisy,' His Royal Highness explained.

At Arundel, when the Duke of Norfolk was showing Keith and several other Australian players around his home, one of them asked, 'Excuse me, Your Grace, but how many rooms would there be in this castle?'

'I'm not sure just how many rooms but I do know there are sixty-two W.C.s,' the Duke replied.

Keith's acquaintance with Norfolk continued when His Grace managed Mike Smith's M.C.C. team to Australia.

In 1948 at Windsor Castle Lord Gowrie, the former Governor-General of Australia, was the Australian team's escort. During afternoon tea he introduced Keith to Air Marshal Lord Tedder. After a few minutes' conversation England's senior ranking airman disappeared and returned carrying a tea-tray.

Advancing towards the former Pilot Officer Miller he said, 'Excuse me, Sir. Your tea, Sir.'

Finding the courage to enter into the spirit of the moment, Keith replied, 'Thank you, boy,' and then, 'Here you are, laddie,' as he handed Lord Tedder a tip.

It was Keith's love for classical music that led to his lasting friendship with Sir John Barbirolli who, in 1953, contributed the foreword to one of the books, *Straight Hit*, which Keith and I wrote together.

This love, indeed passion, for music—especially the compositions of Ludwig Beethoven—also helped to enrich his association with Sir Neville Cardus.

Whenever possible they attended Beethoven concerts together. When none such were available they would repair to Neville's quarters and spend hours listening to his collection of the great composer's works, especially Keith's favourite, the Emperor Concerto.

Yes, despite his low place on the Australian batting averages in 1948, his failure to gain more than 57 wickets, and his brushes with Bradman, Keith gained a great deal from that English summer. His off-the-field experiences consolidated his belief that cricket is 'only a game' and helped to frame it in what he regarded as proper and balanced perspective.

Nine years later and from 1957 to 1973 he was to make England his home from each May to September.

No overseas cricket team toured Australia during the summer of 1948–49, the summer that is most memorable for Don Bradman's retirement and his testimonial match in Melbourne. In this Don held Keith back in the batting order until the crowd arrived. When he did send Keith in he batted light-heartedly and got out trying to hit 6s.

Says Miller, 'When I was out I saw Bradman looking at me with disgust written all over his face and clearly he thought I had not concentrated and did not care. My feeling about this was that Bradman, like so many others, took the game too seriously. Cricket was meant to be enjoyed at all levels and I certainly enjoy it as such.'

Keith's performances for New South Wales also fell far below doing justice to his ability and his adventures in the Kippax–Oldfield Testimonial at the Sydney Cricket Ground almost proved calamitous.

The most successful players in the Sheffield Shield games and the Bradman and Kippax–Oldfield testimonials at the M.C.G. and S.C.G., which preceded the selection of the 1949–50 Australian tour of South Africa and Rhodesia, were Arthur Morris, Jack Moroney, Bill Brown, Lindsay Hassett, Ron Hamence, Ken Archer, and Sam Loxton with the bat and Alan Walker (a hostile, new left-hander), Lindwall, Geff Noblet, Ian Johnson, and McCool with the ball.

Those who contributed most to the success of the Bradman (Don netted about £10 000) Testimonial were Lindsay Hassett, Lindwall, Bradman himself, Morris, Meuleman, and Tallon, who all scored centuries.

In the last hour of play 100 runs were scored and Tallon hit 91 of them to be 146 not out when the match finished as a tie on the last ball of the fourth day.

Captains in the Kippax–Oldfield Testimonial were Hassett and Morris, now rivals for the leadership of Australia. Moroney scored 217 for Morris' team and Hassett 159 for his own. In this match Bradman and Miller were opposed to each other and the duel between Bradman, the batsman, and Miller, the bowler, was eagerly awaited.

Until the 'bodyline' series in 1932–33 Don had been one of the most devastating executants of the hook stroke in the history of cricket. As a captain he had shown in Australia in 1946–47 and in England in 1948 that he considered the bumper, unless bowled to a 'bodyline' field, was a fair delivery.

Under his leadership, at times at his instigation, Lindwall and Miller had used the bouncer frequently, even persistently, against Hutton and Compton and others.

The hook, it is important to stress, is an instinctive stroke and, as batsmen grow older, it grows ever-less instinctive. Even in 1948, however, when he was rising forty, Bradman used to indulge in it against all but the fastest of bowlers.

Against Yorkshire (the second game) in 1948 he hooked successive deliveries to the boundary, smiled, walked along the wicket and said to Keith, 'Looks as if we are going to have a bit of fun. This Aspinall's going to keep bowling bumpers—those terrible bumpers.'

While batting for the Gentlemen of England that year at Lord's, Walter Robins, the former England captain and now England selector, had to face Miller. Robins had been criticising England's Test batsmen for the manner in which they tackled the bumper. Though Robins was forty-two years old Bradman decided to have some fun. 'Give him a bouncer, Keith,' he said as Walter came out of the Long Room towards the wicket.

Keith's first ball to Robins was one of the fastest he ever delivered. Though it pitched short, it failed to rise as much as Keith had intended and almost parted Walter's hair.

Bradman has an odd, rather sadistic, sense of humour. He laughed openly at the discomfort of the man who for long had regarded him as his friend.

Keith remembered that incident at Lord's when he began to bowl at Bradman on the much faster Sydney Cricket Ground wicket six months later. He believed Bradman would be expecting a bumper and he gave him one—one which would be easy to hook.

Bradman stroked it with power and precision to the boundary forward of mid-wicket.

Don seemed grateful to Keith for giving him the opportunity of demonstrating that he had no physical fear of the bumper, could still deal with it as well as he did in his halcyon days. He did not anticipate what was to follow.

Keith's very next ball was much faster and shorter. It reared like a rocket and this time it was the Bradman cranium, not the Robins cranium, that was endangered.

Keith insists that he bowled that second bumper 'for the amusement of the crowd, who expect the emphasis to be on entertainment in a match of this kind'.

This time, he continues in *Cricket Crossfire*, '"Braddles" did not laugh. He looked daggers at me so, for sheer devilment, I decided to give him a third bumper. Bradman matched me in the battle of wits by getting into position to hook. He obviously expected another bumper but when he got it he hit a catch to mid-on and was out.

'Whether that bumper at Sydney or my apparent couldn't-care-less attitude at Melbourne was responsible I don't know, but the sequel to all this was that I was not selected for the next tour, which was to South Africa in 1949–50.

'There were three selectors—Bradman, Jack Ryder, and "Chappie" Dwyer. Dwyer managed the team which went to the Union. After the team had left "Johnnie" Moyes showed me a letter he had received from Bradman. A postscript to it said, "I hope Keith doesn't think I had anything to do with his omission from the team to South Africa".'

I covered that tour of South Africa and can take the matter a deal further. In a letter to me early in the tour Moyes told me what Bradman had written to him—quoted that postscript.

Miller's omission from the Australian side had caused a furore in Australia and in England and great consternation in South Africa.

Nobody in their right senses believed Keith was a less talented all-rounder, for instance, than Sam Loxton. Almost everyone believed Keith had been omitted for what the Board of Control is pleased to call 'reasons other than cricket'.

One theory, which I believe to be unfounded, was that Lindsay Hassett, Australia's successor to Bradman as national captain, did not want Keith in the side on the ground that he was 'difficult to discipline'.

I put this to Lindsay personally and he gave me a forthright and unequivocal denial which, knowing Lindsay, I accepted and published.

The selection of Australian teams is supposed to be confidentially conducted. Though 'Chappie' Dwyer had been a close and intimate friend of mine for many years he had never disclosed even a whisper of what had transpired at Australian selection committee meetings.

I had received that letter from Moyes just before boarding the train from Durban to Johannesburg. It was in my pocket when I entered the old brown-pannelled dining car as the electrified express wound its way upward through what the Zulus so beautifully named the Valley of a Thousand Hills.

'Chappie' was sitting alone by a window gazing out towards Shaka and Dingaan's old stamping grounds. I joined him and handed him Moyes' letter.

As he read it he grew livid and began a fit of coughing that I feared might end in a stroke. Recovering, he downed the remainder of his whisky and sat staring me straight in the eyes as if trying to decide whether I had placed any credence upon Bradman's allegation. To his eternal credit 'Chappie' never uttered a word, but I had formed my opinion and it survives to this day.

During that spring of 1949 Keith was invited to join a social tennis six-some of a Sunday afternoon at former Australian Test cricketer Dr Roy Minnett's home at Manly. The six-some comprised Keith, my brother Alec, General 'Tubby' Allen (GOC 7 Division A.I.F.), General Jackie Stevens (GOC 6 Division A.I.F.), Victor Trumper, Jun., and, until I left to cover the South African tour, myself.

Keith's tennis in no way matched his cricket. Even 'Tubby' Allen was his superior.

Eventually, after my departure, my brother decided Keith, too, would have to be replaced. And he was—as diplomatically as possible.

Later at the N.S.W. Cricketers' Club Keith was heard to say, 'I didn't mind being dropped from the South African tour, but being dropped from Alec Whitington's tennis squad *was* a little too much.'

Fortunately for South Africa's cricketlovers and for Australia and Miller, but unfortunately for Bill Johnston, 'Big Bill' took the wrong turning when driving home one evening to the Edward Hotel in Durban early in November. His borrowed car collided with the entrance to a concrete subway; his forehead struck the frame of its windscreen and he suffered severe abrasions and concussion.

The frontal part of Bill's scalp resembled a golf tee from which a divot had been taken. His doctor doubted whether he would recover in time to take any further part in that South African tour.

Concerned about Lindwall and Walker's lack of form, Hassett and Dwyer cabled the Australian Board of Control seeking a replacement.

Learning of this the South African cricket authorities urged that a second cable be sent containing a special request for Miller to be the player dispatched.

Hassett and Dwyer acquiesced.

Back in Australia Keith had begun the Australian season well and, in Arthur Morris' absence, had been appointed captain of New South Wales. In the first game against Queensland (under Arthur Morris) he had scored 201 not out. In the second (also under Morris) he had scored 63 and 138 not out.

The Australian cricket correspondents covering the tour began a campaign in support of the second Hassett–Dwyer cable, stressing the volume and strength of the support for Miller crescendoing in South Africa.

South Africans had never seen, never would see, Bradman. They wanted to see Miller. In the outcome Miller was swiftly chosen and his passage booked to Cape Town on the *Dominion Monarch*.

13
Table me a mountain – South Africa 1949–50

When Hassett and his men stepped down the gangplank of the S.S. *Nestor* on to the dock of Durban Bay in mid-October of 1949 they were greeted by a huge and flattering gathering of Durban's élite, despite the absence of Keith Miller.

Keith's omission originally had been treated as something of an insult by some sections of the South African Press. Australian Test batsman and cricket writer Jack Fingleton, a highly-successful member of Vic Richardson's all-conquering 1935–36 team, had become a regular contributor to the South African Argus Group of evening papers. And following Miller's omission from the team Fingleton had cabled his own very strong disapproval at the selectors' decision and some outspoken comment from Stan McCabe, Alan Kippax, and Bert Oldfield.

McCabe: 'I'm really shocked. The selectors must consider they have chosen a really strong team if they can afford to drop a player of the calibre of Miller.'

Kippax: 'The omission of Miller is a great shock to me. Any team that can afford to do without Miller must be tremendously strong. I consider him one of the finest cricketers in the world. His lapse of form could only be temporary.'

Oldfield: 'What a bombshell. Keith Miller in form is our greatest all-rounder playing the game today.'

And so when Hassett and his side arrived in Durban the sports editors of the *Mercury* and *Natal Evening News* questioned Australian Pressmen covering the tour. Just why, they asked, had a run-of-the-mill all-rounder like Sam Loxton been preferred to Miller?

Among the gathering on the pier in Durban Bay that mid-October morning was a former Australian named Murray Little. Murray was one South African who was particularly interested to discover the true reasons for Miller's omission. And, as he was the most generous of all our hosts in Durban, he was given the inside story.

Ironically, it had been Murray Little who provided from his new firm, a piston-ring-equipment business in Natal, a fleet of cars for the regular use of Lindsay Hassett, manager 'Chappie' Dwyer, and members of their team. Ironically, I say, because it was while driving one of these cars that 'Big Bill' Johnston suffered the accident which severely injured his head and opened the way for Miller to join the Australian team.

Johnston's accident had occurred after the opening game of the tour against Zululand at Eshowe and just before the first first-class match against Natal at Durban on 28 October.

Upon learning of Johnston's mishap and the unlikelihood of him being fit to take any further part in the tour, the Australian Board of Control asked Ernie Toshack, though he was suffering from a chronically weak knee, whether he was available for selection.

It was, as we have seen, upon receipt of the second request, the specific request for Miller from Hassett and Dwyer, that the Board changed its mind and informed Keith he would be chosen if he could get leave from his employers, Australian Associated Newspapers Limited, and was prepared to make the trip.

Keith's wife Peg was expecting their second child early in 1950 but, after 48 hours' consideration, he gave the following statement to the *Sydney Sun*:

'I am going to South Africa because it seems that the selectors and the team feel that I can help Australia at this time. My wife agrees with me that it is my duty to go. Actually it would suit me better to stay in Sydney. But, if the boys think I can help, I'll be with them.'

The Board and their selectors, of course, had little option but to send Miller after receiving that specific request from their captain and Dwyer, one of the three selectors of the original side.

There were no commercial flights across the Indian Ocean from Perth, via Cocos Island, Mauritius, and Madagascar in those days. Eventually it was announced that Miller had boarded the S.S. *Dominion Monarch* and would arrive in Table Bay about the end of November. This would allow him time to qualify for selection for the First Test due to begin at Ellis Park, Johannesburg, on 24 December.

In the meantime the Australians were scheduled to meet Natal at Durban's historic Old Kingsmead Ground, scene of the 'Timeless Test' of 1939; North-Eastern Transvaal at Willowmore Park, Benoni, where Denis Compton had scored 300 out of 399 in 181 minutes the previous summer; Southern Rhodesia at Bulawayo (Matabele: 'Place of Slaughter'); a South African XI at Salisbury; the Orange Free State at that 'Fountain of Flowers', Bloemfontein; and Western Province at what used to be the world's most beautifully situated Test cricket ground, Newlands.

Hassett's 1949–50 side was the fourth from Australia to tour South Africa. Joe Darling's 1902–03, Herbert Collins' 1921–22, and Vic Richardson's 1935–36 teams had lost none of their matches there—Test or Provincial. Collins' First A.I.F. side was also undefeated there in 1919.

Conscious of his responsibility as successor to the invincible Bradman, Hassett was hoping to preserve Australia's unblemished record, provided this did not interfere *too* drastically with the enjoyment of the fabulous hospitality his team was receiving along the trail over the veld and via the Victoria Falls through what is now Zimbabwe.

During October and November the outstanding performances from Australian batsmen were Sam Loxton's century at Eshowe, Arthur Morris and Jack Moroney's centuries at Durban, Hassett and Harvey's centuries at Benoni, Morris and Moroney's centuries at Bulawayo, and Harvey's 145 not out at Bloemfontein. The most, indeed only, successful bowler had been off-spinner Ian Johnson with 36 wickets from six matches. Johnson's bowling figures at this stage were 36 for 461 at 12·8.

The Australians had drawn their game against Natal, beaten Zululand by an innings and 280, NE Transvaal by 10 wickets, Southern Rhodesia by an innings and 161, a South African XI by an innings and 72 runs, and the Orange Free State by an innings and 139 runs when Hassett and Dwyer drove down Cape Town's stately Adderley Street to meet their reinforcement all-rounder.

So far Hassett's main causes for concern had been South African Test captain Dudley Nourse's undefeated 104 for Natal and the difficulty his pace bowlers, Lindwall, Alan Walker, Geff Noblet, and Sam Loxton were having in adapting to the slow South African pitches.

Would Miller be able to succeed where they had failed he was wondering during the drawn game against Western Province at Newlands?

Keith began his tour a week later by scoring 49 and taking 2 for 9 against Western Province Country Districts at beautifully-situated Wellington. His first stroke was a superbly executed late-cut which sped to the boundary like a sable antelope, carrying with it the message for all to read that classic grace had at last joined the Hassett cricketing caravan in this land of the voortrekker ox wagon laager.

The Australians next took the now Blue Train through the sprawling vine-clad Hex River Valley and across the Great Karoo to Kimberley and the 'City of Gold and Glitter', Johannesburg, to meet the stocky and volatile Eric Rowan, his younger but far taller brother Athol, and Transvaal at the venue of the Christmas Test—that citadel of Springbok Rugby, Ellis Park.

The giant Athol Rowan was probably then the finest off-spin bowler in the world, a cross between Ian Johnson and Jim Laker.

Sent in on a sodden pitch, taking centimetres rather than millimetres of spin, the Australians were dismissed for 84—Miller 7, Athol Rowan 9 for 19.

Transvaal closed its first innings at 125 for 9; 41 in front; and Athol Rowan had the Australians out again for 109—Miller 1, Rowan 6 for 49, or 15 for 68 all told. Only one Australian batsman, Ken Archer, 20 not out in the first innings, had reached a score of runs in either innings. Miller, playing in his first important match of the tour, had managed only 7 and 1, Morris 15 and 12, Harvey 7 and 13, Loxton 6 and 3.

When Athol Rowan's more-than-suspect knee gave way in the second innings he was pronounced unlikely ever to bowl again. A young off-spinner down in Durban named Hugh Tayfield began to lick his lips in the wings.

On the final day on an improving wicket Transvaal, with all its wickets intact, needed only 69 to create history by becoming the first side to defeat an Australian team in South Africa.

Transvaalers and Natalians in those days held about as much love for one another as New South Welshmen and Victorians. Eric Rowan was a cockily confident, but likeable, egotist. He firmly believed that he, not Natal's Dudley Nourse, should be appointed Springbok captain for the approaching Test series.

Before Transvaal's second innings he gloated to Miller, 'We're going to do something to you Australians even a South African Test side has never done in this country. We're going to thrash you hollow.'

He was wrong. Miller, who had delivered 18 overs to take 2 for 48 in Transvaal's first innings 125 for 9, now dismissed that great Springbok batsman Bruce Mitchell for 4, Ian Johnson got Eric Rowan for 11 to make it 22 for 3, and then proceeded on to 6 for 22 from 13·3 overs from a total of 53. The Australians won by 15 runs.

But those who arranged their visitors' itinerary apparently still placed great faith in South Africa's 'secret weapon', hospitality. The preliminary to the Christmas Test at Johannesburg was a match against a South African XI back in Durban from December 16 to 19 and some of the Australians were invited to visit Lourenco Marques and sample its famous prawns piri-piri between this game and the Test.

The Springbok selectors, believing another experienced batsman was required to support Nourse and Eric Rowan in the Tests, sent the 40-year-old Bruce Mitchell, who had scored eight Test centuries including 120 and 189 not out against England at Kennington Oval in 1947 and 120 against it at Cape Town in 1948–49, down to Durban with instructions to 'take a good look at the Australian attack'.

Bruce did. He scored 8 in 95 minutes—out of a two-day total of 329. Bill Johnston, unexpectedly back in harness, but not driving any of Murray Little's limousines, delivered 32·1 overs to take 2 for 81 and Miller 22 overs for 2 for 63. Loxton, who had scored 230 in six first-class innings, but had not taken a wicket on tour to that stage, now produced the imposing analysis of 18/7/32/4.

Jack Moroney 160 not out and Neil Harvey 100 (their second centuries for the tour), and Ken Archer 58 as an opener, helped the Australians to 344 for 4. But Miller 6, and Loxton 4, failed.

Australia was at full strength for the First Test. The South Africans omitted Mitchell on the grounds that 'aggression was needed'. Interviewed back on the Rand a very perplexed Bruce said, 'They told me to have a look at the Australian attack and I did—for more than an hour and a half.'

Hosts of prospectors have trekked the 652 kilometres from Durban to Johannesburg since the great gold rush of the early 1880s. Thanks to Murray Little the London *Daily Express*'s cricket, boxing, and tennis writer Frank Rostron, his wife Barbara (daughter of one of the proprietors of the South African Argus Group), and I did the journey in a 1949 model Hudson sedan at an average touring speed of 110 kilometres an hour.

Fortunately there was plenty to see. The South African veld provides far more beautiful and far less monotonous scenery than does the greater part of gum-tree-straddled Australia. It also has considerably more historic significance.

As we roared up to Pietermaritzburg, and on past the battlefields and bastions of the Boer and Zulu wars Colenso, Weenen, Ladysmith, Majuba Hill, and Spion Kop, black, orange-collared, and long-tailed widow birds (South Africans called them flop or sakabula birds) and white, yellow-billed tick birds were 'flopping' over or squatting peacefully upon the backs of huge oxen; high-breasted Zulu 'maidens' stood like sculpted bronze statues on the crests of the Valley of a Thousand Hills, white and black people, mocking apartheid, mingled in the market places of the towns and villages, and native chieftains lazed in the sun among their wives, children, cattle, and goats around and about their mud-hut kraals.

Among the huge crowds watching the First Test match at Ellis Park from 24 to 28 December were two of the greatest opening batsmen of all time. One of them was John Berry (later Sir Jack) Hobbs, of Surrey and England, scorer of 197 centuries and some 61 000 runs in first-class cricket. Alongside him was the still-puzzled Springbok discard Bruce Mitchell, who had scored that 120 and 189 not out at The Oval in 1947 with a bat Hobbs had presented to his, Mitchell's, sister.

Alongside him, too, might have been Australia's captain Lindsay Hassett, had he not decided to disobey his doctor's very earnest orders to undergo an immediate operation for the removal of his tonsils.

Because of his now-chronic indisposition Hassett, who had rested during the game against the South African XI at Durban, promoted Miller to Number 3 on the batting list, after winning the toss, and placed himself at Number 4.

Lindsay was not to know, of course, that both his opening batsmen, the so-far-very-successful Morris and Moroney, would be out without scoring, with the total 2 for 2. He was not to expect that had he and Keith been caught, as they could well have been off fast bowler Cuan McCarthy before either of them scored, it would have been 2 for 4 or, as we say in Australia, 4 for 2.

As it was, Hassett and a short-of-match-practice and very scratchy Miller, 21, took the total to 71 for 3; Hassett and Neil Harvey, 34, took it on to 163 for 4; and Hassett and McCool, 31, to 200 for 5.

At stumps on that Christmas Eve of more than thirty years ago a very weary Hassett, now partnered by Sam Loxton, was 100 not out. Having watched Loxton being missed off McCarthy when 24 and 'morally' bowled by him at least half-a-dozen times, Lindsay during the last two overs of the day could hardly lift his bat. That night he went straight to bed after dinner for the first and last time on a Christmas Eve during his adult life. And he stayed there for most of Christmas Day while his suite-mate, an anxious and solicitous 'Chappie' Dwyer, acted as his nurse.

Hassett was dismissed for 112 early on Boxing Day, but Loxton, 101, and Ian Johnson, 66, were well supported by the 'tail' and Australia, instead of being 2 for 4 (or 4 for 2) finished with 413. Miller 5 for 50 from 15 overs in the first innings, Bill Johnston 6 for 44 from 20·1 overs in the second, and Ian Johnson 6 for 91 all told, had South Africa out for 137 and 191 and Australia won by an innings and 85.

A week later, some 6500 metres nearer to sea-level at Cape Town, Hassett again won the toss and again decided to bat. This time the Australians, having received that first day danger signal on the Rand, made every post a winning post. Morris, 42, and Moroney, 87, paved the way for Miller, 58, and Hassett, 57. Then

Harvey, unfolding the most glorious display of stroke-making I have watched even from him, chimed in with 178 of an eventual 526 for 7 declared.

It was on the following morning in the team's hotel below Table Mountain that an old Negro paid the ultimate tribute to Harvey. As he sat on the floor outside my bedroom door cleaning boots, and listening to a recorded Chopin concerto, he said with an unforgettable light in his brown eyes: 'Daat very beautifool music, Mastah—beautifool as daat young Mastah Harvey's batting.'

On the third morning of the match Nourse, who had scored a magnificently memorable 231 in the Johannesburg Test of 1935–36 against O'Reilly and Grimmett, was 65 not out of 169 for 3.

Dudley had shown imposing, nay ominous, form on the previous evening and the last thing the Australians wanted him to do was to repeat his performance of fourteen summers before.

Test match play used to begin at 11 a.m. in South Africa. It was 9.50 a.m. when Keith Miller greeted me on the stoep of the International Hotel. 'That's my car down there. Hop in and I'll drive you to Newlands,' he said, pointing to a huge, black, and somewhat dilapidated limousine.

Newlands is a good 19 kilometres, around what is known as Devil's Peak, from The Gardens where we were staying. Traffic along the main road to it (the De Waal Drive had yet to be constructed) was usually congested.

Miller steered the car down Adderley Street and then to my concern turned left towards the Cape of Good Hope, not right towards our destination.

'It's almost 10 o'clock,' I said.

'I have to collect someone between Sea Point and Clifton,' Keith explained.

'Between Sea Point and Clifton! We'll never make it,' I exclaimed.

'Don't panic. There's plenty of time.'

'I'm not panicking. There's no hurry from *my* point of view. I was thinking of *you*. Nourse is 65 not out, remember?'

'Leave it to me.'

I did. I rarely argue with Miller. My wristlet watch was pointing to 10.10 a.m., however, as we took what proved to be a wrong turning into a narrow side street just beyond Sea Point. While attempting a U turn Keith, who is no Jack Brabham at the best of times, headed the huge and heavy car into a deep gutter.

'Damn and blast,' he said. 'We'll have to try and push it out.'

'Why don't you reverse it?'

'There's no reverse gear, or rather it's not working.'

You would have needed a team of oxen to get that car out of that drain, even to have budged it.

'Where did you *get* the car?' I asked.

'From some garage out near here.'

'I'll go and look for one. You'll break that back of yours.'

Two streets away I found a garage.

'What sort of car is it?' the garage proprietor asked.

I did my best to describe the black monster.

'It wouldn't be Keith Miller's car, would it?' the fellow asked with a grin.

'How did you guess?'

'He hired it from *us*!'

That Miller luck again.

'The Test's due to begin in three-quarters of an hour?' the man said.

'Less than that.'

'Hop into that truck then, while I find some rope—that one over there.'

By the time we had the car out of the drain and heading in the right direction, it was 10.25 a.m.

'You'll have to step on it, Keith,' I said, feeling I might be signing my death warrant.

'I still have to collect my friend. Can't leave him stranded.'

I won't dwell over that drive to Newlands. The very thought of it still gives me the horrors. Enough to say it was 10.56 a.m. when we stormed up to the narrow entrance gate to the Kelvin Grove Club, which acts as a parking lurk for Newlands.

By a masterly piece of piloting Keith managed to nose straight between two resplendently polished limousines with pennants on their bonnets. In the rear seat of the first of them I recognised the Governor-General of South Africa; in the second the Australian High Commissioner.

'Go for your life, Keith. You've only got three minutes to be on the field. Leave this to me.'

For once in our long association I was obeyed. The chauffeurs of the two cars and their distinguished occupants proved most understanding and considerate. They probably had recognised the tall, dark, ruggedly-handsome figure dashing past them on his way around the famous Oaks of Newlands towards the Members Pavilion.

That non-functioning reverse gear was no help, of course, but Miller's bewildered pal and I were just passing the scoreboard when Lindsay Hassett led his men, all of them but Miller, out on to the field.

The umpires were already in position when Nourse and his young partner Jackie Nel appeared. Still no Miller.

Hassett was very good at times like these. He began stationing and re-arranging his field-placings like a chess champion.

Nourse, like most South Africans a superb sportsman, took guard for the second time, then strolled down the pitch to chat with Nel.

At long last when the pavilion clock was pointing to two minutes past the hour an easily-recognisable figure came sprinting out of the players' gate making vital adjustments to his shirt and trousers. They didn't have zip-fasteners then.

Hassett had already posted 'Big Bill' Johnston a few metres in front of Nourse at silly mid-on. As Miller approached the pitch Lindsay tossed him the ball as if to say 'Here's your chance to redeem yourself'.

I fancy it was the second ball of the morning that landed exactly where its deliverer intended it to do, reared sharply from that slow wicket towards Nourse's left armpit, and caused that formidable hooker of a bumper to prop it gently into Johnston's hands.

Nourse caught Johnston bowled Miller 65; South Africa 169 for 4.

Though Lindwall and Johnston failed to take a wicket from a total of 29 overs in that innings, Miller 3 for 54 from 17, and McCool 5 for 41 from 11.4, had the Springboks out for 278 and Hassett was able to enforce the follow-on.

In the second South African innings Nourse made 114 and showed what he might have done in that first innings but for that amazing intervention by the man whom Australia's Board of Control and two of its selectors had decided they could do without.

This time Lindwall, 5 for 32 from 15.4 overs, discarded his newly-acquired nickname of 'Wraith' Lindwall and Bill Johnston took 3 for 70. Australia won by eight wickets and led two Tests to nil with three to play.

The tourists travelled around the spectacularly beautiful French Corniche-like Garden Route via fashionable Hermanus, Knysna, George, and Plettenburg Bay to Port Elizabeth (or 'Pollockville' as it is now known because of the deeds of Peter and Graeme Pollock). Here on a rain-affected pitch against Eastern Province Miller struck six 6s and seven 4s while top-scoring with 131 of a match-winning 418.

It was during the last day of the following game against Border at East London that a very dignified, white-haired patriarch, who migrated to South Africa after the Boer War, approached the Australian end of the Press Box and said:

'I have watched most of England's great professional and amateur cricketers of the past sixty years, seen W. G. Grace, Ulyett, Shrewsbury, Ranjitsinhji, Archie Maclaren, Sir Stanley Jackson, and Sydney Barnes. Luckily I was driven to Port Elizabeth last weekend and was able to see Miller score that century of his. I say luckily because he is not playing here and I would have hated to have missed seeing him. He is the one player in your team who measures to the stature of the great olden time players—both for ability and presence.

'Forgive me for interrupting you, but I should be grateful if you would tell Mr Miller what I have said when next you see him,' the old man added and walked away.

Having defeated Eastern Province by an innings and 39 runs and Border by an innings and 293 runs, the Australians took the train up through what is now the Transkei Bantustan and down through the Drakensburg Mountains to their favourite South African city, Durban, and the Third Test.

Top: Keith Miller is met by Len Hutton on board *Himalaya* in the 1950s. *Bottom:* Miller and Ian Johnson arriving at Buckingham Palace in 1956 to receive M.B.E.s for their services to cricket (*Photos—Central Press Photos*)

Top: The Lord Mayor of London, Sir Cuthbert Ackroyd, greets Keith Miller at a Mansion House reception in 1956. In the centre is Eric Mitchell, a friend of the Lord Mayor (*Photo—United Press*). *Bottom:* Miller hits out at Laker during the Third Test at Headingley, Leeds, in 1956 (*Photo—Sport & General Press Agency*)

14
Test cricket's greatest hoax

The Third Test of that 1949–50 summer at Durban's Old Kingsmead Ground is remarkable and memorable for many things. Among them are Dudley Nourse's still controversial decision not to enforce an Australian follow-on immediately before the third day's play, Hugh Tayfield's sensational Test bowling debut on the second day, and perhaps the finest of all Neil Harvey's 79 Test innings—innings from which he scored 6149 runs with 21 centuries—on the fourth.

Its most remarkable and decisive feature, however, the Miller–Hassett bluff on the second day, has received little attention. I say 'most decisive' because it was this piece of Australian deception which fashioned the tapestry of the gruelling and gripping contest.

For the most part, be it noted and remembered, Keith and Lindsay got on extremely well in South Africa that summer and co-operated extremely well. But for this co-operation between them Australia must have lost that Durban Test before it was two days old.

Batting first on a firm wicket on the Friday, South Africa were 240 for 2 at stumps. That formidable strokemaker Nourse was then 64 not out, following his 65 and 114 at Cape Town. His vice-captain and most outspoken and persistent critic, Eric Rowan, was 133 not out (his first century against Australia).

Rowan had scored 156 not out against England the previous summer, was determined to better that performance, and had confidently claimed overnight he would do so, that he probably would get 200.

Rowan and Nourse already had taken the South African score from 75 to 240 for 2. If they became set again a formidable total was inevitable.

Heavy sub-tropical rain fell on the uncovered wicket, however, in the early hours of Saturday 21 January, penetrating deep.

Hot, morning sunshine threatened to make the wicket treacherous when, or soon after, play resumed at high noon. Sunday was to be a rest day; the events of the Saturday's play promised to be crucial.

If the Australians were forced to follow-on and bat twice, if they lost important batsmen in their second innings on the Saturday their fate would be sealed. Australia's almost fifty years' avoidance of defeat on the veld would have ended and they would lead 2–1 in the series with two Tests to be played.

Under the laws applying during that series a team could not enforce a follow-on, make its opponents bat twice in succession, unless it led by 200 runs on the first innings. Even on a truly difficult wicket South Africa could not expect to dismiss the strong Australian batting line, one which had totalled 413 in the First Test and 526 for 7 in the Second, for much less than 100.

The Springboks needed at least another sixty runs and the hard-hitting Nourse seemed the most likely batsman to get them and to get them swiftly.

'Our first task is to dismiss Nourse as soon and as cheaply as possible,' Hassett told his team in the dressing-room.

Even if this were achieved, however, the Australians' position would be alarming and Athol Rowan's 15 wickets for 68 on that soft, turning wicket at Ellis Park early in December was prominently in the minds of Hassett and his batsmen as they followed the white-coated umpires, Hart-Davis and Malan, on to the drying, green field—on to the field on which Charles Macartney's stroke-making brilliance in 1921 had been said to 'mock the summer lightning'.

The younger of the two Rowan brothers had been ordered to have the cartilage removed from his knee after his triumph for Transvaal on the Rand. He was not among the Springbok ranks. But this Kingsmead wicket under the scorching Natal sun could already be, or soon become, far worse than the one at Ellis Park, the one on which the Australians had totalled 84 and 109.

The Australians would be confronting the contrasting off and leg spin of the superlatively accurate right-handed Tayfield and left-handed 'Tufty' Mann now.

Was the deeply-soaked wicket already treacherous? How long would it take to become so? These were the crucial questions.

Remembering Miller's dismissal of Nourse in the first over of the day at Cape Town, Hassett decided to give him the ball.

Many people who have met Keith Miller, many even who have felt they know him well, have not regarded him as a deep thinker. In this judgment of him they have been wrong. He is a deep and intuitive thinker and when Keith's interest was fully aroused he was a cricketing genius. And it was fully aroused now.

Rowan, not Nourse, was the batsman facing him when play began. He had received no instructions to dismiss Rowan as soon as possible. He had six balls with which to experiment. He delivered the first four of them at medium pace about 30 centimetres wide of the off stump, taking care not to impart any spin. All four of the balls cut through harmlessly.

He had established one premise upon which Australia's strategy could be based. The wicket could be *made* to look easy—at least for some time. But was it really easy? Did he dare try and discover, to risk revealing to the South African captain and vice-captain what right now would be its reaction to spin?

If the pitch was shown to be difficult the obvious tactics for the Springboks were to hit for hell and high water and, when another fifty or so runs were on the board, declare. Nourse was just the batsman for the occasion. He had even mastered O'Reilly and Grimmett—albeit fourteen years before.

Miller, ever a gambler, decided to accept the risk without reference to his captain. Nourse could hardly declare right away with only forty runs up his sleeve. If he did, Australia could hardly fail to avoid the follow-on.

Rowan would do his utmost to dissuade his captain from closing. He was a selfish, highly-egotistical man and his sights were on that 156 and beyond.

The Australians needed to know the exact state of the wicket before they formulated their plan for the remainder of that vital day and decided how to implement it. All these considerations flashed through Miller's mind.

Keith delivered the fifth ball of that first over to Rowan with the gentlest amount of spin he could manage. Even so, it turned sharply and ominously—so ominously that Keith glanced anxiously at Rowan and then at Nourse to ascertain their reaction.

Rowan, to his relief, seemed oblivious to the import of that delivery—either oblivious to it or determined to ignore it. Nourse, to his even greater relief, seemed unmoved.

Keith bowled the sixth and last ball of that pathfinding over without a semblance of spin, aimed it well outside the off stump, and it cut through slow and straight.

Miller, now fully informed of the situation, had made up his mind as to what should be the Australian policy. The wicket *was* already bad and would grow worse before it recovered. The only tactics which could save Australia from a crushing defeat were to try and prolong the South African innings for as long as possible and, while doing so, contain the scoring.

Fortunately the implementation of this twofold objective could be pursued through the same tactics. The policy of reducing the scoring rate could help to conceal the bluff.

Miller decided to have a talk to his captain—immediately and as inconspicuously and casually as he could. He must get him, if he was not already, onside.

Luckily they were to pass one another during the change of ends.

As they were about to do so Keith bent to re-tie the laces of one of his boots. Lindsay had noticed how sharply that one off-spinner had turned and he was noted for his ingenuity. He halted alongside Miller, took a handkerchief from his pocket, and held it out to test the direction of the wind. This, of course, was the least of his worries.

Swiftly the two players agreed upon a plan. The problem was just how best to put it into execution. Which bowlers to use.

Lindsay knew Keith could be depended upon to play his part from one end. Who should he use at the other, use right now?

His other bowlers were Lindwall, Bill Johnston, Sam Loxton, Ian Johnson, and McCool. If Lindwall bowled at half pace so as to avoid gaining abrupt lift, the plan might become transparent. If either of the spinners, Johnson and McCool, were used and kept delivering straight-breaks, the Australians' motive would be crystal clear. Johnson and McCool also were the most vulnerable to all-out attack.

Loxton's line and length had usually been erratic. He could not be trusted in such a crisis.

By the time Keith had attended to his bootlaces and Lindsay had completed his meteorological experiment, it was agreed that Bill Johnston must be Keith's partner and confederate: 'Con-man' if you like.

Johnston already had been used as a medium-pace stock bowler as well as a fast-medium new-ball bowler in the preceding Tests. No significance would be attached if he, like Miller, bowled at medium pace. He was accurate in the extreme and could be depended upon to conform to instructions.

But the best-laid plans of cricketers, as well as those of mice and other men, are apt to go awry.

During Johnston's second over Nourse, doubtless finding concentration difficult, flicked at an offside ball and was caught for 66 by the wicketkeeper Ron Saggers at 242 for 3.

The Australians' feelings about Nourse's swift dismissal were understandably mixed. The main threat, the one batsman capable of launching a devastating onslaught upon the innocuous bowling, had departed. But with what thoughts in mind? He *was* the Springbok captain. Had he read the situation rightly? How, and when, would he act? There were some fine cricketing brains up in the Old Kingsmead Pavilion—men who had played against and knew their Australians.

Billy Wade, the South African wicketkeeper-batsman, joined Rowan and, to the relief of the Australians, seemed intent upon settling in.

As over after lifeless off-side over followed from Miller and Johnston, Hassett moved his fieldsmen one by one into positions to which catches were least likely to come. Rowan went on slowly but safely towards 156, that highest Test score of his.

Invaluable and vital minutes were being saved as the sun grew hotter overhead. Anxious minutes, albeit.

Even Rowan's uncontrived dismissal, caught Johnston bowled Miller for 143 at 264 for 4, passed without seeming to arouse suspicion as to the real state of the pitch.

Nourse and the huge crowd appeared to have decided that the

Australians' over-riding objective was to contain the scoring rate and thus on the Monday and Tuesday be able to achieve a draw.

An hour passed as Miller and Johnston bowled on at half pace mostly outside the off stump under the midday sun. Up in the pavilion, however, Alan Melville, the 1948 England-tour Springbok captain, had begun to smell a rat.

Melville had learned a lot about Australians from English cricketers and cricketing connoisseurs while at Oxford University, and while captaining Sussex. His several years in England had also taught him a deal about the behaviour of drying wickets.

Just what *were* these representatives of that 'nation of confidence tricksters' up to at the moment? Alan believed he knew. When Wade snicked a ball from Johnston straight and knee-high to Miller at gully Keith half grasped the easy chance, stumbled, fell, and allowed the ball to drop to the turf. Even though Miller (later that day to be nicknamed 'Larry Olivier') shook his head and wrung his hands in mock disgust, Melville decided to take action.

He hastened to the South African dressing-room and urged Nourse to send a message to Wade and his new partner Mann instructing them 'to hit out or get out'.

South Africa had entered the 280s. Ninety of the vital 300 minutes had passed but still Nourse dallied. No message was sent. Melville, the South African representative for Gordon's gin, retired in exasperation and anger to the Members' stand bar and downed several Johnny Walker whiskies with Natal Cricket Association Secretary, Doug Geddie.

Eventually, despite the efforts of Miller and Johnston, and Hassett's well-calculated field placement, wickets began to fall more rapidly. The pitch was approaching its worst.

Two and a half hours, half the day's play, had passed before South Africa were all out for 311. Miller, 24 overs, 5 maidens, and 1 wicket for 73, had done his job impeccably. Johnston, 31·2 overs, 5 maidens, and 4 wickets for 75, had been what in the circumstances might be called less successful. Statistics, you see, do not always tell the true story.

Australia now needed 112 to avoid being forced to follow-on. Hassett had the right to use the heaviest roller between innings and this would draw the sub-surface moisture upward, prevent the pitch from again becoming treacherous for a time.

Wickets are at their worst, as the Australians well knew, when soft underneath and baked on top. Under such conditions the ball has something to grip on as it lands and even the most innocent deliveries are apt to rise and turn quite unpredictably.

The only Australian batsman in all history who had managed to succeed on them at all consistently had been the immortal Victor Trumper, who had scored 18 of Australia's lowest-ever Test total, its 36 against England on the Edgbaston 'gluepot' in 1902.

Hassett had no wish to be remembered as the captain of a team which eclipsed that all-time low. The ten minutes between innings were anxious and exacting ones for him. Should he rearrange his batting order? Should he send his hardest hitters, Miller, Lindwall, and Loxton, in first against the new ball so as to get as many runs as possible on the board before the pitch again began to form a crust?

The sun was at its hottest now; the sky still a dome of blue. The odds were that Australia would fail to avoid the follow-on. If it lost several of its best batsmen twice that day all hope of forcing a draw, let alone of staging a recovery on the Monday and winning on the Tuesday, would have vanished.

Lindsay decided upon a compromise. He would open as usual with Morris and Moroney, promote Ian Johnson to Number 3 above the exhausted Miller, bat himself at Number 5, and promote Saggers, McCool, and Lindwall above Harvey and Loxton.

Johnson had had considerable experience as a batsman on wet, early-summer pitches in Melbourne club cricket. If the situation grew really desperate, Lindwall, Harvey, and Loxton could fling the bat in a last frantic bid for runs. Alternatively, if the wicket had begun to recover under a declining sun they could stall for time; they had the technique to do so. There is a lot more to cricket than meets the unknowledgable eye.

Nourse opened his attack with the genuinely fast and lively Cuan McCarthy and the steady, fast-medium, swing bowler John Watkins. The heavy roller had achieved what Hassett hoped it would, had drawn water to the surface of the pitch. Though far from being normal the wicket was not yet impossible and, during the first forty-five minutes, Morris and Moroney scored 31 of the initially required 112 runs. Eighty-one needed, just over 100 minutes of play remaining for the day, and all ten wickets intact.

Nourse had received a verbal blast from his predecessor Melville; had been told he had allowed South Africa's long-delayed chance of defeating Australia to diminish through his procrastination. Dudley was worried and he called upon the experienced left-handed spinner Mann, perhaps the most accurate and economical bowler in the world at that time, to deliver the tenth over.

Mann immediately began to turn the ball sharply and to lift it from a length. Nourse introduced the 21-year-old Tayfield, who had yet to bowl in a Test match, at McCarthy's end.

Perhaps no bowler in Test match history has achieved so sensational a debut as did Tayfield. He bowled Moroney for 10, dismissed Johnson leg before wicket for 2, had Morris caught for 25, bowled Miller for 2, and had Hassett leg before wicket for 2.

Five wickets had fallen for 11 runs—all of them to Tayfield. Australia 42, was less than half way to temporary sanctuary with half its batsmen gone. Then Mann took a hand to dismiss Saggers for 2 and McCool for 1. It was 46 for 7 now with Lindwall, Harvey, Loxton, and Johnston left.

Harvey had scored 178 and 23 not out in the Cape Town Test and Loxton a century in the one at Johannesburg. But those performances seemed just part of a dream now, part of another cricketing world.

The batsmen who had fallen during that crash of seven wickets had not surrendered without a struggle; most of them, however, had saved precious time.

The hands of the clock on the old-fashioned mound scoreboard beyond the southern end sightboard had crept past 5 p.m. There would be another ten-minute interval between innings. Hassett could take that heavy roller again. All was not yet lost.

Lindwall dead-batted and stalled for 7 and, though Harvey was caught and bowled by Tayfield for 2, Loxton, 16, and Johnston took the total to 75 while the time snailed its way towards the asylum of 5.50 p.m.

The ground clock was dead on that time when Cheetham caught Loxton to make Tayfield's analysis 8·4/1/23/7. Australia's second innings was intact. It had lived for another day. The greatest bluff in the history of Test cricket had worked.

I was sitting, mentally drained, on the stoep of Durban's superb, white, sea-fronting Edward Hotel after dinner that night when an unusually excited and surprisingly cheerful Miller joined me and ordered drinks.

'I hope you haven't been stupid enough to write off our chances in your story to Australia?' he exclaimed, running his fingers through his hair.

'I haven't cabled it yet,' I replied. 'It's the most difficult story of a Test day's play I've ever had to write.'

'You gathered what was going on, of course?'

'Yes. So did Alan Melville, by the way.'

'I'm sorry for Dudley Nourse,' Keith said. 'He's going to have the whole nation down on him like a ton of bricks when South Africa lose.'

'*When* they lose. *If* they lose, you mean. You're still 236 behind.'

'We're going to win and you'd better say so. You'll probably be the only Pressman who does. Just think of the feather that will be in your cap.'

'You must be joking?'

'I'm dead serious. Want to bet?'

Keith's luck as a punter was too well known for me to accept that £5 wager, but I modified my story—quoting the optimism of the Australian team.

Everything now would depend on the weather and the state of the wicket on the Monday. No rain fell that Saturday night, nor throughout the next day and night. On the Monday morning the sun was brightly shining from a clear, Indian Ocean sky.

Half an hour before the third day's play began I walked out to inspect the Old Kingsmead pitch. It had set hard, but there were indentations on or about a good length at both ends. Most of them were in line with the stumps or just outside that line. They revealed just how accurate Tayfield and Mann had been.

The depressions were as much as 125 millimetres deep 380 millimetres in diameter. They reminded me of those cups in the green baize of old-time billiard tables.

I noticed the glee on the faces of the cock-ahoop Tayfield and Mann as they, too, examined the wicket.

Dudley Nourse was also inspecting it and walking worriedly up and down. It was obvious that he had read his morning newspapers.

The Durban and Johannesburg Press, the entire nation, was hungry for victory, for victory by an innings over the most powerful cricketing country in the world. The Johannesburg Press had been particularly unkind.

'Would you bat again or make Australia follow-on?' he asked, to my surprise, as he came towards me.

Such a question from a national cricket captain to an 'enemy' Pressman was new in my experience. I regarded it as extremely flattering in more ways than one.

'I'm an Australian, Dudley,' I said.

'I know that. I'm asking you for your honest opinion. If you're not prepared to give me that, there's no need to answer.'

Naturally I had expected Nourse, as had almost everyone, to enforce the follow-on. South Africa led by 236 runs, trailed by two Tests to nil in the series—half-way through the series. It had the Australians down and 'Hold that Zulu down, Chief, hold that Zulu down' was one of Natal's most popular songs.

Suddenly the reasons for Nourse's indecision struck me.

'What's the weather forecast?' I asked.

'Fine for the rest of the match,' Dudley replied.

'You believe the wicket can only get worse as the edges of those pockmarks crumble and widen?'

'Yes and, if I bat again, I can take the heavy roller and help to accelerate this. I can study what happens and declare, if and when I care to.'

This all made sense. Maybe Dudley was right, I thought, and said so.

South Africans have never forgiven Nourse for his decision to bat again, but I still believe he had sound reasons for making it. He could hardly have anticipated that his batsmen would perform as feebly as they did. He had perhaps even less reason to think Neil Harvey would play the greatest innings of his life, an innings entirely out of character and utterly in contrast with his effortless display of stroke-making at Newlands—that gloriously free 178 under the shadow of Table Mountain.

On that Monday which South Africans remember much as they recall Dingaan's Day and their expulsion in the 1970s from international cricket, Bill Johnston, bowling orthodox left-handed spinners, and Ian Johnson, turning in the opposite direction (except when he pitched the ball on the inner side of a pockmark) took 4 for 39 and 5 for 34, respectively.

South Africa 311 and 99, led Australia 75, by 335 and nobody, except Hassett and his batsmen, believed they would get the runs. Those who had inspected the wicket gave them no hope even of approaching their goal.

Victory seemed even less likely when Morris 44, Moroney 10, Hassett 11, and Miller 10, were out with the total 95 for 4.

But Harvey, batting with unbelievable skill and judgment, with monumental patience, and unrelaxing concentration for five-and-a-half hours, was 151 not out when victory came on the final day by the surprising margin of five wickets.

Australia, thanks to Harvey and the sterling support he received from his friend Sam Loxton and from Colin McCool, had travelled from 95 for 4 to 336 for 5 on that wearing and marked pitch.

Several times as they approached their target the mentally and physically drained 19-year-old Harvey had walked up the wicket between overs and asked his partner 'Can I get out now?'

'No. Hang on,' McCool had replied.

This is the first time I have confessed my involuntary and innocent contribution to another Australian Test match victory.

Probably this is because I still believe it was that magnificently inspired and executed piece of bluff on the Saturday, not Nourse's reasonably-based decision on the Monday morning, which gave Harvey the chance to play on the Tuesday the finest innings of his life.

I hope that those of you who have read this chapter will realise, if you haven't already, that cricket can be as intricate a game as chess, as gripping as a Shakespearian tragedy—that only for the uninitiated, for those who do not understand its finer points, is it apt to become boring.

The game, as now we shall see, can also provide its comedy.

From Durban the Australians took the 1899 Boer War trail through that Valley of a Thousand Hills to Pietermaritzburg and on upward through Nottingham Road and across the 'river of blood', the Tugela, to Ladysmith, which is still famous for much the same reasons as Mafeking.

Here (a month after Australia had drawn the Fourth Test at Ellis Park) most members of the Natal Country XI were farmers—

some of them, and one of the umpires, descendants of the gallant Boer commandoes.

On the first day of this second-class game Miller was bowling from the river end of the willow-bordered ground to a particularly stubborn batsman. A tiny umpire, whose face was half concealed by the unstarched and unironed brim of a white washing hat, had refused appeals for leg before wicket from two consecutive balls.

On his way back to his mark Miller turned to the umpire, stooped to his level, and demanded, 'Which stump would they have missed, Ump—the off or the leg?'

The little umpire wasn't saying so Keith playfully lifted the frontal part of that brim which was drooping over his eyes.

The brim stayed up and Keith strode back to his mark.

His next ball was an exact replica of the preceding two. It contacted the batsman's pad almost in the identical spot and went on to break his wicket.

'How's THAT?' exclaimed Keith.

Up went the little umpire's hand and forefinger. Grinning broadly Miller tossed back his hair, walked to the umpire, and restored that brim to its original position.

By this time everyone, except the departing batsman, were in hysterics. Few of the spectators, however, may have realised how difficult it is for a bowler of Keith's pace to deliver three balls of almost identical line and length in succession.

During the second game against Transvaal before the Fourth Test Miller had gained less popularity, was accused of delivering far too many bumpers at the 40-year-old Springbok batsman Bruce Mitchell. Admittedly, Mitchell was past his prime but the way in which he dealt with the bumpers left no doubt among the knowledgable that he was in no physical danger.

The Australians had watched Mitchell score eight runs in 95 minutes for the South African XI against them in Durban in mid-December. They had no wish for him to be chosen for the Fourth Test. Miller dismissed Mitchell for 7.

In the Fourth Test Morris 111 ('Nelson's number'), Moroney 118, and Miller 'an attractive 84', led Australia to 465 for 8 declared. South Africa replied with 352.

In Australia's second innings Moroney began a tedious passage towards his second century for the match and the only interest on the final day lay in whether he would get it.

The least interested person of all as he dawdled and dithered through his fifties and sixties seemed to be Moroney himself.

So unconcerned did he appear that an Australian journalist who did a deal of yachting in South Australia's St Vincent's Gulf, described the burly Moroney as 'a purposeless porpoise'. The writer was unaware that Jack, a Sydney schoolmaster who specialised in English literature, had appeared on a radio quiz programme before his departure from Australia, that he had been asked, 'Who was Hamlet's lover?' and, to the delight of his listening pupils, had replied 'Othello' instead of 'Ophelia'.

Jack, conscious he would soon again have to confront his English classes, was not amused. He even threatened legal proceedings.

Moroney was meandering through his seventies when Miller joined him. 'Do you know how many Australians have scored centuries in each innings of a Test match Jack?' he asked.

'I haven't a clue,' Jack replied.

'Only three—Bardsley, Morris, and Bradman. If you want to be the fourth you'd better get on with it. I don't want to be out here all the afternoon waiting for you.'

Moroney did get on with it and was 101 not out of 259 for 2 at the close of the drawn Test.

During a career which lasted from 1946 to 1959 Ray Lindwall only twice was 'dropped' from an Australian Test team. The first of these occasions came before the Fifth Test of 1949–50 at Port Elizabeth and the team selectors were Dwyer, Hassett, and Morris—two of them, like Lindwall, New South Welshmen.

Lindwall, reports his friend Miller in *Cricket Crossfire*, 'was so riled with Hassett that he threatened to flatten him'. Ray so far in first-class games on the tour, had taken 22 wickets for 426 at an average of 19·36.

Geff Noblet, the South Australian new-ball bowler who gained Lindwall's place, said, 'Naturally I am thrilled to be chosen for the first time to represent my country but I would be far happier about it if my inclusion had not meant the exclusion of Ray.' I understand that Noblet was sufficiently upset even to offer to stand down.

Believing the omission of Lindwall was but part of a plan to groom several other members of the side who had not gained their Test caps, Keith's first reaction was, 'Fair enough. Who else is out?'

Learning that the replacement of Lindwall by Noblet had been the only change in the side, his views took a dramatic change.

'If it was decided not to take any chances in a Test but to play our strongest eleven, it seemed madness to leave out Lindwall,' he has written. 'I thought this was pretty thick,' he added. 'It was as though Hassett did not know the form and value of a chap like Lindwall, especially on an overseas tour.'

Discussing Lindsay, he went on, 'Hassett is a very human character, which means he has his share of faults and failings. He is also a charming, gay, witty person with a tremendous zest for life and a full knowledge of where he is going and what he is doing. For so tiny a frame he carried more than his quota of courage . . . A Lindsay Hassett in the 1956 Australian batting order in England might have changed the flow of cricket history.'

At Port Elizabeth Australia, 549 for 7 declared thanks mainly to Morris 157, Hassett 167, and Harvey 122 (his fourth century in the five Tests) defeated South Africa 158 and 132, for the fourth time that summer—equalling the record of Vic Richardson's 1935–36 side.

Though yet again Miller had shown scant interest in his position on the tour averages—had reserved his best for the critical occasion—he had left no doubt as to his right of selection in Australia's Test teams, had shown himself both a happy and invaluable member of a well-captained and superbly-managed side. All told he scored 651 runs at 36·16 and took 55 wickets at 14·07. His Test figures were 246 at 41·00 and 17 wickets at 23·00.

My most lasting memory of him on that South African tour is his final gesture at Port Elizabeth. When Australia had won by an innings and 259 he whipped the bails from the stumps at the bowler's end (most cricketers like to keep such tokens as souvenirs). As he strode from the ground Keith hurled them high into the throng of delighted Africans on the mound reserved for non-whites.

15
Some battlements are built

Throughout the 1940s, while progressing from twenty to thirty years of age, Miller had spent only one winter, the winter of 1949, in Australia. Following his return from abroad in 1945–46 he had lived his summers in Australia but they all had been devoted to cricket and the continual travelling it involved.

Rarely had he been in one place for more than a week at a time, had a chance to pause, to survey, and plan. In consequence, what foundations he had managed to lay for his future needed walls and a roof—even ramparts, his original omission from the South African tour suggested.

Keith's original non-selection for that tour had shown him just how vulnerable he was. He realised he had been living, at times irresponsibly, in a whirlwind for ten years and had learnt just what kind of harvests reapers of whirlwinds are prone to collect. He must decide how best he could protect himself and his growing family, and take appropriate action.

Those few ill-timed bumpers at that ill-chosen and angry target at the Sydney Cricket Ground in February of 1949, and the repercussions they had wrought, were like red danger signals in his brain. Though he had scored 363 at 45·37 for New South Wales during the 1948–49 season he had been ruthlessly rejected, stood in a corner like a jester who had dared to joust with his master.

Because of Bill Johnston's accident in Durban his luck had held. He had received a chance to regain his position in international cricket and he had taken it well. Once more he was recognised as the world's outstanding all-rounder.

So far so good, but his had been a narrow and salutary escape.

Cricket, his success as a cricketer, his name and aura as a cricketer, was vital to his future. It would remain his Excalibur throughout his life.

Well, like a good golfer, he had replaced his divots and was back on the fairway. Summer was six months off. He had time to turn his attention to other problems, to those of his home and his work.

He was too much of a realist to be unmindful of the pitfalls that still lay ahead on the cricketing front, but he knew now just who were his enemies and who were his friends there.

Cricket could wait.

When he returned to Sydney from Cape Town in April of 1950 Keith had been married for three-and-a-half years. For his attractive young American wife cricket was as mystifying as the flight of a boomerang or the mockery in a kookaburra's laughter. She had seen precious little of her husband during those forty-two months. She had forsaken her American parents and friends. She was lonely but she hadn't complained.

Fortunately the Millers had started a family and Keith, who three sons later was to assert that children 'should be born seven years old', was looking forward to the chance of planting his feet before a hearth of his own. There was far too much foreign dust on his shoes.

Adam had four sons and, despite that feud between Cain and Abel, Keith had ideas about out-scoring him. He named his first boy Bill, had him christened Bill, not William Miller. The lad would be addressed as Bill, not as William, Keith reasoned, and this frowner upon formality acted accordingly when he called at the registry office alongside St Mary's Cathedral.

As usual the sensible and placid Peg Miller offered no resistance.

'Keith's too big to argue with. And, anyway, what's in a name?' she explained with her bland, philosophical smile.

When a second son arrived Keith again had his way and Miller Tertius was christened Denis, after Denis Charles Scott Compton.

During that winter of 1950 I spent the occasional Sunday at

Top: Miller, caught Trueman, bowled Laker, Third Test, Headingley, Leeds, in 1956 (*Photo—Sport & General Press Agency*). *Bottom:* Keith Miller goes down on one knee to pull a ball during his innings of 238 n.o. against Leicestershire in May 1956 (*Photo—Associated Press*)

Top left: Sir Donald Bradman (*Photo—London* Daily Express). *Top right:* Keith Miller plays his mighty pull-shot during one of his seven Test centuries. Note the eyes still watching the ball to see whether it will score four or six (*Photo—News Ltd*). *Bottom:* Miller falls after hitting a ball from Jim Laker in the Fifth Test at Kennington Oval in August 1956. This was Miller's last appearance against England (*Photo—Central Press Photos*)

Keith and Peg's home on the outskirts of Manly, that Pacific 'paradise' which boasts of being 'a short distance from Sydney and a planet away from care'. It did then, anyway, when blaring juke boxes, mini-bikes, motor-scooters lacking silencers, and mobile promotional microphones were either non-existent or rare.

If Keith was finding his new domesticity a trifle restrictive after his years with the R.A.A.F., and his cricketing expeditions, it did not show. The Miller home was a happy place, despite the obduracy of the 'confounded, infernal, new-fangled contraption' Keith had installed as a chip-and-coal heater and could not get to glow.

The former Margaret Wagner, of Boston, Massachusetts, clearly adored her husband. Over a quarter of a century later in her sun-bathed, sprawling, two-storey mansion at Newport (New South Wales, not Rhode Island) she obviously still does.

In the prelude to *Cricket Crossfire* Keith confessed 'I have never set myself up as a shining example of propriety'. But it is true to say that, even against such competition as race-meetings at Gosford, nights with his favourite cronies at the Cricketers' Club, and the lure of the outside world Keith's wife, his four sons, and his home have been kept paramount and unassailable.

If I know him, and I feel I can claim to do so better than most, they always will be. Keith has never been a romantic (always a realist) and he has his solid share of philosophy that will serve him as a bulwark in his old age.

His most outstanding quality in my judgment, however, is his utterly uncluttered honesty. He has always had the courage to speak his mind and has constantly reserved the right to conduct his life as a completely open book. Both men and women may have envied, no doubt have been aggravated, by his frankness and fearlessness. But deep down they must have admired him for it.

You have always known exactly where you stand with 'Nugget', whether you were a Prime Minister or a postman, whether he agreed with you or not. Such men are rare and seem to grow rarer with the years in this increasingly complex, increasingly devious, at times alarming age in which we live.

If Keith Miller had been thirty years old and at the peak of his cricketing career in March of 1977 there is little doubt he would have been the first player Kerry Packer would have sought to sign for those professional pantomimes of his. He would have been the John Barrymore of the Travelling Cricket Theatre.

But the opportunity of earning some $30 000 a year directly or indirectly from cricket in 1950 was just not on. In 1948 even Don Bradman's testimonial had netted only $20 000, the reward for a career that must have raised a million or more for cricket between 1926 and 1948.

By 1950 Keith was getting on in years—if not for a batsman, certainly for a lightning-pace bowler with a suspect back. His main hopes of achieving and retaining financial security lay in his journalistic job.

Under the guidance of 'Johnnie' Moyes he made a serious attack upon the intricacies of his trade. Success at it, he was advised, would be achieved only if he could develop what journalists know as 'news sense'. He sought, and was given, reporting assignments on the company's daily newspaper, the Sydney *Sun*, in addition to his magazine work.

The diversified apprenticeship of factual reporting and feature writing was to benefit him greatly when, some six years later, he became the senior sportswriter for the London *Daily Express* at a salary of some £10 000 sterling a year, and he held that appointment for the best part of twenty years.

In 1950 Moyes' magazine *Sporting Life* was rising towards a monthly circulation of 250 000. Maybe the amount of sub-editing involved was interfering with his punting—his and Keith's punting on the strength of those encoded tips. Moyes applied for additional staff and was told he could seek a junior assistant.

It so happened there was a blue-eyed blond named Richie Benaud working in the Accounts Department of Australian Associated Newspapers Limited at that time. The boss of that department was a cricket fanatic named Bert Scotford and Richie, then nineteen, was showing considerable promise as a hard-hitting batsman and googly bowler.

With Scotford's consent Richie joined Moyes and Miller on the staff of *Sporting Life*.

His cadetship there was to have remarkable results, as anyone who has followed Richie's progress in journalism, in radio, and television in Australia and Britain over the past decade must have noted.

In his middle teens Richie had developed an admiration verging upon idolatry for Keith Miller, had endowed him with a halo which sat a little incongruously and uncomfortably about that glossy, black mane.

In his late teens Richie displaced his father, also a googly bowler, from the Cumberland First-Grade Sydney District competition side. By the autumn of 1950 he was a well-established member of the New South Wales practice squad and had already represented his State five times.

Finding Richie's hero-worship of him a trifle embarrassing at times, Keith was apt to try and temper it a little when opportunity came.

One winter afternoon, as Benaud was about to leave the office, he crossed to Keith's desk.

'Can you spare a minute, Mr Miller? I have a question to ask you,' he said.

'Fire ahead, but make it brief, Richie,' Keith replied. 'I'm late for an appointment with a few beers at the Carlton Bar.'

Richie was a teetotaller then, still is remarkably abstemious.

'I've begun calling at a kiosk in Martin Place of an evening on my way to Wynyard Station,' he said.

'At a milk bar, I suppose,' Keith grunted.

'No, at an apple bar. I buy a Grannie Smith to eat on the train. Do you think this will help me with my cricket next summer?'

Believe me, those of you who have known only the mature and sophisticated Benaud, this is *all* true. I was present.

'I don't know whether it will help your cricket, Richie. I'm no expert on apples, but it shouldn't do your health any harm,' Keith replied.

Apparently they didn't for Richie became Australia's Test captain, perhaps her greatest captain, scored 2201 runs and took a then record 248 wickets for an Australian in Test matches.

Richie was to remain one of Keith's most stalwart supporters in the New South Wales and Australian sides, and there were to be times when he needed friends.

During the 1948 Australian tour of Britain Clifford Gibbs, the proprietor of the London publishing firm Latimer House, had suggested to Keith that he find a collaborator and embark upon a series of cricket books.

The first of these, *Cricket Caravan*, was begun during that winter of 1950 and successfully released in 1951. *Catch*, *Straight Hit*, *Bumper*, *Gods Or Flannelled Fools?*, *Cricket Typhoon*, *The Keith Miller Cricket Companion*, and *Cricket Crossfire* were to follow inside seven years and that doyen of cricket writing Sir Neville Cardus saw fit to praise them all.

Those who contributed forewords for these books included Sir Robert Menzies, Maharaj Duleepsinhji, Sir John Barbirolli, and Denis Compton.

It was in his foreword to *Bumper* that Sir Robert described that photograph of Keith, to which I have referred, as 'The finest action picture of a cricketer I have ever seen', as 'In two dimensions a beautiful piece of sculpture, one that would have provoked immense joy in ancient Athens'.

Miller, as we have seen, had put that winter of 1950 to good purpose; had fortified himself on most fronts. More importantly, he had found something nearer to peace of mind.

But summer was coming. The spring flowers in the garden he and Peg, mostly Peg, had planted were beginning to bloom. Increasingly his thoughts began to turn back to cricket and the, for him, vitally important season that lay ahead.

Club games were about to begin. The Sheffield Shield season was due to start in six weeks' time. Freddie Brown's Marylebone Cricket Club team was about to sail from Southampton.

What did he want from cricket? What could he still achieve at it, and derive from it, in his thirties as a batsman and fast bowler with a suspect back?

So far he had survived without becoming anybody's sycophant or slave, except perhaps Australia's when she needed him most. He had insisted on playing the game in the spirit in which he believed it should be played. By doing so he had gained a name in certain quarters for being anti-government and unmanageable, been branded as a rebel, not 'one of the club'. By indulging in those defiant gestures of his in that match against Essex and in the Test at Lord's in 1948, by giving rein to his feelings at Adelaide in January of that year and at Sydney during the Kippax–Oldfield Testimonial, by not paying full court to Bradman in his Testimonial at Melbourne, where he scored 2 and 14 and did not bowl, he had endangered his international career.

Most dangerously of all he had put Bradman in the wrong, inflicted upon this man (who so dearly always wanted to win) one of his rare public defeats. Had 'The Don' accepted this much-publicised reverse, had he written it off, or would he be waiting and looking for the chance for reprisals?

Don had retired from the game as a player, but he was a member of the Australian Board of Control, ambitious, and likely to become its Chairman. He was also Chairman of the national selection committee.

Ever since the formation of the Board of Control in 1905 there had been conflict between it and Australian players and almost invariably the Board had won. In 1912 when Australia's three greatest cricketers, Trumper, Hill, and Armstrong had flouted its authority they had failed. Ironically only Bradman himself, after his triumphant tour of Britain in 1930, had bucked it with any success.

Many of the present members of the Board, as Keith well knew, were conservative and cautious men, jealous, and protective of their authority, of the only public authority they were ever likely to wield.

They would be looking upon him, he imagined, in much the same manner as, after the murder of Julius Caesar, Gaius Octavius and his followers looked upon Mark Antony in ancient Rome.

The analogy, indeed, grew more apposite, all the less exaggerative the more it was explored. They would have to go along with him as a player or risk another tussle with Press and public opinion, one they were again likely to lose.

But they would be anxious to prevent him from gaining a more powerful and influential position in the game than he already held. The last thing they would want was for him to become Australia's captain when Hassett retired.

Did Keith have ambitions to one day become captain of Australia as far back as the spring of 1950? The answer, I believe despite his denials, is 'Yes'.

What then were the chances of this? He had proved himself an excellent and popular leader of the Manly Cricket Club, had shown he had enjoyed himself far more on the field when leading a team than when merely performing as a player, had put more into his own performances.

Noticing this the New South Wales Cricket Association had promoted him to the leadership of its State side, during Arthur Morris' absence, for the first two Shield games of the 1949–50 season against Queensland and Western Australia.

Under his captaincy New South Wales had won both of those games and under Ron James leadership after Keith's departure for South Africa had gone on to win the Shield. Keith had topscored with 80 and taken most wickets, 6 for 73, as his contribution towards the fifteen-run victory over Queensland.

New South Wales officials at State and club level were very happy about Keith as a result. Some of them were far less so about Bradman. Few of them had forgiven Don for what they regarded as his 'desertion of his home State' when he moved to Adelaide in 1935.

This smouldering resentment had flared into anger, ironically enough after Don compiled his one hundredth first-class match century on the Sydney Cricket Ground against India in January of 1948. To meet him on the field as he came from his triumph towards the old Members' pavilion, the elderly and long-term president of the N.S.W.C.A., Mr Sydney Smith, had walked alone and with his hand outstretched.

Instead of taking that conciliatory hand Bradman had ignored the white-haired president, had brushed brusquely past him on his way to the dressing-room. This formed but one of the reasons why many years were to pass before Don's portrait joined that of Victor Trumper in the precincts of the N.S.W. Cricketers' Club.

Yes, the one gap in Bradman's armour lay in New South Wales, the State where Keith was winning considerable support.

No doubt Morris would regain the captaincy for the 1950–51 season. But Keith was in no hurry. He and Arthur were close friends, had a deep liking and respect for one another, and would co-operate well. They had much the same approach to and outlook concerning cricket.

Strong proof of this was soon forthcoming.

Arthur, unlike Bradman and to a lesser extent Hassett, believed Keith's greatest worth to a team lay in his batting, not bowling, ability and, with Keith's agreement, decided to put this to the test by limiting his demands upon him with the ball.

He could hardly have chosen a better time—for Keith or for his

State. Interest in Sheffield Shield cricket was regenerating at the beginning of the 1950s. Australia had not lost a Test match since 1938. Since peace had 'broken out' it had defeated England three–nil and four–nil; India, and South Africa, both four–nil, inside four years.

Australia's cricketlovers were surfeited with victory, especially with the crushing kind of victories Bradman's teams had inflicted. In those then chief citadels of Australian cricket, Sydney and Melbourne, followers of the game anticipated no serious threat to the nation's world supremacy for years to come.

Freddie Brown's men would be outplayed as Hammond's, Amarnath's, Norman Yardley's, and Nourse's had been.

The battles between those traditional rivals New South Wales and Victoria, however, promised to be far less predictable, far more competitive. Cricketlovers north and south of the Murray River were intrigued as to how Hassett and the new young batting star Neil Harvey would fare against Lindwall, Alan Walker, and Miller; how Morris and Miller would cope with 'Big Bill' Johnston and that meteoric 'mystery spinner' Jake Iverson.

Batted at the fall of the first wicket in the opening match against Queensland at Brisbane on 20 October Miller scored 201 not out of a total of 529 for 9.

The significance of that innings, that initial first-class innings he played that season, lay not so much in the size of his score as in the manner of its compilation.

When Keith began New South Wales were 134 for 1. His partners contributed almost as many runs as he did. His old desire for manhandling the bowling was disciplined. He batted far more like his boyhood idol Bill Ponsford used to bat than as he, himself, had become accustomed to batting—building and advancing his innings on sound and scientific lines.

Like Victor Trumper, Keith had more often than not disdained the double century. This time he set his sights on it and kept them there.

It was a superb as well as significant start to what was to be the most successful Australian season of Keith's entire career, something nobody could ignore down south.

Following it, Morris gave Keith only 17 overs in the two Queensland innings—and these as the sixth bowler used.

16
A summer message for 'The Don' and Jack Ryder

That 201 not out of Keith's at Woolloongabba proved to be but a pipe-opener for what became a volcano as runs flowed like lava from his bat. In his first four innings for New South Wales that season Miller scored 201 not out, 63, 138 not out, and 214—616 runs at an average of 308.

This was real Ponsford and Bradman stuff and Don and his co-selectors must have got the message. In this form Miller was threatening to eclipse even Don's own record aggregate for an Australian season, his 1690 at 93·88 in 1928–29.

On the Sydney Cricket Ground on 3 November New South Wales had met Queensland again and this time the *Bananalanders* batted first. Morris had Lindwall, Walker, and the young Alan Davidson in his ranks and, adhering to his new policy, gave Miller only four overs with the ball.

Keith responded by contributing 63 of a second-wicket stand of 133 with his captain and then, when New South Wales were set 225 to score in 131 minutes for victory on the final day, Morris chose him for his opening partner.

Together they got those 225 runs at a rate of 104 an hour. Miller contributed 138 of them at above 60 runs an hour, Morris 78 at 35. It is interesting to recall that when Alec Bedser first visited Australia in 1946–47 a Western Australian told Bradman in Adelaide 'Bedser's a very fine bowler'. 'I'll decide about that,' Don rejoined, 'when I've seen him bowl at Arthur Morris.'

On 10 November of 1950 Morris and Miller figured in another

huge partnership for their State, this time against Freddie Brown's M.C.C. side. Facing an attack which included Bedser, Trevor Bailey, Douglas Wright, and Eric Hollies (the man who had bowled Bradman for nought in his last Test innings at the Oval in 1948, and thus by four runs prevented him from retiring with a Test match average of 100·00) they added 265 for the second wicket.

When Morris left for 168, scored in 261 minutes with one 6 and thirteen 4s, Miller shared a stand of 138 with Jim Burke and finished with 214, scored in 305 minutes with three 6s and fifteen 4s. This time he had travelled at over 42 runs an hour before being bowled by (you guessed it)—Hollies with the total 509 for 3.

Bedser from 24 overs had taken one wicket, Jack Moroney's, for 127.

Down to Melbourne the following Thursday flew Morris and his men to take part in the first of the summer's 'grudge matches' between Victoria and New South Wales.

For the reasons that have been stated the traditional cricket rivalry between these States, a rivalry which had been born in the days of Murdoch and Spofforth, Blackham and McDonnell, a rivalry which matched that between Yorkshire and Lancashire, was intense.

New South Wales held the Sheffield Shield and wanted to keep it. Victoria wanted to regain it and, with six of Australia's recently-selected Test team—Hassett, Harvey, Bill Johnston, Loxton, Ian Johnson, and Iverson—in their ranks, expected to do so.

Victoria batted first and Lindsay Hassett played a 'particularly brilliant' innings for 179 of 374 'with Miller, Lindwall, and Walker in full cry'.

So hostile and persistent was the rain of bumpers Hassett had to face that at one stage he asked the umpire at the bowler's end, 'If this does not constitute intimidatory bowling under the rules, perhaps you will explain to me what does?'

'Get on with the game. Leave it to the umpire. It's nothing to do with you, Lindsay,' Miller called.

In the outcome Victoria, 374 and 295, defeated New South Wales 346 (Miller an anti-climactic nought) by 28 on the first innings and those temporary adversaries Morris, Lindwall, and Miller and Hassett, Harvey, Loxton, Johnston, Johnson, and Iverson, hastened up to Brisbane (rather like King Harold and his Saxons from Scotland to Hastings in 1066) to join forces against England in the First Test.

Feelings were still frayed and were to become raw during the Australian net practice at Woolloongabba.

When it was Morris' turn to bat he chose the net in which that mystery spinner, 'Wrong-grip Jake' Iverson was bowling. Hassett immediately ordered Iverson into the adjoining net where a Victorian was batting.

Over to Keith Miller: 'The usually placid Arthur was furious. He put on a real show in the dressing-room demanding something be done about this stupidity. "We are representing Australia. It is disgraceful to let interstate considerations be carried to such lengths," Arthur stormed.

'But Lindsay Hassett,' Keith continues, 'seemed to go to even greater lengths in that Brisbane Test to guard against a New South Wales player seeing too much of "Wrong-grip Jake". When I went out to field I took my normal position in slips for Iverson but, to my astonishment, Hassett ordered me to stand at silly-point.'

At silly-point, of course, Keith would have his back to Iverson's hand as he released the ball. Miller was one of Australia's specialist slips fieldsmen, however. Had Hassett put Victoria's interests ahead of Australia's—when he was captaining Australia? Doubtless he had his mind on the return game between New South Wales and Victoria at Sydney in January—*and* on the ordeal he had just undergone as a batsman in Melbourne.

That Brisbane Test of December 1950 was the one before which the whimsical Arthur Mailey had inadvertently omitted to name a wicketkeeper in his forecasted English team, explaining, when quizzed by Denis Compton on the point, 'You won't need a wicketkeeper. You won't get a ball past the bat.'

But Arthur, not for the first or last time I am afraid, was proved to be wrong. The Englishmen actually played two 'keepers, Godfrey Evans and McIntyre, and Australia's totals were 228 and 32 for 7 declared.

England, thanks to Bedser 7 for 54 all told, and a heroic and dynamic undefeated 62 by Hutton, who kept driving Lindwall and Miller over the head of cover then standing back and hooking them for boundaries, lost that Test by only 70 runs.

In Melbourne over Christmas the margin was narrower still.

Though Denis Compton, whose usually cheery countenance was claimed to have found contact either with a garden spout or an irate husband's fist, was absent, England only lost by 28.

Its captain Freddie Brown scored 62 and took 5 for 52 and when this sunny-haired, rosy-faced, burly 'John Bull' of a man brought his team back to Sydney for the vital Third Test, the hawkers of costercarts in the centre of the city began calling, 'Lettuces with hearts as big as Freddie Brown's.'

When, before the Brisbane Test, a member of the Queensland Club had greeted Brown with the toast, 'To your good luck and victory' Fred retorted angrily 'You're one of those hypocritical and patronising Australian bastards' and stormed from the club precincts.

Brown just could not believe a genuine Australian would ever want England to win. Now he was beginning to change his mind. About the only Australians who seemed anxious for another English defeat were the eleven cricketers representing their country.

The Third Test was to follow another game between New South Wales and the M.C.C.

Following that 214 in the earlier match Miller's batting average had toppled from 308 for 616 runs to 95·8 for 671. It was almost down to Bradman's 93·88 for 1690 in 1928–29.

The slump had to be arrested—and arrested it was. Sharing another century stand with Morris, Keith went on to 98 of a total of 333 before falling to his old bugbear Douglas Wright.

In reply Hutton, a superb 150, and Reg Simpson, a monumental 259, took the Englishmen to 553 for 8 declared and New South Wales, 130 for 6, were in danger of an innings defeat at the end.

Had the tide turned? Would Compton be ready to rejoin the Test ranks? Denis, still nursing the blackest of eyes, had been secreted into his Sydney hotel, the Australia, on the Friday of the game against New South Wales.

On the Saturday morning Blayne Fielder, news editor of the Sydney *Sun*, had asked his cricket correspondent to arrange for

Compton to admit a photographer to his bedroom. When the cricket writer refused Fielder rang Miller who rang Compton.

Over again to Keith: 'Denis was front-page news all over the cricket world. A lot of writers tried to concoct all sorts of gossip out of the mishap . . . The photographer "shot" Denis in his pyjamas just as he was getting up. I had the shock of my life when I saw the picture in the paper. Compton's hair was all over the place, he was unshaven; he looked like a hobo in the picture. Naturally he was upset and so was I.

'If the photographer was lacking in common decency, Denis should have thought for a moment, however, and refused to let him take the picture until he was more presentable.'

Compton, his eye restored to normal, rejoined the England team for the Third Test on the following Friday and England won the toss.

When the score was 34 without loss Keith brought off the most fantastic slips catch of his career, to dismiss Washbrook off Ian Johnson. Anticipating the late cut, he moved several metres to his right, flung himself horizontally until he was four metres wide of the wicket, and held the ball close to the ground with his right hand.

When Hutton and Simpson had taken the total beyond 120 without further loss Hassett brought Miller back at the Paddington End with the old ball. Dismissing Hutton leg before wicket for 62 on 128, he bowled Compton for nought and had Simpson caught by Loxton for 49 to make England 137 for 4 and have the wickets of her three most formidable batsmen for five runs inside four overs.

One brief burst of brilliance, genius if you like, had turned the tide of the Test match—*on a perfect batting pitch with the old ball.*

Facing 290 Australia had lost Morris, Ken Archer, and Hassett for 122 when Miller joined Neil Harvey. By stumps on the Monday night Keith was 99 of 368 for 6.

On the Tuesday morning the photographers of all four of Sydney's daily newspapers waited inside the Members' Gate to snap his arrival at the ground. He had scored 98 against the M.C.C. seven days before. Now he was 99 not out and so far had been the outstanding cricketer of the Test.

Minutes passed on the old clock on the *Showboat* Pavilion. There was no sign of Miller even when the clock pointed to 11.29, a minute before play was due to resume.

The photographers rushed to ring their news editors. No Australian player in history had been missing in the middle of a Test match, certainly not when he was 99 not out, and looked upon as the potential saviour of his side. This was a story, indeed; a story to match that great racehorse Phar Lap's mysterious disappearance before the running of the Melbourne Cup in 1930.

On a previous occasion Miller had almost been late for play at the Sydney Cricket Ground during a match between New South Wales and Victoria. By the time he had parked his car on that occasion the game was about to resume. Only a helpful policeman had managed to escort him through the tremendous throng. There had been the close thing at Newlands during that Test match of 1949–50, too.

News of his absence now had got around and anxiety was at fever heat as the umpires, and then the Englishmen, took the field.

It changed to relief, to audible sighs of relief, as Keith stepped nonchalantly alongside his partner Ian Johnson down the shallow steps of the stand. He had entered the ground inconspicuously through the Paddington gate to avoid the congestion at the main Members' gate. He had been to his eye doctor, he explained, to obtain treatment for conjunctivitis.

On the Monday he had batted in 'unusually subdued fashion' while piloting Australia on to safer ground.

In the words of 'Johnnie' Moyes he was 'now much more like the authentic Miller and by the time Johnson left, just before one o'clock, they had turned the game Australia's way'.

When Australia was dismissed for 426 Keith was 145 not out scored in 354 minutes and he 'had held the side together at a critical stage, limiting himself to one soaring 6 over the sight-board off Warr'.

Few players have played so decisive a part in a Test match between England and Australia as Miller did on this occasion. Indeed, this must be regarded as even his most telling Test performance—that catch, those four wickets for 37, and the undefeated 145.

Iverson did the rest with 6 for 27 in England's second innings 123. Australia won by an innings and 13 runs. It had retained the Ashes three–nil—and Miller's batting average for the season was back above the hundred mark—standing on 114·25 for 914 runs.

During the remainder of this, his most successful Australian summer, he failed only twice with the bat.

In the Fourth Test at Adelaide he scored 44 and 99, yes 99, to help himself towards eventual top position on the Australian averages with 350 runs at 43·75.

For New South Wales he scored 83 in the return 'grudge' game against Victoria, and 122 against South Australia at Sydney, to take himself to the pinnacle of the Sheffield Shield averages (for all States) with 607 runs at 121·40.

In all first-class games that summer he batted twenty times, scored 1332 runs (including two double-centuries, three single centuries and two nineties) at 83·25.

On the Sydney Cricket Ground he batted nine times and amassed 926 runs at 132·3.

As a bowler in the five Tests he delivered 106·6 overs to take 17 wickets at 17·82 and finish above all except Iverson of the Australian attack.

17
A magician is unmasked

The poet Wordsworth's heart was apt to leap, he led us to believe, whenever he beheld a rainbow in the sky. The hearts of Australia's cricketlovers have been prone to soar highest over the past thirty years, their eyes to shine brightest, whenever they have beheld news that a West Indian team was heading for Australia.

Expectations were especially lofty in the spring of 1951 when those 'Three Terrible Ws' Frank Mortimore Maglinne Worrell, Everton Weekes, and Clyde Walcott, that mystifying marionette Sonny Ramadhin, his confederate Alf 'Old Man River' Valentine, and some other velvety black stars from the Caribbean set forth to eclipse the Southern Cross.

According to expert report they would swoop like a band of Captain Henry Morgan's cut-throats upon Australia's cricketing fortresses and whip off with the loot to their lair, that old pirate refuge Jamaica's Port Royal. All very rousing and romantic a prospect—except for the Australian champions who were about to be conscripted for the 'Defence Force'.

We needed, it seemed at the time, either five Ned Kellys, eleven Errol Flynns, or a score of Peter Finches.

Twelve months previously the West Indians had raided and ransacked England's cathedrals and monasteries of cricket and beaten her three–nil. Worrell, *the* most terrible though most suave and stylish of the 'Ws', had amassed 261 in one Test innings at Trent Bridge. Weekes, a 'Black Bradman', had plundered a century there; Walcott, that 'giant Othello' of a batsman and wicketkeeper, had gone towering to 168 not out at Lord's.

At the end of the season England's 'Emperor of Games' Charles Fry had been moved to say, 'If I had to choose one batsman to give an exhibition of batsmanship at the London Palladium it wouldn't be Hutton or Compton, even Bradman or Hammond. It would be Worrell, of Bridgetown, Barbados.'

And had not that magician Ramadhin mesmerised even Hutton and Compton while taking 135 wickets on the 1950 tour of Britain? Had he not caused Compton to confess, 'All you see is the blur of a black hand, a white shirt with sleeves buttoned to the wrist, and a red ball. You have to guess the rest.'?

On top of all this, had not the West Indies captain John Goddard been heard to say of Sonny's fellow conspirator, Alf Valentine, 'Val could turn a ball sharply on a glacier.'?

So concerned regarding Ramadhin and Valentine was Australia's opening batsman and vice-captain Arthur Morris on the morning of 26 October 1951 that he stepped into his car and drove 170 kilometres up the Pacific Highway from Sydney to Newcastle to watch their Australian debut.

This, though Arthur had scored 253 of a New South Wales total of 400 against Queensland the previous Saturday. With him Morris had taken his most powerful pair of field glasses and he spent the afternoon squatting alongside the sightscreens.

His reward for his trouble and this 340 kilometre round trip was the spectacle of Ramadhin concealing most of his conjuring tricks while the bespectacled Valentine took 10 for 113.

He had learnt nothing and in thirteen days time would be called upon to confront the blur of that black hand and that flapping white sleeve from a distance of 18-odd metres in the Brisbane Test.

If Arthur, like the young Richie Benaud, was a worrier, Keith Miller and his 'Jonathan' Ray Lindwall were not. In their bedroom at Lennon's Hotel on the eve of the Test they had a long talk and formed both a bowling and a batting plan.

The menacing machinery of those 'Three Terrible Ws' must be manacled by all-out speed, to which they were unaccustomed. And Ramadhin must be attacked.

Over to Keith: 'None of us knew a thing about Ram and Val. We thought conditions might be to their liking at Woolloongabba and, frankly, almost all of us were worried. Australian batsmen were going about asking, "What the devil do these fellows do?" and there was no one to supply the answer.'

What the Australians *did* know was that Ramadhin had delivered eighty-one overs, a year previously, at Trent Bridge to take 5 for 135, had delivered seventy-two overs, at Lord's, to take 6 for 86, and that Valentine's fifty overs, at Old Trafford, had brought him 8 for 104.

On Friday 9 November of 1951 Goddard won the toss and batted on what promised to become a spinners' wicket before the Test had travelled very far. Hassett issued much the same instructions to his pace bowlers as Lord Nelson had done to his sailors at Trafalgar.

Lindwall obeyed them by bowling the left-handed Alan Rae with his very first ball. Worrell 37, Weekes 35, and Walcott 0, were economically disposed of and Miller bowled Goddard for a fighting 45. Australia confronted the moderate total of 216 when it began its ordeal. It was 129 for 5 when Lindwall joined Keith.

Back to *Cricket Crossfire*. 'I was out of form and I thought, "If Ramadhin tosses it up I will hit him." I did not know whether it was a leg break, an off break, or a top-spinner. I just hit. Ray adopted the same policy; I made 46, Ray 61. We totalled 226, a lead of ten only, but very useful in a low-scoring match.'

Though Weekes, handicapped by a thigh injury, hooked and drove bravely and brilliantly for 70 in the second innings 245, and Ramadhin took 5 for 90 from forty overs, Australia squeezed home by three wickets.

Back again to *Cricket Crossfire*: 'Ramadhin and Valentine had each taken six wickets in the Test and appeared to have the "Indian (West Indian) sign" over many of our batsmen.

'Then we went to Sydney where the wicket was more favourably disposed to batsmen and Hassett and I both made hundreds (132 and 129). It was then I started to pick Ramadhin. I found I could spot his leg break from his off break and top-spinner. I began to tease him, calling him "Shorty".

'"Well, hello Shorty! You're a nice chap but you haven't improved your bowling much since the last match, have you?" I'd say to him. And I could see he was letting it get him down. From that time on he never tried his hardest against me. It still holds good. When I come in to bat he just rolls his arm over for a bit and then gives the whole thing away. He has never got me out yet (NB: This was written after the 1955 tour of the Caribbean, in 1956) and I think he is suffering from a "Miller complex". He also had a lean time against Len Hutton, though the Englishman mastered him more by his great defence and I by attack.'

In the outcome Miller scored 362 runs in that 1951–52 series at 40·22. Though he delivered 232·3 overs, of which 53 were maidens, Ramadhin took only 14 wickets for 695 at an average of 49·64.

It was during the excruciatingly exciting finale of the vital Fourth Test at Melbourne that Ramadhin threw in the sponge and walked from the field.

Australia needed 38 runs to prevent the West Indians from levelling the series when Bill Johnston joined Doug Ring for the final stand. As he did so a score or so of the black-uniformed constables of the Victoria Police Force, believing the end was imminent, a mere formality, took post inside the white railings around the ground.

Long before Australia's Number 9 and Number 11 batsmen had got the 38 runs Ramadhin found the ordeal too much for him and deserted his team.

Miller and Lindwall's plan to hobble the 'Three Terrible Ws' also worked. Though Worrell scored a truly noble century, virtually with one hand, in that Fourth Test, his series average for 337 runs was only 33·70. Weekes contributed 245 at 24·50 and Walcott (from six innings) 87 at 14·50.

Lindwall's Test series analysis was 154/19/484/21/23·04 and Miller's 128·3/16/398/20/19·90.

Speed had defeated spin; attack had overcome defence; and Australia, to its surprise and relief, was still on top of the world.

In the Sheffield Shield games of that summer Miller had again captained New South Wales on the one occasion when Morris was unavailable, had led it to an important and decisive victory over Western Australia, and helped it to regain the trophy.

All told that summer he scored 584 runs at 36·5 and captured 32 wickets at 21·25. He was to gain his reward, rather unexpectedly and perhaps embarrassingly, the following spring.

18
A rift in the Australian cricket lute

The New South Wales Cricket Association empowers its State selectors to appoint its Sheffield Shield captains. From and including the 1947–48 season Arthur Morris, whenever he was available, had been entrusted with the leadership, had been honoured with the role that such respected characters and champions as William Lloyd Murdoch, Montague Alfred Noble, Herbert Collins, Alan Kippax, Stanley McCabe, and William John O'Reilly (alias 'The Tiger') had filled.

Under Arthur's captaincy New South Wales had won the Sheffield Shield in 1948–49 and 1951–52.

In his four seasons as State captain Morris had built an imposing record as a Shield batsman. It was:

1947–48—9 innings
81 highest score   401 runs   44·55 average.
1948–49—13 innings
177 highest score   858 runs   71·50 average.
1950–51—7 innings
182 highest score   498 runs   83·00 average.
1951–52—4 innings
253 highest score   508 runs   127·00 average.

This adds to 2265 runs at 73·06 (with 2 innings not out).

As a batsman in Sheffield Shield cricket he was getting better and better, more and more devoted and reliable.

He was leader of the State which held the Sheffield Shield, of the State which six months previously had regained it by a margin of twelve points and a percentage of almost 35.

In 1949 the Australian Cricket Board had appointed him vice-captain (under Lindsay Hassett) of the Australian team to tour South Africa. They had re-appointed him to that role for the Test series against England in 1950–51 and the West Indies in 1951–52.

Morris seemed almost certain to lead Australia when the already 39-year-old Hassett retired from Test cricket.

Perhaps understandably no explanation came from the New South Wales Cricket Association or from its Selection Committee when Morris was deposed and Miller replaced him as State captain for the 1952–53 season.

I have found it impossible to extract one today.

Any outsider's ideas about the reasons for this dramatic change in leadership, I have been officially informed, would be based upon pure conjecture. So the best I can do is to conject.

There certainly was much conjecting, or conjecturing, done at the time in question—October of 1952. And when, in December of that year, the Australian Cricket Board retained Morris as Hassett's vice-captain for the 1952–53 Test series against South Africa, it multiplied. It revived when the Board named Morris as Hassett's vice-captain for the 1953 tour of England in late February of that year.

The 1952–53 season New South Wales State Selection Committee was manned by Messrs E. A. 'Chappie' Dwyer (the manager of the 1949–50 Australian team to South Africa and a national selector of twenty-two years' standing), Albert Vincent, Selby Burt, Billy Wells, and Dudley Seddon.

Members of the Australian Cricket Board for 1952–53 were:

New South Wales delegates—R. A. Oxlade, F. M. Cush, K. O. E. Johnson (the manager of the Australian Services Team) and, after Johnson's resignation from the Board on 11 November 1952, E. G. 'Scoutie' Macmillan;

Victorian delegates—Dr A. Robertson, W. L. Rush, and G. A. Davies (manager of the 1953 Australian team to England);

South Australian delegates—R. F. Middleton (Chairman), Sir Donald Bradman, and H. H. Bridgman;

Queensland delegates—J. C. Hutcheon, Q.C., and T. J. Burge;

Western Australian and Tasmanian delegates—A. C. Randell and H. C. Smith.

There may, or may not be significance and relevance in the fact that Keith Johnson resigned only months after his appointment and that 'Chappie' Dwyer ceased his twenty-two-year term as an Australian selector after the 1952–53 season though he remained a New South Wales selector until 1954.

It is unquestionable that Sir Donald Bradman had gained considerable influence on the Board by the spring of 1952. And it should not be forgotten that Roy Middleton, his South Australian colleague, was then its chairman.

It is also intriguing to recall that the last occasion when a similar situation to the Miller–Morris one occurred in Australian cricket was in 1936–37. This was when Vic Richardson, though he had just led Australia to a four–nil series victory over South Africa and had led South Australia from 1921 to 1934–35, was not reinstated as State captain in 1936–37. Bradman, who had led South Australia in 1935–36, while Vic was abroad captaining his country, retained that position.

It is far more probable than improbable that both in 1936–37 and in 1952–53 Bradman and Middleton had their strong say.

Certain it is that the Australian Cricket Board, or a majority of its members, must have believed it had compelling reasons for retaining Morris as national vice-captain, despite his deposition in favour of Miller as New South Wales captain.

Possibly the Victorian, South Australian, Queensland, Western Australian, and Tasmanian representatives were having what is called 'a shot' at the N.S.W.C.A.; maybe one at Miller—probably at both. Maybe they had their reservations about placing Keith in a position of authority at the national level.

But, firstly, let us try and deduce why the N.S.W.C.A. made its change in the State leadership. Press opinion in Sydney at the time was that the New South Wales authorities had come to regard Morris as a 'somewhat unimaginative and undynamic leader, as one whose captaincy was hardly calculated to attract big, or bigger, crowds to games at the Sydney Cricket Ground', that they believed Miller, 'the more positive and magnetic cricketer and character', would have this effect.

If this was so, action would have had to have been taken

through the N.S.W.C.A. Executive and Finance Committee to bring pressure upon the State selectors, and I can find no evidence that this occurred.

The conclusion I have come to is that the five selectors were allowed a free hand and decided, probably for the reasons advanced by the Press, to give Miller a chance.

I am certain that Miller played no part behind the scenes. Morris was (still is) his friend, and Keith is not the kind of person to have rallied against him.

In my opinion, Miller must have been deeply embarrassed, despite the gracious and sportsmanlike manner in which Morris accepted and adapted to the situation, and the loyalty he gave to his successor—the kind of loyalty Keith had given him.

Keith was ambitious to one day become a State, and maybe even national, captain. But he would have preferred his promotion to have come under far less invidious circumstances.

It was, indeed, because of the exemplary behaviour of Keith and Arthur that little harm was done, that the probable object of the State selectors was achieved, and that, from the point of view of cricket in New South Wales and of the New South Wales cricketloving public, only good resulted.

One of the members of the New South Wales team in 1952–53 and from then until 1955–56 (the season after which Miller retired) was the future Australian captain, perhaps the outstanding captain Australia has had, Richie Benaud.

His views upon Keith as a cricket captain are contained in his book *Willow Patterns*, Hodder & Stoughton, which was published in 1969.

He has written: 'I always found Keith a good captain of the unorthodox variety and I learnt a lot from him in this department of the game—particularly by way of trying something a little unusual, if all orthodox methods failed.

'He produced some unusual moves in the time he was captain of New South Wales, but there was always plenty of thought behind everything he did.

'Basically a nervous character, his suggestions would be proffered boldly but with a characteristic cough and much hand waving. But the players who took his advice or asked for it invariably benefited.

'He was prepared to buy wickets if his bowlers would cooperate and I took many wickets in first-class cricket that in some way could be traced back to a pointer produced by Miller. It may have been a change of pace or some little weakness in a batsman, undetected by myself, or it may have been something to do with the pitch or the amount of zip being gained from the surface. But it happened that his advice suited me because I was always keen to try something a little different.

'Once Keith was settled in New South Wales his attacking brand of cricket brought him many admirers for potential leadership of the State side. Morris was always a quiet skipper but a very thoughtful one who led the side just as well as did Miller when he became captain, but Arthur led it in much less flamboyant manner.'

Keith began his career as regular New South Wales captain with a 253-run victory over Queensland in Brisbane. To this he contributed a century, but gave himself only 17 overs from which he took 1 for 51. As a matter of interest, Morris scored 95.

Because of the demands of Test cricket Miller led New South Wales only six times that summer—in four Sheffield Shield encounters, and twice against Jack Cheetham's lively young South Africans.

During a busy November New South Wales won the return match against Queensland by 9 wickets, defeated the Springboks by 5 wickets, beat Victoria by an innings and 35 runs, and lost to South Australia by 3 wickets.

The second game against the South Africans, played at the New Year, was drawn.

In these six games for his State Keith scored 335 at 41·87 and took 21 wickets at 21·9. It is notable that his finest performance —93 runs and 9 wickets for 125—came in the closely-fought loss against the eventual Shield winners South Australia.

In the absence of Miller and Morris that attractive strokeplayer Sid Carroll led New South Wales on to second place in the Shield competition.

Cheetham's 1952–53 Springboks are remembered as the finest band of fieldsmen ever to tour Australia. It may be forgotten, however, that they were the first fieldsmen to introduce the practice of duck-diving Rugby fashion along the turf to intercept strokes that seemed certain to elude them—a practice which is common all over the cricketing world today and which has been accepted as a great boon by those who make their living from dry-cleaning.

On his arrival in Perth Cheetham was shown some outstanding specimens of the Westralian wild flower, the kangaroo paw.

'Before we leave your country,' commented this super-optimist, 'it will be a case of the poor kangaroo.'

Just how Cheetham's young and inexperienced cricketers were going to topple Australia from its cricketing throne seemed a mystery until Cheetham explained.

'Very few batsmen have scored centuries in Test matches without giving at least one chance,' he said. 'We don't intend to miss any.' In the event they missed very few and held many that verged upon the miraculous. This is mainly why they drew the Test series 2–2 against much the same sides as had outplayed England and the West Indies in the previous two summers.

Perhaps the outstanding catcher of a cricket ball, even in this South African side, was Russell Endean. Certain it is that Endean caught Miller three times from what seemed impossible chances that summer, the most unbelievable of them being that held on the brink of the boundary of the Melbourne Cricket Ground during the Second Test.

Batting in his most masterly fashion, Keith had just passed his half-century when he lofted a ball from Tayfield with tremendous power and on a flat trajectory towards the seats just to the left of the Richmond end sightboard. The power behind the stroke was awesome. Spectators at the Jolimont end of the ground were expecting to read 'Death at the Test' as one of the headlines in the following morning's newspapers. The spectators in the seats behind Endean had similar and more personal fears. They all either scattered or ducked.

Standing a metre or so inside the white rails on the edge of the minor precipice that then existed there, Endean set himself for what he alone believed possible. Then he leapt upward with right arm outstretched like a falling passenger leaps for a strap in a Melbourne tram.

There was no need for those spectators to scatter. To the amazement of everyone Endean was seen standing on the edge of the dip like the Statue of Liberty with the ball in his right hand, striving to prevent himself from falling back under the force of the drive.

From all over the ground Springbok fieldsmen dashed to wring the stinging hand that had held perhaps the most amazing catch that can ever have been held.

Keith's own astonishment and admiration overcame his dismay and he strode smiling from the field.

His reward and compensation were to come on the following day when he captured the wicket that made him one of six cricketers who had taken 100 wickets and scored 1000 runs in Test matches.

After scoring 55 and taking 5 for 81 in the Third Test at Sydney, Miller's normally robust and resilient health began to fail him. He delivered only 3 overs in South Africa's first innings of the Adelaide Test and was not fit enough to bowl in its second.

Following four strenuous and exacting summers of Test and other cricket in South Africa and Australia, he and his friend and fellow fast bowler Ray Lindwall were feeling the strain. A tour of England lay a few months ahead and the national selectors wisely decided to omit these key players, these now 33- and 31-year-old all-rounders, from the final Test at Melbourne.

In six Test innings Keith had scored only 153 runs at 25·50 but, with 13 wickets from 91 overs at 18·53, he managed to head the series bowling averages for either side.

With Miller and Lindwall resting the Springboks won the Fifth Test by six wickets and drew the series. If it was not a case of 'the poor kangaroo', as Cheetham had predicted, it certainly was a very sore old marsupial that tramped from the field on 12 February 1953.

For three summers Australia's bowlers had rescued her, Test after Test. Now what had proved itself to be perhaps the most penetrative and versatile attack in Test history seemed to have been shorn of its menace and mastery. Hutton and Compton were soon to be confronted again on their home heath, and this time Australia would have no Bradman.

19
Coronation Year crusade – England 1953

'Oh to be in England now that April's there.'

Browning's words carried an even more plaintive ring during the Australian autumn of 1953. In that Coronation Year they sounded like mission bells—particularly to seven young Australians who had not been to Britain before, who had never seen Big Ben, St Paul's Cathedral, Piccadilly Circus, Windsor Castle, or the gentle, white-framed greenery of Lord's Cricket Ground on a sunny summer day.

Thus it was with high expectation and high, young hearts that the 17-year-old Ian Craig, 19-year-old Ron Archer, 22-year-olds Richie Benaud and Graeme Hole, 23-year-old Alan Davidson, 24-year-old Colin McDonald, and 25-year-old Jim de Courcy boarded the Orient liner *Orcades* at Port Melbourne in late March of that year.

None of them had been north of the Equator. All of them were reasonably handsome as well as young. They soon would have the Old World, that new Old World for them, at their toes. Their one cause for concern was their cricket, whether they would succeed at their cricket on what, for them, would be strange and foreign fields.

Nor did they have to worry even about cricket right now.

During the next four weeks they would be seeing beautiful, if crowded, Colombo, the minarets and bazaars of Bombay; they would be steaming through the Suez Canal, calling at Naples and at Edmond Dantes' old haunt Marseilles.

And, what's more, there would be gay and glamorous girls and young women to sunbake, swim, dance, and maybe to skylark with along the 19 000-kilometre ocean road.

Even those now-fatherly figures of Australian cricket, the near 40-year-old Lindsay Hassett, his vice-captain the 31-year-old Arthur Morris, the 33-year-old Keith Miller, the 31-year-old Ray Lindwall, and the still only 24-year-old but Test-chastened Neil Harvey felt lighter in the mind and about the heart.

This was the way to travel; the way to see the world. It was deemed a great honour then, a cause for great congratulation, to be a chosen representative of one's country at cricket, especially to be representing it in the Old Country which had cradled the game. Young, even middle-ageing, Australians were not so materialistic then. The amount of money they received for playing five months' cricket mattered no more than the proverbial hoot, so long as it saw them through.

Richie Benaud could chew those daily apples of his with gusto. And had not the editor of Debrett informed the swarthy young Jim de Courcy of Newcastle, New South Wales, that, because of the heroic deeds of one of his ancestors at Crecy, Poitiers, or Agincourt (maybe it was Camelot) he might have the right to stand 'hatted' before his beautiful and soon to be crowned young Queen?

During the 1952–53 Australian summer Keith Miller and his collaborator had completed their fourth cricket book. It was to be entitled *Bumper* and to be published in London to coincide with the arrival of the Australian team. For reasons unanticipated by its authors, it was to emerge with a resounding bump.

That sagacious Australian Prime Minister Sir Robert Menzies had written a beautiful foreword to the book. In this, with almost uncanny foresight, he had said: 'The authors were cautious enough not to send me a copy of the manuscript. This masterly move was greatly admired by one who has devoted some portion of the last twenty-five years (little as critics will believe it) to keeping out of avoidable trouble. Its result is both obvious and comforting. From my point of view I can hereafter wash my hands of any responsibility for the indiscretions which some industrious reviewer is bound to find in this book. Even Miller (though this seems improbable) will be able to maintain an unblemished reputation for not embarrassing Prime Ministers.'

Sir Robert must have been psychic.

On page 26 of *Bumper* appeared the following paragraphs—paragraphs upon which Fleet Street pounced: 'Without wishing to be disloyal to a man who has been our constant friend and delightful companion on many tours around the English-speaking world, we must say, in the cause of sincerity of opinion, that we believe Len Hutton could develop an advantage for England in the sphere of captaincy.

'Lindsay Hassett's captaincy has been too much influenced by an increasingly cautious outlook in recent years.

'Lindsay is apt to miss the recurring opportunity when it comes and is also apt to do nothing about it for fear that whatever steps he takes may prove to be the wrong ones. Daring captaincy demands willingness to accept blame if the bold stroke goes astray. Lindsay is no lover of criticism . . .

'The great difference between the captaincy of Hassett and Bradman is that Bradman made his plans half an hour ahead of the changing plot of the game, whereas Hassett deals, or fails to deal, with things as they occur.

'Next to Bradman we believe Len Hutton to possess the shrewdest cricket brain since "Gubby" Allen. Hassett can be a good captain when at his best and concentrating. Hutton could become a great captain during this coming series.'

The balloon went up and the bombs exploded in the London morning papers on the day following the Australians' arrival at Southampton. 'Keith Miller Criticises His Captain' read the 72-point-type headline across the front page of the city's top circulation evening newspaper. There were other more startling ones.

It so happened that the Australians were guests at a welcoming luncheon that day in the banqueting hall of the Savoy Hotel. Between 500 and 1000 English sportslovers, the cream (some of it a little curdled) of English sporting society, were present. Before responding to the opening address Hassett was asked to introduce each member of his team to the gathering. As he did so each player was obliged to rise at his particular table.

'This is my vice-captain Arthur Morris,' Lindsay announced as the handsome Arthur rose shyly from his chair.

Maybe it is as well Arthur was appointed vice-captain. I remember thinking at the time as Keith, the third-most-senior member of the side, was signalled to his feet in the centre of the hall.

Lindsay Hassett, at times, can match Alfred Hitchcock as a master of suspense.

He knew most Londoners, certainly most of this type of Londoner, devour their morning newspapers, tackle the pages even of their broadsheets, *The Times*, *Telegraph*, and *Express*, on their way to their offices in crowded tubes. He knew the first editions of the *Evening News* and *Evening Standard* ('Everyone needs standards' as the sandwich boards still say) had just gone on sale outside and inside the Savoy.

He waited while Keith scrambled awkwardly from his chair and stood erect in the huge dining hall, running his fingers through that unruly shock of hair.

'There is Keith Miller, whom you all know well,' Hassett eventually said. '*I hear he has written a book.*'

This masterpiece of droll diplomacy raised a belly laugh all over the banqueting hall, but it did not quieten the Press.

Feeling the situation needed to be set in proper perspective, Neville Cardus rallied to the side of his friend and fellow worshipper of Ludwig Beethoven in the *Observer* that weekend.

'I have read Keith Miller's book and find nothing objectionable in it. His comments on Hassett as a captain are, in my opinion, just darned good dinkum Aussie criticism,' he said.

The tour began with a match against Prince Philip's XI at Kingston-upon-Thames and it was noticeable that His Highness went out of his way to greet Keith, and spent more time with him than with any of the other Australians. That surely most graphic, if gravelly-voiced, of all sports broadcasters and telecasters, John Arlott, also helped.

The Prince, of course, had suffered a deal of embarrassment himself at times—including that occasion in the United States when an excited radio commentator announced his imminent arrival with the words, 'You'll recognise Prince Philip when you hear the twenty-one ton galoot.'

Miller's own reaction to the now-simmering situation was typical of the man.

He began the team's first-class match programme by doing a 'Bradman' at Worcester—scoring 220 not out of a total of 542, after Morris 17, and Hassett 22, had failed. After being run out for 42 against Leicestershire he contributed 159 not out of a total of 453 for 6 under Morris' leadership in the important game against Hutton's county, Yorkshire.

He thus had amassed 421 runs for one dismissal during the first seven days of this, for him, perhaps not merriest but certainly most satisfying of Mays. Five years previously, it will be remembered, he had begun Bradman's last tour of Britain with 50 not out at Worcester, 202 not out at Leicester, and 9 wickets for 91 against Yorkshire within the corresponding week.

Keith's problem in 1953, as in 1948, was to sustain the degree of incentive required to maintain this kind of momentum.

Though Arthur Morris chose him as his opening partner, even allowed him to take strike, against Cambridge University on that batting paradise that is Fenner's, he scored only 20 and then dashed off to Newmarket Racecourse to back a succession of 'cert's'. All of them failed. So, from then on, did Miller as a batsman.

His chance of scoring 1000 runs in May disintegrated along the trail to the First Test as scores of 0 at Lord's (of all places), 19 at Oxford, 20 at Old Trafford, 48 at Nottingham, and 6 against Sussex at Hove followed.

I began to wonder whether I should whip out another jointly-authored book, this time criticising Sir Winston Churchill, maybe even God, and inserting a foreword by that agnostic Sir Bertrand Russell.

Despite occasional trouble with his back, Keith was doing rather better with the ball. He had taken 4 for 47 against the Marylebone Cricket Club at Lord's and 4 for 27 against Oxford University.

Early in the tour he and Lindwall had decided to have a serious talk with Lindsay about the advisability or not of using the Carmody 'Umbrella' field of four off-side and three leg-side slips in England, where boundaries are shorter and more penetrable than on Australian grounds. Both Keith and Ray believed the stationing of seven fieldsmen in an arc about the wicketkeeper might have vital influence on the outcome of a series in which the issue was expected to be closely-run.

Their brief conversation proceeded as follows:

Hassett: 'If the ball penetrates the "umbrella" it goes for four runs.'

Miller and Lindwall: 'If a man catches the ball, it's out'.

Though Hassett, as usual, took time to make up his mind, the Carmody field was used at Trent Bridge, at Lord's, and at Headingley. In the Tests there Lindwall returned innings analyses of 5 for 57, 5 for 66, and 5 for 54—and seven of his fifteen victims were caught.

Miller, again plagued with his back problem, did not bowl in the Trent Bridge Test but he contributed 55 towards a vital fourth-wicket stand of 109 with his captain, who made a superbly sound 115 against a belligerent Alec Bedser.

Captaining the Australians in the absence of Hassett and Morris in the return match against Yorkshire at Sheffield, Keith topscored with 86 of 323 in pursuit of 377.

In the Lord's Test (another drawn game) Keith scored 25 and 109—sharing in what was described as a 'gallant second-wicket stand of 165' with Morris after Hassett, who had scored another fine century in the first innings, was dismissed by Brian Statham for 3.

Only six centuries were scored in that rain-dogged Test series. Hassett got two of them and Miller, Harvey, Hutton, and Willy Watson one each.

During the Fourth Test at Leeds which, like the first three, was drawn, Australia had to contend not only with the English climate but also with some highly controversial (indeed indefensible) decisions from that former 'Chief Justice' of English umpiring Frank Chester.

Earlier on the tour Keith and Chester had got on well together. Whenever Keith was fielding at square-leg the two of them used to discuss horse-racing together, to exchange fancies for the Derby, the Oaks, or whatever blue-riband event was in the offing.

Before the summer had proceeded very far, however, both Keith and Ray Lindwall noticed a significant change in Chester and decided he had developed an anti-Australian complex. They were surprised that this should have happened to the umpire whom Bradman had classed as the finest of his experience.

Miller has written that during that 1953 tour when he and Lindwall appealed Chester often responded with a snarling, 'Naht out'. 'OK, Frank, but I don't appreciate that snarling manner of yours,' Keith eventually was provoked to reply.

Cricketers are entitled to appeal to umpires when they believe, or are in doubt as to whether, batsmen are out. All they seek is a straight and civil answer. And that is what umpires are paid to give.

Whenever Keith complained to Chester about his snarling responses the latter would turn his back and walk away.

'Frank,' Miller called loudly on one occasion, 'I want an answer.'

During a vital stage of the Leeds Test Reg Simpson hit a ball from Lindwall wide of mid-on. Hassett chased it and Miller ran from mid-off to take the return at the bowler's end. Hassett's return was right above the bails. Miller broke the wicket and turned to find Simpson still some distance from the completion of his third run from the stroke.

'You've got him, you've got him,' called an exultant Lindwall from a few metres along the pitch.

Keith regarded the appeal as a mere formality. 'How's that, Frank?' he quietly asked.

Over to Miller: 'Chester seemed to be having some bother with his balance, but at length he looked up and mumbled "not out", shaking his head from side to side. We were astounded, dumbfounded; we just could not believe our ears. In fact I found it so unbelievable that Chester could allow Simpson to continue his innings that I made four appeals. When he continued to shake his head I nearly went berserk. And so did others in our team. We were so angry we could not talk.'

I well remember Lindwall throwing himself on the turf and rolling over and over in astonishment. Later, when Miller was fielding near him, Chester raised the matter of that run out. 'You must realise I had to get into position in a hurry,' he said.

Miller gasped with amazement. The batsmen were on their *third* run.

Australia, battling to retain the Ashes it had held since 1934, led by 99 runs on the first innings in that Test at Leeds. Compton injured his right hand while batting in England's second innings but was not out overnight. His hand was so badly bruised on the fourth morning that he could not hold a bat and retired 'hurt'. After Laker, 48, and Bailey had helped England to a precarious lead of 140 Compton agreed to continue his innings with a bandaged hand. Shortly after its resumption he played gingerly forward to Lindwall and edged the ball to Graeme Hole at second slip.

Miller, who was fielding at first slip, believes Hole made the catch cleanly about 30 centimetres above the turf. He, Hole, Lindwall, and Hassett all appealed when Compton, who had not turned his head to follow the flight of the ball, stayed what is known as 'put'.

The umpire at the bowling end, Frank Lee, claimed Lindwall had obstructed his view of the ball and referred the decision to Chester at square-leg.

I was watching Chester at the time. He appeared to be in either a daze or a dream. When he eventually realised the decision was now up to him, he strode like a somnambulist towards the pitch, then began calling 'Naht out, naht out' and vigorously shaking his head.

Compton's 61 in that second innings (his stand with Bailey) undoubtedly prevented Australia from winning that Test and preserving its hold on the Ashes. At the close it needed only 30 runs with 6 wickets in hand.

So angry was Hassett that he wrote a letter to the appropriate officials at Lord's stating that the one umpire he would not tolerate for the decisive Kennington Oval Test was Chester.

As Keith and Ray were climbing the steps of the Headingley pavilion after stumps that evening, a group of members began to boo. One of them was so persistently rude that Keith retraced his steps and stood challengingly in front of him in the aisle. The member declined the opportunity of indulging in a bout of fisticuffs—as Keith had anticipated he would.

So far those seven young crusaders, those twentieth-century D'Artagnans of ours had failed to set the Thames, or the Trent, on fire with their performances in the Tests. Only Graeme Hole had done reasonably well with the bat and Alan Davidson with the ball. Wet weather and Alec Bedser, who took 39 wickets at 17·51 in the series, were proving far too much for them to overcome.

An additional burden had fallen upon the 'fathers' of the side in consequence. Hassett, 302 runs in the unaccustomed role as opening batsman, Morris 295, Harvey 319, Miller 222 and 8 for 214, and Lindwall 22 wickets for 374, had shouldered their responsibilities well, helped to keep the issue open for the final gambit at The Oval.

Though Keith had always contended (rightly as time was to prove) that Bobby Simpson held a more promising future as a Test batsman than Ian Craig, the teenager's long string of failures, punctuated only by a 47 against Cambridge University, aroused this perennial champion of the underdog's sympathy and compassion.

Ian had won his place in the touring side by scoring 213 not out of 416 for 7 for New South Wales against Cheetham's South Africans and 53 and 47 against them in the Fifth Test of 1952–53. In his first and only Shield innings in 1951–52 he had scored 91 against South Australia at the age of 16 years and eight months.

He was now only just eighteen and Don Bradman had been rising twenty-two and Stan McCabe rising twenty when they first toured England in 1930.

Remembering that McCabe's early run of failures had been ended by batting him as an opener, Keith promoted Craig to Number 1 when he captained the Australians against Yorkshire. Ian scored 19, but at the time of the Fourth Test he had batted 16 times for 207 runs and finished the tour with 429 runs at 16·50.

Keith, like many others, attributed the continuing Craig catastrophes largely to the unimaginative (to use a kindly word) managership of the side by Australian Cricket Board member George Davies.

Just why Davies had been preferred to men like 'Chappie' Dwyer, Bill Dowling, of Victoria, or Alec Baker, of South Australia, as manager of an Australian team to England during a Coronation Year became more and more mystifying as the tour progressed.

If Davies in 1953 was not what is known as an alcoholic he approached dangerously to being so, and the effect of his often-embarrassing behaviour upon young men like Craig, Archer, Benaud, Davidson, and Hole is not hard to imagine. They also needed a bit of 'mothering' at times and that role falls to the manager not the captain of a touring team.

Davies' most unfortunate performance occurred at Lord's during the opening by Prince Philip of the ground's cricket museum.

Before his address Prince Philip informed Davies he would like to meet all members of the Australian side in the Long Room after the ceremony. Fortunately Keith Miller overheard the Prince's request; Davies either forgot or ignored it and took all members of the side back to the Park Lane Hotel—all of them except Miller.

Keith, by some strange coincidence parading another blackened eye, came rushing to me to see if I would help him placate Prince Philip.

'How's her husband?' was the Duke's immediate question.

'I fell down some stairs, Sir,' Keith insisted.

'*You* don't believe that, do you?' Prince Philip said, turning to me.

That evening Keith and I decided to have some fun at George Davies' expense. We telephoned him in his hotel room and, mustering the nearest approach we could to the ducal accent, managed to alarm him for some minutes before that cough of Keith's gave the show away.

At the beginning of the 1953 season Freddie Trueman was being hailed by the English Press as 'another Larwood' and tipped to become the decisive figure in the Coronation series.

During May, after watching Trueman bowl at Edgbaston in a Test Trial Match and conferring with Miller and former England captain Charles Burgess Fry, I wrote for both the Australian and English Press: 'To call Trueman, "another Larwood" is unfair both to him and to Larwood.'

Miller was reported as saying 'Trueman is just another bowler'. Yorkshiremen are apt to have long memories. Three years later Trueman bowled Miller for 28 in the Lord's Test. 'Just another batsman I see,' he called along the pitch.

Fry's comment upon Freddie in 1953 was 'He doesn't tie his bootlaces properly'. Asked to elucidate, he added, 'Detail *is* important'.

England's selectors had omitted their 'white', though very brunette, hope from all four Tests. For reasons best known to themselves or, perhaps, England's selectors, Yorkshire had not played him in either of its games against the Australians.

He was chosen as Bedser's new-ball partner for the final Test on 15 August, the match England had to win if it were to regain those long-elusive Ashes. After watching him bowl in an inter-services game at Lord's I repeated my earlier, published views on Trueman.

By taking 4 for 20 on a rain-wettened wicket after lunch on the opening day, however, Trueman gave England its chance. Though he took no more wickets in the Test England were victorious by 8 wickets.

Some mysteriously bulky packages began to arrive for me at the Park Lane Hotel. They bore Yorkshire postmarks and contained (besides very uncomplimentary notes) quantities of cow manure. When I showed them to Miller he was mightily amused but refrained from comment.

On the second Saturday after the Test I arrived at Kingston-upon-Thames to find the Australians 89 for 3 and Trueman bowling for the Combined Services XI against Keith and Jimmy de Courcy. Keith was approaching his century and de Courcy was past fifty when the players came off for lunch. Trueman had none for 55.

I walked across to greet Miller and de Courcy and suggested the situation called for a bottle of champagne in the marquee.

'We were thinking of you,' Keith grinned.

'I hope you'll keep doing so,' I said as we downed several glasses of Moet. The clerk in the reception desk at the Park Lane had been complaining about my unaromatic mail.

When Morris closed the Australian innings that evening the total was 592 for 4. Miller was 262 not out. De Courcy, after sharing in a fourth wicket of 377, had left for 204 and Ian Craig, with an undefeated 71, had helped Keith to carry on the good work.

Trueman, who only with great difficulty had been persuaded to share the second new ball, had delivered 14 wicket-less overs for 95.

Freddie, of course, was to develop into a great fast bowler. No man who has taken 307 wickets in 67 Tests on an average 21·57, who has on 17 occasions taken 5 or more wickets in a Test innings, can be denied that accolade. But Freddie was still at a very formative and untidy stage of his career in 1953.

Major interest in the remaining games of the tour revolved around speculation as to whether Australia's normally Number 11 batsman, Bill Johnston, would head the first-class match batting averages. On the final day of the English part of the tour 'Big Bill's' aggregate was beyond 100. So far in 17 innings he had been dismissed but once and the impish Hassett wanted him to finish the tour with an average higher than any Bradman had achieved in England.

He even sent a message to Norman Yardley, the England XI captain at Scarborough, asking him to ensure Bill was not dismissed. He wasn't, and finished top of the Australian first-class match batting figures with the following probably-unique figures: 17 innings, 16 not outs, 102 runs at 102·00.

Miller finished third to Johnston and Harvey with 31 innings, 3 not outs, 262 not out highest score, 1433 runs at 51·17. With the ball he delivered 492·2 overs, 161 of them maidens, to take 45 wickets for 1014 at 22·53. As always he had been extremely economical.

His Test match figures were:

9/0/109/223/24·77 and 186/72/303/10/30·30.

They look more presentable when it is remembered that Hassett, 365 runs at 36·5, topped the batting averages and only Lindwall, 26 at 18·92, took more Test wickets than Keith for Australia.

They would have been better, however, but for Keith's failure in the Fifth Test. In this match he scored 1 and 0 and took only 2 wickets from 45 again-remarkably-economical overs.

England fittingly regained the Ashes in Queen Elizabeth's Coronation Year under her first professional captain—the Ashes which Australia had held since 1934. Lindsay Hassett announced his retirement from Test and first-class cricket, leaving the questions as to who would lead Australia and Victoria to be resolved.

On the lighter side it is interesting to report that Jim de Courcy's entitlement to appear 'hatted' before his newly-crowned Queen was never established by Debrett. The tracing of his ancestry collapsed during a search of the family tree at either Bradford or Sheffield—much to Jimmy's relief.

As he himself said, 'Just imagine me parading through Buckingham Palace or Windsor Castle in a bowler, let alone a top hat.'

Soon after the Australian team returned to Australia the New South Wales Cricket Association re-appointed Miller as State captain for the 1953–54 summer, though Morris had been Hassett's 1953 tour deputy. The Victorian Cricket Association appointed Ian Johnson as Hassett's successor.

20
Why not the Australian captaincy?

The arrival of Len (later Sir Leonard) Hutton's Marylebone Cricket Club side in Australia in early October of 1954 created even greater interest than is customary on such occasions.

England had regained the Ashes after almost twenty years.

For the first time in history a professional cricketer was to lead England on an overseas tour. This, though Lord Hawke, a former England captain and, like Hutton, a Yorkshireman, had exclaimed, 'Pray God England will never be led by a professional.'

The nearest approach to such an 'aberration' had occurred when Denis Compton acted as Freddie Brown's vice-captain of the 1950–51 tour of Australia. And it had not escaped repercussion.

The most embarrassing of these came on the team's arrival in Adelaide. Here the conservative committee of the class-conscious Adelaide Club issued its usual invitation for the amateur members of the team to become honorary guests of their exclusive sanctum—either ignoring or overlooking the new status of the still-professional Compton.

This snub, or oversight, caused the half dozen or so amateurs and their manager Brigadier M. A. Green to decline (somewhat icily) the club's proffered hospitality. And they stuck to their guns even when the club's secretary, Colonel 'Dickie' Wills, who had been away on leave when the invitations were extended, did his utmost to repair the damage.

Another cause for the stimulation of exceptional interest among

Australians that spring was the inclusion in the English side of three fast bowlers, Frank Tyson, Brian Statham, and Peter Loader, all of whom had been clocked delivering cricket balls at speeds ranging between 130 and 145 km/h—Tyson, alias 'The Typhoon' at above that velocity.

Their selection, the Press claimed, had resulted from an ultimatum from Hutton to his co-selectors. Len, who had endured a deal of physical discomfort and mental travail when confronting Lindwall and Miller in recent years, was anxious, like Bradman in 1948, to have his revenge. He also believed Australia's batsmen could be unnerved into error by real pace; he was annoyed, it was said, that a fourth fast bowler (that 'New Larwood' and Yorkshireman, Frederick Trueman) had not been sent.

Even so the Test series promised to develop into a two-sided blitzkrieg and a strong divergence of opinion arose among Australians as to whether that blitzkrieger Keith Miller or the placid and peace-loving Arthur Morris, who had been Hassett's vice-captain for the past five years, should be appointed to lead and launch the Australian broadsides.

So readers who were unborn or in diapers in 1954 may be able to measure the intensity of the interest in this question perhaps I should emphasise that sport comfortably eclipsed even sex and rock music in Australia at that time as a topic for discussion—that it certainly did so among the males of the community.

I *think* 'comfortably' is the word. We were a more outdoor-minded people then, still rather coy about what are now boobs—bare or brassiered—even bikinied buttocks. The arousal of national interest in these had begun (thanks to Dr Kinsey, and Marilyn Monroe) in the United States, but not in Australia, despite the efforts of *Man Magazine*.

Sport, as a topic for discussion and debate in Australia, also had politics beaten to a frazzle. A Gallup poll had revealed that over 80 per cent of Australians read the sports columns of the newspapers and periodicals and that less than 20 per cent of them made a habit of perusing political news and comment.

We Australians of the 1950s left politics to the professionals, mainly to that extremely polished professional Sir Robert Menzies, our apparently impregnable Prime Minister. It seemed reasonably safe to do so.

For these reasons it was the question as to which of Miller and Morris would captain Australia against England that captured both the headlines and the public imagination that October and was of most concern to the often unfraternal sporting fraternity of the nation.

Miller had long replaced Don Bradman as Australia's sporting idol, had become a species of cricketing Churchill. Though the likeable Morris would have to be side-stepped the majority of Australians were adamant that the time had come for Miller to be given his unruly head—that he was the man to put those now unruly 'Poms' back in their proper and, for twenty years, customary place.

The New South Wales Cricket Association clearly believed so. It had again preferred Miller to Morris as its captain. The Australian Board of Control, whose task it was to appoint the Australian leader, was expected to fall into line.

But the Board had proved in the past that it was a law unto itself. So had the chairman of its national selection committee, Sir Donald Bradman. And it was to be a section of the Board and at least two of its selectors who now set about creating a cricketing commotion.

There was an uneasy air as to who would wear the crown. Just when the Press had come to stamp Miller as 'a good thing', 'an odds-on shot' if not quite a certainty, signs began to emerge which suggested that we were in for an almighty shock.

An outsider named Ian Johnson, who was thirty-five years of age, far more of an Attlee than a Churchill, whom the Board's selectors had not deemed worthy six months previously to send to England even among a team of seventeen players, was filtered (rather surreptitiously) into considerations.

Ian, not Miller or Morris, was dispatched to Perth to take part in the second first-class game of the M.C.C. tour, the game between the Englishmen and a Combined Eleven.

This move certainly required explanation, especially as it was thought that the Western Australian Cricket Association would greatly have preferred to have had Miller as a crowd-puller—that it would have preferred that attractive stroke-player Morris to the rather pedestrian Johnson.

Those who delved at all deeply decided that the move to

dispatch Victoria's captain, not New South Wales' captain or vice-captain, across the Nullarbor must have been instigated by the Australian Cricket Board. With what motive? Cricketing critics in the Eastern States began to wonder and then demand.

If that motive was to place Johnson in the running for the Test captaincy, why had the Board not insisted upon him being made captain of that Combined Eleven in Perth? It was all what the King of Siam would have proclaimed as 'a puzzlement'.

To the relief of the Miller and Morris factions Johnson contributed only 2 and 10 with the bat and 3 for 44 with the ball to the Combined Eleven's cause under the leadership of Keith Carmody, the Western Australian captain, from 22 to 26 October. Nothing here to set the Swan River on fire or provide ammunition for those who may or may not be members of a pro-Johnson plot.

As the M.C.C. were not programmed to play Victoria on their way through to the Brisbane Test (scheduled for 26 November) and as Victoria had no Sheffield Shield game to contest until 19 November, Johnson would have little further chance to establish his claims for inclusion in Australia's team before the start of the series, let alone to justify his appointment as national captain.

The Board now would be obliged to renounce, or at least postpone, whatever it, or a section of its members, had had in mind.

Undeterred by Johnson's unspectacular showing in Perth, however, the controlling body—through its selectors Sir Donald Bradman (South Australia), Jack Ryder (Victoria), and Dudley Seddon (New South Wales) swiftly produced a far more significant and resounding bombshell.

Johnson, not Miller nor Morris, was named captain of the Australian Eleven to meet the M.C.C. in Melbourne from 5 to 9 November.

Miller and Morris, though sadly short of match practice, were not even chosen to play. New South Wales was to be represented by Ronnie Briggs, a comparative nonentity and those 1953 tour pilgrims Richie Benaud and Jim de Courcy.

The cat was out of the bag now. It loomed like a Bengal tiger. Speculation gave way to condemnation, except in a then (even more so than today) parochial Victoria.

The Melbourne *Age*, Melbourne *Argus*, and Melbourne *Herald* and *Sporting Globe* began campaigning for Johnson to become Test captain. In Sydney the *Daily Telegraph*, the *Sun*, and the *Mirror* began insisting that Miller was the obvious man for the formidable task; the ideal leader for this crisis in Australia's cricketing affairs.

Only 'Grannie', the *Sydney Morning Herald*, crossing her elderly legs and guarding her voluminous skirts, perched (as was her wont) on the fence.

One cannot help thinking that the Board's now obvious intentions would have met with far more volatile reaction from the public had the young who are at large today been on deck. Our modern militants must have leapt at this chance of parading the streets of Sydney and Canberra, Adelaide and Brisbane (there was no Joh Bjelke-Petersen then), Hobart and Perth and brandishing posters proclaiming 'We Want Miller', 'Down With the Board', 'Banish Bradman', and even 'No Miller, No Test Wicket'.

A more youthful Dr Jim Cairns could have led others of them in countermarches along Collins and Bourke streets in support of Johnson and a twenty-five-year-old Bob Hawke may have stepped in at the last moment and resolved the issue—probably in Miller's favour.

It all, come to think of it, would have been excellent net practice for the anti-Vietnam and anti-uranium (anti-just-about-everything) demonstrations of the late 1960s and 1970s.

Certain it is that, had 1979 style demonstrations been staged in November of 1954, those who campaigned for Miller would have been armed with the overwhelmingly more imposing brief.

Under Miller's leadership in 1953–54 New South Wales had regained the Sheffield Shield. It had defeated Queensland and South Australia (holders of the trophy) twice each. It had beaten Western Australia in their one match and had won one and lost the other of the 'grudge games' with a Johnson-led Victoria.

During that season Miller had topped the New South Wales batting averages with 510 runs from ten innings at 63·75 and captured 14 wickets at 28·92. His outstanding Shield game performance had been his 143 and 4 for 91 in the losing match against Victoria, who finished second in the competition with 24 points to New South Wales' 26.

Miller had been the cricketer who did most to recover the Shield for New South Wales, to prevent his old State, Victoria, from winning it.

For Victoria Johnson had made only 98 runs from nine innings at 12·25 but, enjoying one of his best Australian seasons with the ball, he had taken 37 wickets at the impressive average of 16·43.

The only other first-class match of the 1953–54 season had been the Lindsay Hassett Testimonial game at the M.C.G.

This contest, organised by the Victorian Cricket Association (in consultation, no doubt, with Hassett) had been played between teams captained by Hassett and Morris. There was no move at this stage by the V.C.A., it should be remarked, to advance the claims of its new State captain at the national level—to put him in the running for the national captaincy in 1954–55.

Playing for Hassett's side Miller became the man of the match by scoring 100 in his first innings and 101 in his second. Also playing under Hassett, Johnson scored 17 and 14 and took 4 for 182 and 4 for 86.

Admittedly, this was not the ideal kind of occasion for a high-trajectory off-spinner. During its four days 1801 runs were scored and twenty 6s and 181 4s were struck. Four of the 6s came in five balls off Johnson from an unexpected source—from the bat of young Ian Craig, who compiled 106, one of the four centuries of the game.

Miller's thrilling batsmanship failed to win the day for Hassett, but it helped the man who had scored 6935 runs for Victoria and 59 centuries in first-class cricket (10 of them in Tests) towards a reward of some $11 000.

During Bradman's $20 000 Testimonial at the same ground in 1948, it is perhaps pertinent to remember, Miller had scored 2 and 14 and delivered not one solitary over.

Certainly it is pertinent to remark that Miller had done more, both as a captain and a player, during the 1953–54 season than Morris or Johnson to stake his claims for the national leadership.

And so when October ended in 1954 he appeared, all other things being equal, to have a strong advantage, indeed an indisputable one, over Johnson. But all other things were *not* equal; most other things anyway. *They, too, were heavily in Miller's favour.*

He had represented Australia in 40 Tests, Johnson in 27. He had represented Australia on three tours of England and on one each in South Africa, India, and New Zealand. Johnson had made only two tours abroad—one to England in 1948 and one to South Africa in 1949–50.

The disparity between the Test match records of the two players was monumental.

These then were:

Batting:

	Innings	*Highest Score*	*Aggregate*	*Average*
Miller	62	147 not out	2117	37·8
Johnson	42	77	533	13·66

Bowling:

	Overs	*Maidens*	*Runs*	*Wickets*	*Average*
Miller	990·5	219	2519	117	21·52
Johnson	713·4	170	1903	60	31·71

To that time only Miller and the great England all-rounder Wilfred Rhodes had scored more than 2000 runs and taken more than 100 wickets in Test matches. Miller had done so from forty Tests, Rhodes from fifty-eight.

The Sheffield Shield records of the two candidates were:

Batting:

	Matches	*Innings*	*Highest Score*	*Aggregate*	*Average*
Miller	44	66	206 not out	3354	56·84
Johnson	43	59	132 not out	1287	23·83

Bowling:

	Overs	*Maidens*	*Runs*	*Wickets*	*Average*
Miller	692·2	85	2412	85	28·14
Johnson	1152·4	199	3874	154	25·15

Mightily in Miller's favour would appear to have been the long-standing Australian predilection for appointing batsmen as national captains and for ignoring the candidature of bowlers.

Of the eighteen men who had led Australia against England to that time fourteen (Dave Gregory, Murdoch, Horan, Scott, McDonnell, Trott, Darling, Hill, Sid Gregory, Collins, Ryder, Woodfull, Bradman, and Hassett) had been specialist batsmen, three (Giffen, Noble, and Armstrong) had been all-rounders, and one (Blackham) had been a wicketkeeper.

Not one specialist bowler had filled the role and Ian Johnson (on his record as stated above) scarcely qualified as a Test match batsman or all-rounder. His claims for inclusion in the approaching Test match in Brisbane rested almost entirely upon his ability as a bowler.

Once the Australian team was named by the selectors it was the Board's duty to appoint its captain, simply to appoint the man whom it believed would make the best leader against the team it would have to confront.

It held the right, of course, to disapprove of any member or members of the selected twelve 'on grounds other than cricket'. But it was hardly likely to exercise this privilege against Miller whether or not it had done so in 1949. Only once was the Board known to have acted in this fashion. This was in 1951–52 when Sid Barnes was chosen in the Australian team for the Adelaide Test against John Goddard's West Indian side.

Its action had rebounded against it and jeopardised Australia's chances of victory when Hassett, the Australian captain, became unfit to play.

Australia was forced into the Test with one bowler too many, one batsman too few, and the unfortunate Hassett, though injured, had to act as twelfth man.

In his *Australian Cricket, A History* 'Johnnie' Moyes described this as 'an absurd state of affairs which caused many verbal and written condemnations of the controlling body'. It was, he said, 'the kind of situation in which the originator of Mr Bumble would have delighted'. It also led to a libel case in which members of the Board were embarrassingly involved as witnesses.

By November of 1954 Miller, as we have seen, had been chosen to represent Australia at home and abroad in 40 Test matches. The Board, as far as is known, had never seen fit to disapprove of his selection 'on grounds other than cricket'.

It was unlikely to 'Bumble' again now.

Before returning to the events of the 1954–55 Australian cricket season it should be stated that Sir Donald Bradman, when he accepted a contract to cover the 1953 Test series for the London *Daily Mail* and a group of Australian newspapers, resigned as one of the three South Australian delegates to the Board and that when, in December 1953, one of that State's delegates, Hughie Bridgman, died, Sir Donald was immediately reinstated.

I should like also to state at this stage that anything I have said, or am about to say, in this chapter is in no way intended to reflect upon Ian Johnson, who was to prove himself in the West Indies in 1955 one of the finest captains Australia has fielded and, in England in 1956, one of its outstanding sporting ambassadors.

When the Australian Cricket Board sent Johnson, and not Miller or Morris, to Perth in late October of 1954 it did not insist upon him being made captain of the Combined Eleven. That it had the power to do so is unquestionable. The Board is the responsible body for international cricket and this was an international match.

Its reasons for not demanding that Johnson be captain are debatable. Possibly the pro-Johnson or anti-Miller 'plotters' felt they should proceed as cautiously and unostentatiously as possible —keep what cards they held close to their chests.

Following his 2 and 10 with the bat and 3 wickets for 44 in Perth, Johnson scored 5 not out and took 6 for 66 for his Australian Eleven against a Hutton-less M.C.C. in Melbourne on 5 November.

You may be recalling that 5 November is Guy Fawkes Day and, basing their case upon that 6 for 66, the 'plotters' went on with their plan. They would have been happier, of course, had the M.C.C. 205, not been leading Johnson's Australian Eleven 167 for 7, when rain washed out play in that Test preliminary.

Because of that bowling performance Johnson was now well in the running for selection among the eleven players who would take the field for Australia in Brisbane on 26 November. He could be chosen without causing an uproar. But one nigger in the woodpile still remained. On 12 November in Sydney the M.C.C.

had to meet New South Wales, *captained by Miller*.

In this game Keith top-scored with 86 to help New South Wales to a lead of 130 on the first innings. When the match ended New South Wales needed only 119 runs for victory with eight wickets, including those of Miller and Morris, standing. The M.C.C. side contained eight of the players who were to begin defending the Ashes for England less than a fortnight later and this time was led by Hutton.

The case for Miller to be appointed to the leadership in Brisbane, indeed for the entire Test series, now appeared complete —unanswerable.

On 19 November Johnson, for Victoria against South Australia in Melbourne, scored only 4 and took 2 for 36 and 2 for 87. But the pro-Johnson (or anti-Miller) members of the Cricket Board lacked nothing on the score of determination. Though faced with all the facts I have tabulated, and now a mostly hostile Press, they went ahead with their project.

Who were they and why, ever since the beginning of this vital season (probably before then), were they so determined to act as they did? They must have had a powerful and obdurate spokesman. Where do we look for him?

The Board consisted of thirteen delegates—three each from New South Wales, Victoria, and South Australia, two from Queensland, and one each from Western Australia and Tasmania.

The New South Wales Cricket Association (through its delegates) had shown its support for Miller for two years and had maintained it in the face of the Board's retention of Morris as the national vice-captain. It had done so simply because it believed Miller was a more inspiring leader than Morris and its opinion had been confirmed.

We can accept that the three New South Wales delegates voted for Miller late that November. Indeed I know that they did, that they were opposed to the campaign for Johnson from the very beginning, and that they kept expressing strong opposition to it.

We can also accept that the Victorian Cricket Association wanted Johnson to be captain partly because Miller had left his native State to join the ranks of its inveterate enemy north of the Murray River in 1947.

Was the move for Johnson initiated in Victoria? My most

Top left: The great Gary (later Sir Garfield) Sobers leaving the field happily after one of his numerous Test-match centuries. *Top right:* Frank Mortimore Maglinne (later Sir Frank) Worrell, the acme of elegance, executing his leg-sweep (*Photos—Advertiser Newspapers Ltd*). *Bottom:* Miller talking to Mrs Clement Attlee at a dinner held at the Mitre Hotel, Hampton Court (*Photo*—Evening Standard)

Top left: Keith Miller, the journalist, shown in 1957 typing his sports column for the London *Daily Express*. He still contributes regular articles for newspapers, including Sydney's *Daily Telegraph* and *Mirror* (*Photo—Adelaide News & Sunday Mail*). *Top right:* A typical glare from Keith Miller after sending down one of his fiery deliveries (*Photo—Associated Press*). *Bottom:* Sir Donald Bradman (in hat) amuses fellow-members of the Australian Cricket Board at a meeting in the 1970s. Many people consider Bradman, though now retired, still controls the policies of the ACB (*Photo—Advertiser Newspapers Ltd*)

authoritative information is that it was not. It can have come, therefore, only from South Australia, Queensland, Western Australia, or Tasmania.

You will already have formed your opinion and, if you have decided upon South Australia, you are, according to those authorities of mine, absolutely right. A move such as the one we are investigating, one which could be expected to, and did, arouse strong opposition and create nation-wide controversy, required as I have said strong promotion.

South Australia's three delegates to the Board were Messrs R. F. Middleton (Chairman of the Board), A. J. Baker, and Sir Donald Bradman. Its representative on the national selection committee was Sir Donald Bradman.

Of these three delegates Bradman was incomparably the most powerful figure, the obvious leader, the man who, with the support of the Victorian Jack Ryder (that 'King of Collingwood') was in a position to handle the first hurdles, those at the selectorial level.

It had been Bradman and Ryder who had omitted Miller from the originally chosen team for the South African tour in 1949–50. Assuming therefore, as I have indestructible grounds to believe we can, that Bradman not only instigated but played the leading part in executing this move, we turn to the motives which inspired him.

Were they purely personal ones? Was he, as many contended, still resentful regarding those unhappy and embarrassing experiences he had had with Keith at Adelaide, Sydney, and Lord's? Was he, as many contended, still unable to forget or forgive the kicking of that ball back to him at the Adelaide Oval in 1947–48, the bowling of those two bumpers too many at him on the Sydney Cricket Ground in 1948–49, that deliberate duck against Essex, that refusal (when unfit) to bowl in the Lord's Test of 1948, and that disappointing contribution to his Testimonial?

Having played for four seasons under Don, I believe he was. I also believe he must have forgotten, or overlooked, the fact that he, himself, had been quite a 'bad boy' at times—had broken his contract with the Board during the 1930 tour of England, had been fined for so doing, had been the one Australian batsman to defy his captain Woodfull's (and I have Woodfull's own word for this) orders during the Bodyline Series of 1932–33, and had broken the confidence imposed upon him as a national selector in 1949.

But, also knowing Don, I do not believe he would have used his own quarrel with Miller as the basis of the anti-Miller case he put to those colleagues of his on the Board, the ones whom he believed would be open to persuasion. For one thing, he could hardly have expected such arguments to be effective.

My belief is that Bradman was genuinely convinced that Miller was not the man the Board should appoint to lead Australia on an overseas tour and that, if he were appointed to lead her now at home, this would be the inevitable and unavoidable consequence.

This was the case, as I have good reason to believe, Bradman put first to the two other South Australian members of the Board and then, with their support, to its Victorian members who, naturally, could be expected to welcome the chance of helping to install their own State captain.

This was how Miller could best be prevented from becoming Australia's leader on the imminent tour of the West Indies and the 1956 tour of England. The outside support the South Australian and Victorian delegates needed could only be enlisted by such arguments.

Members of the Board were mostly untravelled, unworldly, conservative, cautious, and unimaginative characters. They would be unlikely to appreciate (as indeed Bradman appears not to have done) that the very qualities of Keith's which had won the admiration of overseas people (from Royalty to ragamuffins) and would help Australia now were the ones being advanced against him—his fearlessness, positiveness, independence of thought and action, and his frankness.

They might also be inclined to regard these qualities of Miller's as a threat, were he appointed national captain, to their own authority, even to their tenure in office—to the long-preserved, absolute authority of the Board.

Facts such as the following either would not occur to, or would be lost upon, them:

1. That Australia's Prime Minister Sir Robert Menzies had recently stated he regarded it as an honour to have been invited to contribute a foreword to one of Keith's books;

2. That the British Royal family and many of the scions of the English hierarchy had shown themselves delighted to form and develop Keith's acquaintance and friendship;
3. That Sir Neville Cardus had described him as 'The Australian *in excelsis*';
4. That South Africans, deeply disappointed at his original omission from the 1949–50 Australian side, had clamoured for his addition to it when the chance presented itself; and
5. That Keith's wartime wing-commander had called him 'the bravest and most willing (I should like to stress "most willing") pilot I ever had under my control'.

These other members of the Board would lack the imagination (as indeed Bradman, himself, seems to have done) to see that Keith, once given the captaincy, might be inspired to even greater efforts than he already had performed for his country—as he indisputably had been for his adopted State, New South Wales.

So I believe was unquestionably the greatest all-round cricketer this country has produced (still has produced during a century of years) prevented from gaining the honour of becoming its captain—either at home or abroad.

And the Board's less-than-unanimous vote of late November 1954 becomes all the less comprehensible when it is remembered that only a few months later it appointed Miller as Johnson's vice-captain for the 1955 tour of those turbulent islands in the Caribbean, realising (as it must have done) that any injury or mishap to Johnson would place Keith in command.

21
Summer of 'The Typhoon' – Australia 1954–55

Though Australia's north-eastern coastline is no stranger to tornadoes, most of them with female names, its Test batsmen had not faced a two-legged 'Typhoon' until the summer of 1954–55.

Two-legged 'Typhoons', when armed with a cricket ball, can place testing demands upon courage.

Australia, itself, had produced a two-legged 'Demon' named Spofforth in 1877 and a two-legged 'Terror' named Turner in 1886. In 1925 it introduced a 'Scarlet Pimpernel' in Clarrie Grimmett to Test match cricket, and in 1931 a 'Tiger' named Bill O'Reilly.

But a two-legged 'Typhoon', as an adversary, was quite unprecedented—a scary prospect. It could become as ogrish as had the 'Bodyline' of Harold Larwood and Bill Voce twenty-one years before.

This cricketing freak and phenomenon of the mid-1950s was a 24-year-old named Frank Tyson. Like Larwood he was not (by Australian standards) a tall man, but he had shoulders and arms that would have graced Oliver Goldsmith's 'village smithy' and hips and thighs to match.

He hailed originally from Staffordshire and bowled for it and, later, for Northamptonshire mainly, he said, to help his widowed and impecunious mother feed her father-less flock.

By 1954, from a run-in that must have aroused admiration in Marathon, he was unleashing cricket balls so swiftly (at around 150 kilometres per hour) that the Polish born Joseph Conrad, were he alive to watch them, might have embarked upon a sequel to one of his best-remembered books. You guessed it—*Typhoon*.

On his arrival in Perth at the beginning of October 1954 Tyson, who had played in one Test match (against Pakistan on his way to Australia) began a sustained effort to ensure he would participate in another—at Brisbane on 26 November.

Owing to the ultimatum his captain Len Hutton had delivered to his co-selectors back at Lord's in August, Tyson had six rivals to contend with—those fast and fastish bowlers Brian Statham, Peter Loader, Alec Bedser, Trevor Bailey, Bob Appleyard, and Bill Edrich.

All of them, as he realised, held an advantage over him. All of them could *swing* a ball. His only asset was sheer and frightening pace. Well, races, he had read, were apt to go to the swift. He added another yard or two to his run and concentrated upon achieving rhythm.

Given his first chance against that Combined XI in Perth, Frank dismissed the Australian Test batsman Graeme Hole for 4 and, from 20 much-publicised overs, took 3 for 27.

Allowed to open the bowling for the M.C.C. in Adelaide he took 5 for 62. Again given the new ball in Sydney he dismissed four batsmen (including Keith Miller, Richie Benaud, and a youngster named Bobby Simpson) for 98.

Only Miller, who scored 86, consistently toed the line of his fearsome deliveries and it was during this match that a Sydney writer with a liking for alliteration christened him 'Typhoon' Tyson.

Even typhoons can blow their gaskets, however, and from 29 overs in the First Test at Woolloongabba Tyson took only one wicket, Richie Benaud's, for 160 runs. Between them he, Statham 2 for 123, and the 36-year-old Alec Bedser 1 for 131, dismissed only four batsmen while Australia amassed 601 for 8. The colossal cost of those dismissals was 414 runs. Hutton's fourth pace bowler, Trevor 'Barnacle' Bailey, took 3 for 140 to complete this Capricornian calamity.

Hutton, the captain and chairman of selectors of England's crusade, reacted by spending the Sunday morning of the Test miserably in his hotel bed. Here he seemed mesmerised by the caustic comments in the national newspapers concerning his leadership. His decision to send Australia into bat after winning the toss, and his exclusive reliance upon his four-man fast attack, had aroused universal criticism.

Arthur Morris, known in Australia in 1950–51 and in England in 1953 as 'Bedser's Bunny', had scored 153 of that 601 for 8, Neil Harvey 162, Miller a 'crisp and confident' 49, Lindwall 64 not out, and Hole 57 before being thrown out from the boundary by Tyson.

When the Test ended on 1 December in a victory for Australia by an innings and 154, Denis Compton, though he had scored 2 not out and nought, not Hutton, was England's hero.

This was because Denis, having broken his finger on the boundary fence during Australia's innings, had insisted on batting against Lindwall and Miller in a vain effort to help Bailey to his first Test century.

'Compton Shows Battle of Britain Spirit on Churchill's Birthday' read headlines in Brisbane and Sydney, but they failed to cheer, even console, his long-term rival and now captain.

Then came the crowning blow: the news that George Oswald Browning Allen, the chairman of the selection committee which had chosen the M.C.C. side, the chairman of just about everything chairmanable in English cricket, was arriving in Sydney in two days time. Allen would be attending the Sydney Test on 17 December and then those in Melbourne and Adelaide, the Brisbane *Courier Mail* said.

Allen had 'vigorously opposed' Hutton's demand for that flock of fast bowlers in August at Lord's. Australia's spin bowlers Ian Johnson 5 for 84, Benaud 3 for 71, and Bill Johnston 3 for 106, had taken 11 of England's wickets in Brisbane. The last thing Hutton, England's professional captain, was looking for was what he disdainfully termed 'amateur interference'.

On his arrival in Sydney that Friday Allen took a taxi to his birthplace at the bottom of Victoria Road, Bellevue Hill. Finding his birthplace had become a block of apartments owned by Sir Frank Packer (the father of Kerry) he knocked on the door of one of them and was greeted by its occupant, former Australian tennis star Adrian Quist, who invited him in for a drink.

'What happened to those fast bowlers of yours in Brisbane, "Gubby"?' asked Adrian, who has a devilish sense of humour.

'Hutton demanded we choose them. It's *his* funeral now,' Allen retorted.

'Will he play them all again in Sydney?' Adrian asked.

'Not if I can prevent it,' said 'Gubby'.

Quist had an Australian Pressman, who was covering the M.C.C. tour, staying with him at the time and he conveyed the gist of this conversation to Hutton in Melbourne.

The M.C.C. side for the match against Victoria over the weekend preceding the Sydney Test had already been named. Tyson, Bailey, and Loader were to provide the pace, Statham and Bedser to be rested.

Tyson drew his own conclusions. He, the newly-named 'Typhoon', had played in his last Test for the tour. Confirmation of his fears came on the second morning of the match in Melbourne while the English team were waiting in the lounge of the Windsor Hotel before taxiing to the cricket ground.

When Hutton entered the lounge he avoided the table at which Tyson was sitting and crossed to one occupied by several members of the Australian Press.

'You don't look happy, Len,' one of them said.

'Would you, after what happened in Brisbane?'

Two of the Pressmen at the table had represented Australia at cricket.

'Which bowlers would you choose for Sydney?' Hutton asked them as an afterthought.

'Tyson for a start,' one of the writers replied.

'I was hoping for a *serious* answer.'

'I gave you one. If you don't believe me take a look at this paper.' The writer had sent a story to his editor in Sydney the previous evening saying Tyson was the one man, the one bowler, who could retain the Ashes for England, the one bowler Australia had to fear.

Hutton read the prominently displayed story and gave Tyson the new ball against Victoria that day. He took six wickets (Neil Harvey's among them) for 68 with some of the fastest and most accurate bowling he had delivered in his young life.

He and his captain were not the only happy men that night at the Windsor Hotel. So, understandably, was that Australian cricket writer and he went to see Hutton and told him of the extraordinary piece of good fortune which had caused that opinion of his of Tyson to gain the banner headlines.

It had gained its prominence, indeed its very appearance, only because the Assistant Sports Editor, the late Lindsay Palmer, had retreated (as was his habit) to the lavatory adjoining the sports room in search of inspiration, as the deadline for his first edition approached. On his way there he had found what was worrying him, the missing cable from his tour correspondent. It was fluttering about the floor of a windy corridor between the sportsroom and the loo.

The headline 'Typhoon Tyson England's One Hope' had fitted perfectly in 72 point Bodoni caps across the top of his main page.

The 1954 Len Hutton was a superstitious as well as canny character. He made up his mind about his Test attack that night before 'Gubby' Allen could get at his co-selectors. Alec Bedser, not Tyson, would be omitted from England's side for the Sydney Test. Tyson and Statham would be retained.

On such slim strings is the course of history, cricket history anyway, dictated. Tyson took 4 for 45 and 6 for 85 in that Test in Sydney and England won by 28 runs.

So it was that the English and Australian teams gathered in Melbourne to ring out the old year and ring in the new with the series standing at what Australians used to call 'Even Stephens'.

So, too, it was that the Englishmen were now favourites to take a two–one lead. Tyson's triple triumph, a recurrence of Keith Miller's back trouble, and grave doubts as to the quality and durability of the Melbourne Cricket Ground pitch had made them so.

Because of his back injury Miller had not played in the Sydney Test. He had been chosen for the one in Melbourne on the understanding that he would not be called upon to bowl; selected on the strength of his 86 and 49 against Tyson for New South Wales and Australia in November.

In his last three bowling spells Tyson had taken 6 for 68, 4 for 45, and 6 for 85, which adds up to 16 for 198 at 12·37. Miller, free to concentrate on his batting, was the man with the courage and technique to defy him. So it was claimed. Several of Australia's leading batsmen had shown a tendency to retreat from the line of flight when facing Tyson. Miller had not done so and could be counted upon not to do so now; counted upon to set a timely example to his colleagues.

The need for such an example promised to be even greater because of the uncertainty prevailing regarding the M.C.G. wicket. So anxious on this point had Victorian officials become that they had conscripted the neighbouring Albert Ground curator, Bill Vanthoff, to take charge of the preparation of the pitch. He, if anyone, it was thought, might prevent it from disintegrating into loose bricks of turf and top soil after the first two days of the five-day Test.

Melbourne, as it happened, was undergoing a heatwave and, if deliveries from Tyson landed in the cracks between those bricks, somebody might be seriously injured—even killed.

Australia's Prime Minister at that time was Robert Gordon (later Sir Robert) Menzies. He was an inveterate, one could say passionate, lover of cricket and a patriot among patriots. He lived in Melbourne and never, when he could avoid it, missed a ball of a Melbourne Test.

Half an hour before play was due to begin on 31 December of 1954 Vernon Ransford, the secretary of the Melbourne Cricket Club, invited Sir Robert to take a look at the suspect pitch. While he was doing so Ian Johnson lost the vital toss and Hutton said he would bat first, not second as in Brisbane.

On his way back to his seat Sir Robert came face to face with Miller in one of the dark corridors of the M.C.G. Members' Pavilion.

Sir Robert, steeped as he was in cricket history, remembered how, on the corresponding morning of the Melbourne Test of 1911, a great English bowler named Sydney Barnes (who, like Tyson, had been reared in Staffordshire) had gained immortality in this cricketing colosseum.

Unexpectedly given the new ball by his captain, Johnny Douglas, he had taken four wickets, those of Warren Bardsley, Charles Kelleway, Clem Hill, and Warwick Armstrong while conceding one run. On that morning forty-three years before Barnes had come in to lunch to a mixture of applause and hooting after delivering 9 overs unchanged and achieving an analysis of 9/6/3/4.

'There's a slight ridge on that wicket out there, Keith,' Sir

Robert said. 'I've had a good look at it and it's just where it could help you. Why don't you try a couple of overs? Your back might stand up in this heat and it's vital that we get a good start.'

It is difficult to resist the entreaties of a Prime Minister so persuasive as Sir Robert. Keith had a word with a delighted Ian Johnson on his return to the Australian dressing-room.

The history of Test cricket is crowded with coincidences but with few, if any, as memorable as the one that was now to emerge.

From 9 successive overs, 8 of them maidens, that morning Keith dismissed Hutton, Edrich, and Compton during ninety minutes bowling. Only two scoring strokes were made from his 72 deliveries—both of them, a two and a three, by Colin Cowdrey.

The analyses of Barnes and Miller deserve, I feel, to be set alongside one another.

Barnes: Nine overs, six maidens, three runs, four wickets.

Miller: Nine overs, eight maidens, five runs, three wickets.

When his back grew too painful for him to continue bowling that afternoon Miller's figures were 11/8/14/3. Barnes' final figures had been 23/9/44/5.

In 1954 England reached 191, almost solely because of the first and greatest of Colin Cowdrey's eventual twenty-two Test Centuries.

On the Saturday (New Year's Day) of 1955 and the early part of the Monday Australia responded with 231. To this Len Maddocks, the manager of Greg Chappell's 1977 team to England, contributed 47 and Ian Johnson an invaluable and undefeated 33.

Towards stumps on the Saturday evening the cracks criss-crossing the parched pitch, however, were between 60 and 120 millimetres wide. The wicket had begun to resemble a jigsaw puzzle and promised to become one.

Nine of Australia's first innings wickets had fallen to England's pace bowlers, only one to its dispenser of left-handed 'Chinamen', that whimsical 'tyke' Johnny Wardle. But Wardle's chance, because of those widening cracks, was expected to come. Australia's lead of 40 seemed too slender for confidence.

The unmortared 'bricks' already formed on the surface of the wicket would loosen, it was forecast, some time on the Tuesday, if not before.

Then, to quote poet Alexander Pope, 'All hell and Parnassus would be let out' for the batsmen.

During the corresponding Test of the 1932–33 series England's extremely suspicious 'Iron Duke' of a captain, Douglas Jardine, fearing interference with the wicket, had stationed one of his team's acolytes as a spy in the England dressing-room from the Saturday night until the Monday morning. Had Hutton followed Jardine's example his spy would have had quite a story to tell.

This task was left to a Melbourne cricket writer of considerable repute and unquestioned integrity named Percy Beames, the only Victorian who had captained his State at both cricket and football.

The Sunday was the hottest day of that heatwave, the Fahrenheit temperature soaring well beyond the century. On his way to his office in Collins Street that evening Beames decided to look at the M.C.G. wicket.

To his amazement he found it was being watered, quite heavily watered, *with a hose*.

Beames has never been a sensationalist. He decided to dwell upon events. The watering of a wicket during a Test match was, in his experience, unique. The reporting of it would cause violent repercussion in England and Australia and greatly embarrass the Melbourne Cricket Club.

But, when they came in for lunch on the Monday, members of the Australian team put word around that the pitch, despite the weekend heat, was greener than it had been on the Friday, that those cracks in it had diminished, that they had found wet grass cuttings in the holes dug by the bowlers' feet.

At stumps on the Monday night England, 159 for 3, were 119 ahead. On the Tuesday morning Beames revealed what he had seen on the Sunday evening in his story in the Melbourne *Age*.

Though the watering of the pitch had helped England, officials of the Victorian Cricket Association and Melbourne Cricket Club produced wrathful denials that any such thing had occurred. Later they were to substantiate them with statutory declarations, ones sworn by curator Bill Vanthoff and members of his staff. These officials, of course, were absolutely innocent and simply could not believe that such a 'heinous offence' could have occurred at one of cricket's most hallowed shrines.

The heatwave continued into the Tuesday, but the refreshed

wicket held together while England went on to 279 and a lead of 239, while Australia (for the loss of two wickets) reduced this to 164.

It was on the Wednesday morning that what Australia's batsmen had feared, what Bill Vanthoff had tried to prevent (possibly because he had no wish to become an accessory before the event to murder), transpired.

Play had scarcely resumed when those 5- and 7-centimetre diameter bricks began to work loose under the peppering they received from the lightning deliveries of Tyson and Statham.

Balls which landed on the edges of them nearest to the bowler jumped sharply; those which landed on the edges of them furthest from the bowler shot through low—irrespective of length.

The batsmen who faced them were in doubt whether to react upwards as for lifeboat station drill or downward as for enemy air attack. If they fended downward they might receive one of those bombs on their batting box, their belly-button, their chest, or their chin, even between their eyes. If they fended upward they could lose the ferrules of one of their stumps.

On reaching the wicket Miller bravely decided upon the former course of action. Nobody, not even a triumphant 'Typhoon', was going to cause him to flinch, to give a centimetre of ground before a crowd that had taken the total Test attendance to beyond 300 000 and the takings to a then record $95 866.

For more than half an hour Miller kept his head and bat down, his feet behind the line of flight. The execution of the strokes needed to produce the 165 runs Australia needed to score was another matter, however—an impossibility.

Eventually a goodish-length ball from Tyson reared sharply from a length on the line of the off stump, struck Keith on the right glove, and carried to Bill Edrich at gully. Neil Harvey already had departed, caught low on the leg side by wicketkeeper Evans.

Having seen that orthodox defence was unavailing, Benaud and Archer began blasting at the ball with diagonal, at times horizontal, bats. Inevitably, both of them lost their central stumps and Australia were out on Admiral Lord Nelson's number 111.

Her last eight wickets had fallen in 86 minutes for 36 runs and England led two Tests to one with two to be played.

Tyson, having delivered 12·3 of the 31·3 overs England required to dismiss Australia, had taken 7 for 27. In the Sydney and Melbourne Tests he had captured 19 wickets at 11·84—after taking 1 for 160 at Brisbane.

While the Englishmen were defeating Tasmania by 243 runs and South Australia by an innings and 143, Miller led New South Wales to a nine-wicket victory over Victoria, taking 5 wickets for 38, in a Tyson-like spell, towards it.

When the two Test teams assembled in Adelaide for the Fourth Test over the Australia Day weekend, Sir Donald Bradman and his fellow South Australian members of the Australian Cricket Board can hardly have been congratulating themselves.

So far Ian Johnson, to give him his due, had done what he could as a player to save their and Australia's face. He had taken 5 for 84 and scored 24 not out in the Brisbane Test, missed the Sydney Test through ill health, taken 2 for 45 in Melbourne, and scored 37 without losing his wicket.

What Australia needed now, however, if it was to mount a recovery and regain the Ashes, was a species of cricketing Caesar. In the eyes of most Australians Miller, not Johnson, was cast in that mould.

Sir Donald, Ryder, and Seddon brought in Colin McDonald, in place of Favell, to partner Arthur Morris and Alan Davidson to replace the injured Lindwall. England stuck to all its batsmen and its heavy artillery for what promised (under another heatwave) to become cricket's equivalent of the Battle of the Somme.

Runs came as slowly as metres had been gained during that first World War holocaust in Picardy while Australia struggled to 323 and England to 341 in their first innings. Maddocks 69, McDonald 48, Miller 44, and Ian Johnson 44 not out of a valiant ninth-wicket stand of 92, did best for Australia; Hutton 80, Cowdrey 79, and Compton 44, for England.

Only one of Australia's batsmen had failed to reach double figures in the first innings. Seven of them had passed twenty. Because England were to have last use of the wicket, it seemed the series might be levelled with one Test to be played.

But another cricketing coincidence then occurred. Tyson, who had been forced to bowl 26·1 overs to capture 3 for 86 in Australia's first innings, now took 3 for 47 from 15 and his partner Statham 3 for 38 from 12.

Australia, for the second time in succession, lost all its second-innings wickets for 111. England needed only 94 to win the Test and the series, to retain the Ashes.

Miller, though he had no Lindwall to support him, refused to admit defeat. He dismissed Hutton 5, Edrich 0, and Cowdrey 4 to have England 18 for 3 and his own figures 3 for 12 from 3 overs before Compton steadied his side and steered it to victory.

Rain prevented all but a little over a day's play in the Fifth Test at Sydney, but in the game which preceded it Miller led New South Wales to one of the Englishmen's two defeats of the summer, contributing 82 runs and 2 wickets for 46 towards it.

This was the first time since 1936–37 that New South Wales had beaten an English side. That side of 1936–37 was led by none other than our Sydney-born George Oswald Browning 'Gubby' Allen.

Though New South Wales retained the Sheffield Shield that season it was not one of Miller's best—either with bat or ball. From twelve first-class innings he scored 381 at 31·75. As a bowler he took 19 wickets for 489 at 25·73.

Naturally it came as a surprise to him when, in March of 1955, the Australian Cricket Board appointed him as Ian Johnson's vice-captain for the imminent tour of the West Indies.

22
Caribbean triumph—West Indies 1955

The team which Ian Johnson (with Keith as his vice-captain) led through the Caribbean islands and what then was British Guiana from mid-March to late June of 1955 was the first Australian cricket side to travel to its various destinations by plane. All previous Australian teams had benefited from long voyages as a prelude to operations.

The advantages derivative from team camaraderie on a long voyage before tackling exhausting and demanding itineraries in foreign lands have already been explained.

Ironically it was Ian Johnson's side, his battered, recently-'typhooned' band of 15 warriors, who were called upon to establish this precedent. If ever a cricketing combination needed a rest on an ocean liner to recover from its wounds—physical and psychological, it was this 'demoralised Coterie of Old Contemptibles and Kids' as one Sydney Pressman had described them.

But fate in the form of that Australian Cricket Board and the Australian Treasury had decreed there should be no respite. Only a fortnight after their escape from 'Typhoon' Tyson they were dispatched from Sydney's Kingsford Smith Airport on their 54-hour, 20 000-kilometre journey to Kingston, Jamaica—via Fiji, Canton Island, Honolulu, San Francisco, Vancouver, Calgary, Regina, Winnipeg, Toronto, Nassau, and Montego Bay.

They crossed the Pacific in reverse of the route Sir Charles Kingsford Smith had taken in the *Southern Cross* in 1928, but calling at the same fuelling ports.

Australian tennis star of the 1930s and 1940s Adrian Quist, who has a wicked sense of humour, had lent that dramatic novel *The High and the Mighty* to one member of the Australian team. He suggested he should begin reading it when he left Honolulu on the long hop to San Francisco. As it transpired this player had to vacate his first-class seat for this section of the journey and join some dusky Indonesians in the ill-lit economy-class compartment. He began tackling the novel as instructed, only to discover it dealt with a diabolically hazardous flight from Hawaii to California during which engine after engine had failed and fuel run low.

The player's relief when he sighted the Golden Gate Bridge on a sunny but cold March morning is easily imagined. But the Australians, owing to their country's then need to conserve its reserves of the then 'almighty' U.S. dollar, had been refused permission to dwell along route in the States—even to fly across them in a direct line to Jamaica.

Thus they were denied perhaps the one chance in their lives to explore San Francisco's Chinatown; to board that famous cable car to the summit of Nob Hill and enjoy a pint or two of Schlitz at the Top O' the Mark, the glass-windowed bar-restaurant of the Mark Hopkins Hotel. They missed seeing the dives along the Barbary Coast that author Jack London haunted in search of background and inspiration for his books.

Most of the weary Australians would happily have settled for a sojourn on Alcatraz in San Francisco Bay but they were swiftly moved to another plane and diverted northward over the pine-punctuated, white mountains of Oregon and Washington to Vancouver.

Back in the early 1930s another Australian cricket team, captained by Victor Richardson and containing Don Bradman and the 'inimitable' Arthur Mailey had played a match on Vancouver Island. In March of 1955 most of Vancouver's cricket-minded citizens seemed to be of Scottish extraction, inheritors of their ancestors' fondness for Johnny Walker whisky—both red and black label. Some of them had seen Bradman, Mailey, and Richardson in 1932. They gave Johnson, Miller, and *their* men—few of whom (unlike 'The Don') were teetotallers—a memorable afternoon, then drove them to the airport for their overnight flight to Toronto. Spring had yet to spring and southern Canada

Australia's perhaps two greatest all-rounders, Keith Miller and Richie Benaud, with their close friend Arthur Morris (*Photo—News Ltd*)

Keith Miller in casual attire in his late fifties. The renowned locks, though still luxuriant, are grey-threaded but the even-now sapphire blue eyes are as penetrating as ever (*Photo — News Ltd*)

was heavily blanketed with snow. So, soon, were the wings of the aeroplane, with snow that rapidly became ice. At Calgary, home of the famous stampede, the plane landed on a narrow strip of tarmac framed by walls of snow. And again at Regina.

'Australia's commercial pilots have it easy compared to yours. They don't have to fly through blizzards,' said Miller to the air hostess. 'This isn't a blizzard. Not yet,' she replied. 'Wait till we cross Lake Huron.'

Arriving with the sun in Toronto after their second successive night in a plane the Australians were granted only a four-hour respite in a centrally-heated motel before joining yet another plane for their southward flight over New York, Washington, D.C., and Miami to Nassau.

Once again, thrice again so near and yet so far. And, to increase the mounting frustration, it was announced during the approach over the Bahamas that all transit passengers would be confined to the airport lounge at Nassau while waiting to resume their journey.

Even the arrival on board of the dusky, undeniably lovely 'Miss Jamaica', homing from a beauty contest in Miami, failed to enliven the weary Australians. And most of them were bachelors. Totally neglected, 'Miss Jamaica' joined the extremely handsome captain in the cockpit and stayed there alongside him for the 500-kilometre hop to Montego Bay.

Here in the airport lounge the Australians and their manager Jack Burge—even 'Miss Jamaica'—were handed rum crusters and told they would have to undergo a 'temperature test' before being allowed to disembark at Kingston.

Ironically, the only passenger who failed the test was the dazzling 'Miss Jamaica'. 'Probably,' Keith Miller quipped, 'because of her proximity to that pilot.'

'I always run temperatures in planes,' retorted 'Miss Jamaica', and she was far too beautiful to be disbelieved.

It was almost midnight—midnight of the third day out from Sydney—when we arrived at the Palisadoes Airport and were driven around the harbour under the coastal mountains and through the amber-lit streets of 'Cap'n Morgan's Town' and past his old pirate stronghold, Port Royal, towards the sprawling and fashionable Courtleigh Manor Hotel.

The dusky driver of our bus, Pontius by name, had a passion for pace and somebody (Colin McDonald, I fancy) dubbed him 'Pontius the Pilot'. Certainly he needed a pilot's, not a driver's, licence.

Utterly exhausted and realising that within two weeks they would have to confront those batting 'tornadoes' the 'Three Terrible Ws', Worrell, Weekes, and Walcott, and the spin twins Alf 'Old Man River' Valentine and Sonny Ramadhin, in the first of five five-day Tests, the Australians made a bee-line for the bedrooms surrounding George and Dorothy Phippard's hotel swimming pool.

But 'Uneasy lies the head that wears the crown'. Ian Johnson gained little sleep that night: the spectacle of his dispirited, 'demoralised', and weary troops sitting in the lounge of the Montego Bay Airport with thermometers drooping from their lips like king-sized cigarettes had recalled that remark the Duke of Wellington is said to have made while reviewing his troops on the eve of Waterloo—'I don't know what effect these men will have upon the enemy but, by God, they frighten me.'

It kept haunting him almost until dawn.

Ian Johnson, unlike most former Australian captains, was a public schoolboy. He had learnt about the 'Iron Duke' while studying English History at Melbourne's Wesley College, the school which produced two Australian Prime Ministers, Sir Robert Menzies and Harold Holt.

He also was well aware that no visiting cricket team had ever defeated the West Indies in a series conducted in those 'Cricketing cauldrons', as London *Daily Mail* cricket correspondent Alex Bannister had called Kingston's Sabina Park, Port O' Spain's Queen's Park, Georgetown's Banda Ground, and Bridgetown's Kensington Oval.

He knew, because he always did his homework, that the 'Windies' had held Len Hutton's England team to a two-all draw in the Caribbean during the previous season, thanks considerably to scores of 220, 124, and 116 from Clyde Walcott, of 206 from Everton Weekes, and 167 from Frank Worrell.

That famous Battle of Waterloo had been 'won on the playing fields of Eton' by what is known as 'the public school spirit', Johnson remembered. Sir Winston Churchill, who inspired the

'First of the Few' to victory in the Battle of Britain, had been educated at Harrow.

Collecting his morning newspaper from under the door Johnson found an article on its sports page headed 'Aussies favoured for Tests'. The article quoted George Headley, the West Indies finest pre-war batsman and now chairman of its selection committee. Headley had toured Australia during the Bradman–McCabe–Woodfull–Ponsford–Kippax and O'Reilly–Grimmett–Ironmonger age of the early 1930s. He had a deep respect for Australian cricketers. 'Australia will win because it will establish a moral ascendancy. And hold it,' he had declared.

Johnson could scarcely believe his eyes. Just how did the leader of 'a demoralised and disunited team', 'a band of has-beens and infants', 'A Coterie of Old Contemptibles and Kids', go about welding it into a matchwinning combination within ten days? 'A moral ascendancy.' Those were the crucial words and they made him remember Waterloo and the Battle of Britain—that public school spirit.

Johnson donned his swimming briefs and made for the blue-tiled pool. Here he found some Sydney, Melbourne, and Adelaide Pressmen. His teammates undoubtedly were still in bed. Not up with the lark or, in this instance, the swallows which kept swooping from the telephone wires low over the blue pool.

'How long is it,' he asked the journalists, 'since an Australian cricket side received any real discipline from its captain?'

'You should know, "Johnno". You played under Bradman,' came the reply from Ray Robinson or Keith Butler.

'I'm talking about *real* discipline, the kind you get at public schools. Don never gave us any of that. He led by example. We hardly saw him except on the field.'

'I suppose you'd have to go back to Vic Richardson then. Maybe to Monty Noble in 1909?' somebody said. 'Noble was supposed to be quite a martinet and it seems to have worked for him.'

'Yes. And that's what this team of mine is going to get right now.'

Just how would vice-captain Keith Miller react? we wondered. 'What sort of discipline have you in mind?' one of us asked.

'Three hours net practice morning and afternoon before Friday's game against Jamaica and between it and the Test. Team talks every evening. Maybe a curfew. Can I count on your support?'

'Yes,' most of us said.

About three hours later I met Keith Miller in a corridor of the hotel. 'What d'you think "Johnno's" up to?' he asked.

'How would I know?' I replied.

'We're to have three hours' practice morning and afternoon all the week. They say the average noon temperature here is about 100 degrees Fahrenheit in the shade. He can't be serious.'

'I think he is,' I said.

And Johnson was dead serious. He also got Miller to help him with net coaching to iron out the faults in the Australian batsmen's techniques which had contributed to their downfall against Tyson.

So it was that on the Tuesday, Wednesday, and Thursday of that week fifteen Australian cricketers stood out like so many 'mad dogs and Englishmen' under the fierce Jamaican sun—not only stood there, but batted, bowled, and fielded there while their captain drilled them like a regimental sergeant-major and his vice-captain helped with the coaching.

There was resentment at first and a great deal of grumbling but, as the players found their confidence and form returning, as they sweated towards a kind of fitness which had become foreign to most of them, resentment changed to resolve and criticism to co-operation. Johnson's key bowlers, the now 35-year-old Miller and the 33-year-old Lindwall, the bowlers who had dented the confidence of those 'Three Terrible Ws' in Australia in 1951–52 and contained them to reasonable scores, began to look as if they'd been dining on monkey glands.

So fit and determined were they and the other players on the Thursday evening that Johnson declared Friday a rest day for the twelve men chosen to meet Jamaica.

At Sabina Park on the Saturday morning the red-and-white robed, red-fezzed darkie band of the Jamaican Regiment was blaring the rousing last bars of 'The Jamaican Rhumba' as Johnson walked out with Jamaica's captain Alan Rae to the glassy-fast pitch and won the all-important toss. Back in the dressing-room he reminded his opening batsmen Arthur Morris and Colin McDonald of that famous message Admiral Horatio Nelson had flagged to his fleet off Cape Trafalgar in 1805. And of the effect it had had.

By mid-afternoon the Australians were almost to 150 without loss. After McDonald (73) departed at that total Morris went on to his own 157 and the score, thanks to valuable contributions from all members of the midriff, to 453. By stumps on the second (Monday) night half the home side were out for 81. That initial moral ascendancy *had* been gained. Could it be held?

The answer, but for a youngster named O. G. 'Collie' Smith (an orphan who had copped a fair amount of discipline himself at Kingston's Boys Town), must have been 'yes'. But 'Collie', later to become Gary Sobers' closest friend and to score centuries against England (2), Australia, and India, had been told his main hope of escaping from that Boys Town lay through his batting ability. He began his elopement by contributing 169 to a sixth-wicket stand of 277 with Jamaica's wicketkeeper Binns who made 151.

Trailing by 21 runs on the first innings the Australians had to set about establishing that initial moral ascendancy all over again. This time their first seven batsmen contributed 297 at an average of 42. Australian wicketkeeper Len Maddocks followed his first innings 62 with an 83 and Johnson declared on 319 for 9 to travel to a favourable draw.

Team practices were confined to the mornings on the Thursday and Friday preceding the First Test. On the Thursday night London *Daily Express* cricket writer Pat Landsberg, a native of Jamaica, was permitted to take the Australians to see the fights at the Kingston Stadium. For the two main bouts each combatant received a stipend of £2 10s. During the first of these one of the Negroes collapsed before a blow that would have been classed as a gentle push at Madison Square Garden or the old Sydney Stadium at Rushcutters Bay. The referee began his count. Resting on one elbow the youngster called: 'Don't bother to count, Ref, I ain't a-gettin' up.' Who could blame him?

On the eve of the Test the players dined up in Jamaica's Blue Mountains at an old inn that could have belonged in Shakespeare's England. It was called the Blue Mountain Inn and on the wall of the 'loo' there hung a penny attached to a string. It was the penny, we were told, that Princess Margaret had 'spent' during her

Caribbean tour of the previous year.

Possibly because of his public-school education Johnson conquered his urge to purloin the penny and hand it to West Indian captain Denis Atkinson the next morning for use in the all-important toss.

This time the West Indies had all their biggest guns on deck—Weekes, Worrell, and Walcott as the foundation of the batting and Valentine and Ramadhin of the bowling. Young 'Collie' Smith, who was to be killed four years later in England in a car driven by his cricketing comrade and idol Gary Sobers, had been given his Test spurs at the age of twenty-one and was to bat at the fall of the fifth wicket.

On this second Saturday and Monday of the tour it was even more vital that Australia should mount a massive total—and they did. Missed by British Guiana's opening batsman Gibbs off Barbados' fast bowler King, a bloomer which West Indian Pressmen claimed 'would put the projected Federation of the West Indian islands back fifty years', Morris went lbw to Valentine for 65 of another century stand with McDonald. McDonald was stumped for 50 by Binns off the same bowler, the bowler whom his captain John Goddard had claimed in Australia in 1951 could turn a ball sharply on ice. He was now operating on sunbaked clay that gleamed like glass and Australia was 232 for 2 when Miller joined Harvey.

Playing patient, errorless, and implacable cricket, these normally aggressive and adventurous batsmen were unseparated at stumps; by this time Alf Valentine's spinning finger was bleeding profusely about the nail and Worrell had strained a muscle in his leg. With their total beyond 250 for 2, the Australians spent the Sunday relaxing around the blue-tiled pool of their hotel.

On the Monday when Harvey was bowled by seventh bowler Walcott for 133 Australia were 361 for 3. Ray Lindwall, promoted by Johnson (for the same reasons as Herbie Collins used to promote his great fast bowler Jack Gregory in the 1920s) to allow him time to rest, helped the resolute Miller on to 417 for 5.

By now the gallant Valentine and frustrated Ramadhin had delivered the majority of their exactly 100 overs for the innings. And Miller had not failed to 'congratulate' each of them with a genial grin and a handshake as the runs against their names on the rickety old scoreboard mounted past the century on their way to 113 and 112, or a combined bag of 4 for 225.

After reaching 147, the highest score of his Test career, Miller left at 430 for 6. While he had been batting Australia had advanced by 293 runs. Becoming desperate, Denis Atkinson (whose appointment as captain of a team containing nine Negroes and one Indian, had caused controversy in the politically and racially aroused Caribbean) made exactly the decision the Australians had been hoping he might. He ordered King to begin firing bouncers, even with the third new ball, at Benaud and Ron Archer.

It was a costly mistake as 58 more runs were stroked in 48 minutes and the Australians were now free to retaliate with a bumping barbecue of their own.

In the West Indian dressing-room on the Monday evening after Johnson, 18 not out, had closed on 515 for 9, Atkinson slumped into a chair and declared 'We've had it'. He had used nine bowlers. Of these, Valentine's figures were 54/20/113/3, Ramadhin's 46/12/112/1, and the fiery but futile King's 28/7/122/0. The West Indians' chief bowling hopes for the series had taken 4 for 347 between them—rarely in the whole history of Test cricket can so many have been scored from so few.

But Johnson was to miss the satisfaction of captaining Australia on to its seemingly-inevitable victory. He had been injured by one of King's bouncers and Miller led the Australians on the Tuesday.

Weary after batting through the greater part of the game—after building that pyramid of patience—Keith gave the new ball to Lindwall and Archer and followed them with 'Big Bill' Johnston and Benaud. Archer dismissed Gibbs 12 and Binns (a duck after his 151) to make it 27 for 2. Weekes was run out for 19 at 56 for 3. Then Holt, the cause of this Caribbean calamity, fell to Lindwall for 31 and the limping Worrell to Bill Johnston for 9 to make it 101 for 5.

Miller, captaining Australia for the first time, was doing rather better than well. And, when Walcott and young 'Collie' Smith became associated, he met the giant Barbadian batsman with two silly points as both a trap and a barrier for his offside power. Despite this Walcott and Smith 44 took the total to 239 and Miller had to join the attack himself to get Walcott for 108—the first of Clyde's five centuries of the series. He then dismissed Denis Atkinson for 1 to advance his innings analysis towards 16/5/36/2 and have the West Indies, 259, trailing by 256 and bound, if so ordered, to follow-on. Lindwall 24/6/61/4, however, had been the outstanding bowler.

The climax of the match arrived on the fourth day, the Wednesday. By then Australia's attack, already lacking Johnson, had been further depleted by an injury to Archer. After Gibbs and Binns (his second duck for the Test after his 151 for Jamaica) had failed to score, and Benaud had caught and bowled Weekes for 1, Walcott and Holt began a recovery from 32 for 3.

Miller, playing his greatest of all Test matches, had been on the field throughout, except for the first two hours of the Saturday. Having bowled Binns for his second duck Miller came back to help Lindwall. Again he set silly points and now silly mid-ons around batsmen who had never suffered this humiliation.

The tactics succeeded against all except the fugitive from Boys Town, who blasted two significant boundaries through the barriers. At stumps of the fourth day 'Collie', after 344 minutes in all at the creases in this his first Test match, was 92 not out on top of his first innings 44.

Long before the close of play Lindwall was on the brink of exhaustion; Miller, having scored 147 on the first and second days, had bowled 34 overs on the Tuesday and Wednesday; Walcott, Denis Atkinson, and the injured Worrell still had to be dismissed. Australia were down to four bowlers in this furnace of a cricket stadium and the West Indies still needed 70 to draw level on the final day.

In the morning 'Collie' came to his century like a champion—his second against the Australians within the space of nine days in his first three innings in international matches. His 169, 44, and now 100 not out had given him an aggregate of 313 at an average of 156·5. Already he was being judged fit to wear part of the mantle created by Worrell, Weekes, and Walcott.

Miller decided to join Lindwall in an all-out attack on that Thursday morning and, when Smith was 104, he took the vital wicket. He followed it by dismissing Atkinson for 30 to finish as what nowadays would be known as 'Man of the Match' with 147 runs, an analysis of 44/14/98/5, and his brilliant attacking captaincy as his magnificent contribution towards Australia's nine-wickets victory.

In its last four Tests against England Australia had compiled totals of 228, 184, 231, 111, 323, 111, 221, and 118 for 6. In the last six of these innings Miller had scored 7, 6, 44, 14, 19, and 28—118 runs at 19·6. As a bowler from seven England innings he had taken seven wickets.

In the five Tests of 1953 in England Miller had scored 223 from nine innings, 114 in eight of these, and taken 10 for 303 at 30·30.

Now at the age of 35 and four months and in the most torrid conditions known to Test cricket had come this amazing transformation which later was to bring him two more Test centuries (137 in Barbados and 109 back at Kingston), a series batting record of 439 runs at 73·16, and a series bowling analysis of 188·2/37/649/20 at 32·45. Only Harvey scored more runs.

Even the greatest of champions, two or four-legged, need a touch of the spur at times. Johnson's gamble had begun most profitably.

One Test up; four to go. On to Port O' Spain and its velvety steel bands.

Learie Nicholas Constantine, son of Negro cocoa plantation overseer Lebrun S. Constantine, and later Baron Constantine, West Indian High Commissioner to Britain, was the player who in the early 1930s placed West Indian cricket on the international map.

A genuinely fast and hostile bowler, an electrifyingly talented and adventurous batsman, and perhaps the most spectacular and versatile fieldsman in the history of the game, Learie is remembered as 'Old Electric Heels'. He was born in and played for the island of Trinidad and he covered the Second Test of 1955 for Radio Trinidad at Port O' Spain's Queen's Park.

The beautifully situated Queen's Park ground bears no more resemblance to Kingston's drab Sabina Park than does Cape Town's Newlands to London's Kennington Oval. Its apple-green field is half-encircled by white stands and even whiter sightboards. Behind and beyond the stands, and climbing the green mountains, the golden-blossomed poui trees revel in their rivalry with the sun.

On the mounds, which are reserved for Coloured people, Negroes, East Indians, and Chinese varying in hue from ebony through chocolate to yellow, everyone is hilariously happy, wildly excited, and noisily demonstrative. The Second Test between the West Indies and Australia is about to begin. That biblical Tower of Babel by comparison would resemble a silence room in a West End London club. The male spectators are wearing red, blue, or white shirts which, because of the extreme humidity, they are hanging outside their blue and black trousers. On their curly-topped heads sit old and worn felt hats. The cuffs of their trousers are frayed for these are poor people in a material sense, though far richer than the inhabitants of the Members' Pavilion in humour and the faculty for enjoying life.

Above them birds, mostly giant, black crows, hang stationary in the air and, as the Australian team takes the field, a roar goes up which sends the bird life 50 metres higher into the blue sky as if it has been hit by anti-aircraft flak. The West Indian captain, this time Trinidad's aristocratically handsome Jeff Stollmeyer, has won the toss and he is striding out to open the innings with J. K. Holt, Junior.

'The winning of the toss on this newly laid billiard table of a pitch should give us a great advantage,' claims Learie Constantine in his velvety drawl, over Radio Trinidad. 'It will help compensate for the loss of Worrell who is recovering well from his muscular strain on Accra Beach in Barbados.'

But Ray Lindwall has recently taken six wickets for 41 from 19·4 overs in a drawn game against Trinidad and Miller been rested from it after his tremendous contribution at Sabina Park. A swift, brief shower of rain has 'fired' the surface of the pitch and 'This is the fastest, most hostile bowling I have watched since I last watched Larwood in 1933,' Constantine now can be heard saying over the portable radios on the crowded mounds.

Lindwall and Miller, indeed, have forgotten the years and returned to their fiery youth and pace. The rejection of two lbw appeals has inflamed them still further, as has their knowledge that the early life from the pitch must soon die under the tropical sun. They have begun firing bumpers at Holt and Stollmeyer—and Ian Johnson, stationed at mid-off, has been reminding them of the laws as to intimidatory bowling.

There is no calming them, though, and first Stollmeyer, 14, and Holt, 25, fall before the flame to make it 39 for 1 and 40 for 2. Walcott, the West Indies' cricketing 'Othello', has been promoted to Number 3, and their 'Black Bradman', Everton Weekes, has joined him at the wicket. After each delivery they bowl Lindwall and Miller keep clapping their hands for the red ball and then fling themselves in full flurry at the batsmen. Fielding a drive Johnson approaches Lindwall yet again and addresses him earnestly. Snatching the ball from his captain's hand Lindwall delivers an even deadlier bumper.

An angry, swelling murmur from the mounds changes to an exultant cry of delight, however, as Weekes, pivoting like a Calypso dancer from one of Port O' Spain's dockside cafes, hooks the bumper high into a tamarind tree. The game goes on and the menace is fading from the 33-year-old Lindwall and 35-year-old Miller—dying under an ever-deadlier sun.

Lindwall and Miller have done their utmost; have had their fling. They are men of good humour for the most part, men who honour companionship, and when the giant Walcott calls for drinks they stroll across to share them with him and Weekes.

Hardly have drinks been taken, however, than black clouds shroud the sky and down comes the drenching rain. There is to be no more cricket this day and the West Indies are 73 for 2.

This Test contains no rest day and play continues next morning and throughout the week. After an unforgettably brilliant and devastating partnership of 242 by Weekes 139 and Walcott 126, the West Indies have reached 282 for 3. This is the first time that Lindwall and Miller have come to grips with two of those 'Terrible Ws' together and in top form. They are not accustomed to being hooked high into tamarind trees or over the tops of stands. And they are relieved that Worrell, the third of the 'Ws', is away bathing on that Barbadian beach. Were he present to follow Weekes at 282 for 3 and partner the young Gary Sobers from 323 for 5 the two of them may have handed in their resignations.

Like Jamaica's Rio Grande, the Weekes–Walcott partnership, though flowing swiftly and sensationally, has appeared eternal. Only when it seems to have spewed the baffled and breathless Australian attack on its banks does Richie Benaud strike—thrice. He has Weekes caught by Johnson; he bowls 'Collie' Smith, and then has Walcott stumped by the recent Speaker of South Australia's House of Assembly, the Hon. (and portly) Gilbert Langley.

When Johnson holds the catch given by Weekes, those who have been his slaves, sink gratefully to the ground. When Benaud breaks 'Collie's' stumps with a leg-break, before he has added to the 317 he scored in three innings at Kingston, they rub their eyes in amazement.

Richie Benaud was blooded as a Test match bowler that day. His third victim, Walcott, falls at 323 for 5 and, though tried only as the sixth Australian bowler, Benaud finished with an analysis of 17/3/43/3. And what a three!

Lindwall, four more wickets, and Miller, his first, cut through the second half of the innings to bring 323 for 5 rudely down in the world to all out for 382. Lindwall, 6 for 41 in Trinidad's first innings in the previous game, now has 6 for 95, or 12 for 136 in eight days—following his 8 for 210 in nine days at Kingston.

Test cricket can have few greater contrasts provided than those of the batting of Weekes, Walcott, and the awakening Gary Sobers, 47, on the second day of this match and that of Arthur Morris and Colin McDonald on the third. But that initial 'moral ascendancy' had been arduously won at Kingston. Under Johnson's admonitions it will not easily be cast away. After the batsmen have done what Constantine describes as 'an Australian crawl' to 147 for none by stumps, the halfway mark of the Test, another cause for the slow scoring is revealed: Morris has been crippled by cramps and has to be wheeled into dinner that night at the home of West Indies Board of Control chairman Sir Errol Dos Santos in a bath chair. He hasn't been 'batting on plasticine and got his feet stuck', after all as 'Old Electric Heels' has claimed.

Fair comment by Constantine we had thought, and still think. Morris and McDonald's first 100 had come in 160 minutes; Weekes had reached his own individual century in 165 minutes; and Walcott and Weekes had passed 150 of their stand in 137.

To the amazement of Sir Errol Dos Santos' house servants Morris continues batting on the fourth day. Cold foments and manipulation applied by Jahuda Singh, amateur masseur and Trinidad's Minister for Communications, had improved Morris' condition and he batted infinitely better than on the previous day.

He was dismissed on 'Nelson's number' 111, at 191 for 1, McDonald went for 110 at 259 for 2, Sydney Central Market stall proprietor Willie Watson was lbw to Ramadhin (Sonny's second wicket for the series) for 27 at 328 for 3.

Then Richie Benaud fell to Ramadhin for 5 and Miller, who had delivered 28 very lively overs to get 1 for 96 in the West Indies innings, was run out for 3 to make it 345 for 5.

The swift-footed and left-handed Neil Harvey used to have the same psychological effect upon his running partners in those days as Graeme Wood has been producing more recently on his. So Keith and Arthur Morris will confirm. But Neil followed his 133 at Kingston with an identical score here and Ron Archer 84, Ian Johnson 66, and Lindwall 37 not out, had Australia to 600 for 9, or 218 ahead, when Johnson closed the innings.

Harvey could be excused for Miller's dismissal on this occasion. Keith had descended upon him from the bowler's end—unannounced and uninvited, head down and black hair over his eyes—while Neil was admiring the execution of one of his more exquisitely timed leg glances.

At the close of the fifth day the West Indies, 382 and 40 for 1, trailed by 178. Early on the final day the West Indians showed their opinion of the situation by appealing against the light. Having done so and failed, Holt and Stollmeyer scored 40 in 32 minutes—most of them from Lindwall.

On the sixth day the pitch was still gushing with runs. Said Pat Landsberg, 'If it's not dead its next of kin should certainly be warned.' Said its Negro creator, 'I have no feelin' for dee bowlers. I was a batsman.'

Technically the finest of Clyde Walcott's five centuries for the series, his 110 of 273 for 4, and Weekes' brilliant 87 not out held Australia off, despite Archer's 3 for 37 and, with the home side 25 ahead and Weekes and Gary Sobers at the wicket, the game was drawn.

Cricket's glorious uncertainty was graphically illustrated by young 'Collie' Smith's 'pair of spectacles', following his triumphs in Jamaica. Explained the young refugee from Boys Town, after being caught at slip from Archer, 'The ball doesn't swing in Jamaica, I'd never been out of Jamaica, I'd never seen a ball swing.' This alibi failed to satisfy the worried West Indian selectors. They dropped 'Collie' from the Third Test despite his average of 53·6 for 377 runs against the Australians. Restored for the fourth and fifth Tests he found his confidence undermined.

So far in a series which was to contain an all-time record of 21 individual hundreds, Australia, through Harvey (2), Miller, Morris, and McDonald (one each) had contributed five of these and the West Indies, through Walcott (3), Smith and Weekes (one each), the same number.

Only Lindwall (12 wickets), Archer and Miller (each 6), and Benaud (5) had enjoyed reasonable success with the ball. For the West Indies Valentine 103/32/246/5, Ramadhin 78/20/202/3, and King 65/14/220/1 had combined analyses of 246/66/668/9 at 74·2. Those Calypso singers of the dockside cafes were no longer chanting ad nauseam 'Put Ramadhin on dee ball'.

Consequently the Australians' main worries when they crossed to British Guiana for the Third Test were focused rather upon the political crisis than the cricket. Recent rioting in the Guianan capital, Georgetown, had culminated in the dynamiting of Queen Victoria's statue, the dismissal of Dr Chedi Jagan's Communist Government, and the dispatch to the scene of the disorder of two British battle cruisers and a regiment of the Black Watch.

'My country is a rough little land, but you'll love it' Guiana-born Ernest Eytle, of the British Broadcasting Corporation, told us when we landed at Atkinson Field about 40 kilometres up the mangrove-and-sugar-cane-lined, mud-red Demerara River from Georgetown. And, despite the appalling poverty and squalor along the *Via Dolorosa* between the airport and the capital, we eventually did.

In Georgetown's broad main street, high between the twin towers of a snow-white, wooden cathedral, a pink robed effigy of Christ smiled sadly and compassionately down upon a strange blend of bicycle and black limousine, of night club and church, of saint and street singer.

We were beginning to understand why Jagan, the dental surgeon, his then friend and equally handsome colleague Forbes Burnham, LL.B., and their People's Progressive Party had gained power in 1953. Later Georgetown *Chronicle* cricket writer and political reporter, the dusky and Dickensian-looking Croker, revealed why they were ousted.

'I was sitting at a table near Jagan and Burnham while the votes were being counted on the night of the Election,' he said. 'There are only 24 seats in British Guiana's House of Assembly.

'"The P.P.P. has won twelve seats," an announcer soon called.

'"Twelve seats!" exclaimed a worried and astonished Burnham. Pleasure and concern vied for expression on the face of Jagan. "One more and we're in. God forbid. I never expected we'd win more than six," he cried.

'"Fourteen seats have gone to the P.P.P." came the next announcement.

'"Fourteen!" exclaimed the now seriously alarmed Jagan and Burnham. "Now we'll have to carry out all those promises of ours."

'They did and out they went. The Governor, supported by those two battle cruisers and the Black Watch, took over.'

The West Indies were now one down with three to play. They ordered the Georgetown curator to prepare a pitch 'that would produce a finish'. No secret was made of this move and the Australians thoroughly approved of it. They were cock-a-hoop confident now, anxious to increase their lead, and put defeat in the series beyond possibility.

Worrell's return found the 'Three Terrible Ws' intact; Marshall an accurate right-hand off-spinner replaced the left-handed Valentine whose spinning finger was betel-nut red; Australia made no changes.

Stollmeyer won the toss but only Weekes, 81 of 182, could cope with the green pitch. Miller dismissed both opening batsmen and Benaud, 4 for 15 from 3·5 overs, lopped off the tail.

When Morris and McDonald opened the Australian innings just before the tea adjournment they showed a far better appreciation of requirements. Almost from the start of play the ball had been coming through at uneven pace and uneven height. Weekes had got by with uninhibited strokesmanship. But his had been a rake's progress and his colleagues had behaved like so many fowls with a fox at the fence.

Five of Australia's first six batsmen, McDonald 61, Morris 44, Harvey 38, Miller 33, and Benaud 68, batted soundly and Australia, 215 for 5, was 33 ahead before Sobers, 3 for 20, started a rout.

'You can't play strokes on that pitch,' said Miller at lunch the next day. 'It's dangerous to drive unless you're right to the pitch of the ball.'

'Here comes the poor man's Miller,' called a Guianese cricket writer when Benaud entered. 'I should have called him the millionaire's Miller' the same character said after Richie had smacked 68 of the last 96 (37 of the last 42) including eight 4s and two 6s.

Asked in 1953 which of the world's batsmen past or present he would choose to give an exhibition of strokeplay at the London Palladium, our old friend Charles Burgess Fry said, 'Frank Worrell without a doubt'. On this third day of the 1955 Test in Georgetown Worrell proved that even the most distinguished and delicate of strokes could be executed with grace and security on an unreliable wicket. His 56 in a total of 207 made him the artist batsman of the match.

For Australia Ian Johnson discomfited those who had been calling him 'a non-playing captain' with 7 for 44 from 22·2 overs —this followed his 66 with the bat at Port O' Spain. While Worrell caressed the ball Walcott cracked it before hitting his wicket when facing Lindwall on 73. So far in his six Test innings Walcott had scored 108, 39, 126, 110, 8, and 73 to have 464 to his name at 77·26.

It was during this innings that Keith Miller confided to his captain that every time Ian delivered a leg-cutter as variety to his flighted off-spin he grunted loudly enough to be heard in slips.

'What can I do about it?' inquired Ian.

'Grunt *every* ball, "Johnno", I suppose,' came the reply.

West Indian captain Stollmeyer was waving a white handkerchief as he led the West Indians on to the field for the final session. This, unlike Denis Atkinson's admission at Sabina Park, was no token of surrender. Stollmeyer was merely testing the direction of the breeze before deciding which end his fast bowler King should use.

Shortly afterwards, when putting his foot to a drive by Colin McDonald, Stollmeyer trod on the ball and fell heavily to the ground thus ending his long Test career. McDonald and Morris dashed to his aid, denying themselves (or rather McDonald and Australia) two runs.

Advancing soundly to 31 and 38 respectively they, Harvey 41 not out, and Watson 22 not out, gave Australia an imposing eight-wickets victory and the two–nil lead they were seeking before coming to the batting parlours of Barbados and Jamaica.

So far the introduction of that public school spirit or type of discipline appeared to have paid remarkable dividends for a team containing only three public schoolboys—Johnson, Lindwall, and McDonald.

Keith Miller's perhaps most striking attribute, his phenomenal, almost animal, vitality, can rarely have been more evident than during his sustained and dramatic duel with the dazzling and predatory Everton Weekes in the match between the Australians and Barbados in Bridgetown.

Off a cricket field in 1951–52 and 1955 Keith and Everton were boon companions and shared a tremendous zest for life. On many an evening during the arduous 1955 tour they met in Weekes' room and played Calypso and classical jazz records on the wind-up gramophone which the 'Black Bradman' carried with him wherever he went. One of the records was Nat King Cole's 'Answer Me' which Keith had bought for Everton the day after John Holt, Jun.'s, failure to do just that had caused Weekes to be run out in the Kingston Test.

On a cricket field the extreme brilliance of Weekes, the batsman, usually challenged Keith, the bowler, to all-out attack.

Weekes was in superb form that summer of so long ago, the kind of form he revealed so rarely in Australia in 1951–52 following the injury to his leg in the Brisbane Test.

During his superlative century and second innings 87 not out in the recent Port O' Spain Test Weekes had kept hooking both Miller and Lindwall into the tops of tamarind trees. He seemed to have gained command over both of them. But on the grassier pitch and in the heavier atmosphere at Georgetown Miller had managed to hold Weekes in reasonable check and was unlucky not to dismiss him during his charmed 81.

Weekes chose Barbados and his home island idolators as the venue for the decisive round of this man-to-man battle. The pitch and the hot, dry weather were both in the West Indian's favour as he well knew. Though Miller was aware of the odds against him he accepted the challenge immediately Weekes came in. Keith had just dismissed Colin Hunte for 0 and Smith for 4. His black mane was flying, his tail in the air. The ball still retained some shine when Weekes began from 2 for 8.

His belligerent attitude appeared to add a metre or two to Keith's already-classic, fast pace, yet had no effect upon his consistent line and length. But the 'Black Bradman' disdained any thought of defence. He began driving, hooking, and square-cutting with a flair and ferocity that brought the excitable crowd exultantly to its feet and he was 50 in 44 minutes with ten magnificent 4s.

Believing such adventurousness could not be successfully sustained, Miller maintained his lightning speed and hostility for more than an hour. Wondering, as we all did, at Keith's reserves of stamina, Johnson allowed him his head. When Gary Sobers replaced Colin 'Leaning Tower' Depeiza, run out for 27 at 101 for three, Miller dismissed the 18-year-old for a duck, Weekes was 68 of 102 for 4.

On went Everton's unbelievably brilliant strokeplay until he had reached perhaps even his most dynamic century in just over even time and gone on to 132 out of 214. At this stage the 35-year-old Miller, benefiting from a brief rest, had him caught by Alan Davidson. The next episode of their duel would come in the approaching Test.

Until this savage confrontation in the sun at Bridgetown, the most exciting battle between a great batsman and a great fast bowler I had watched was the Bradman–Larwood affair at the Adelaide Oval in the 'Bodyline' Test of 1932–33. This now had to take second place. Yes, even 'The Don's' meteoric 66 out of 88 —that strange gamble with his fate and fame.

Despite Weekes' onslaught Miller's innings analysis was 17 overs 3 maidens 4 wickets for 51. When Weekes departed at 214 for 5 it had been 15/3/42/4. Honours can be said to have been even, I suggest, between the man who came to be known in London as 'Killah Dillah Miller' and his predatory prey. But there were two Test matches yet to be played.

Australia, or rather the Australians, won that game against what West Indian captain of the early 1950s John Goddard always called 'My l'il Island', Barbados. That island which has produced the 'Three Terrible Ws' (Worrell, Weekes, and Walcott),

Gary Sobers, Basil Butcher, Seymour Nurse, Gordon Greenidge, and Conrad Hunte, and that great fast bowler Wesley Hall. But the margin was only three wickets.

Barbados had become a British colony in 1605, two years after the death of Queen Elizabeth I and about the time Will Shakespeare was producing his *Othello*, and King James (with the aid of some ghost writers, no doubt) was working on his Bible. According to Barbadians, pirate Henry Morgan came to their island as an indentured labourer, worked there for seven years on a sugar plantation, and joined his buccaneers at Port Royal, Jamaica, in about 1660.

Inhabitants of Barbados derive more pride from their association with Admiral Lord Nelson. Their capital city Bridgetown is sprawled about a Trafalgar Square. Built alongside a bridged canal the square is dominated by a statue of Nelson. Each time we passed that statue on our way to the Kensington Cricket Ground our dusky taxi man chuckled and said, 'Don't forget me wan I'se gone.' (Eventually we clicked—'*One eye's* gone.')

Nelson did much of his early naval training when based in Bridgetown. His wife, like Napoleon's Josephine, came from the Caribbean.

Keith Miller, like his prototype Jack Gregory of the 1920s, usually performed better as a batsman when his team batted first. Could Johnson win the toss?

Owing to Arthur Morris' indisposition on the morning of the Fourth Test South Australian batsman Les Favell came into the Australian side, Victorian straight-breaker John Hill replaced Bill Johnston, Denis Atkinson regained the leadership of the home team, and Valentine and 'Collie' Smith were restored to the ranks for this vital match.

Bitter criticism followed Atkinson's re-appointment. Local critics contended that Barbadian-born Frank Worrell or John Goddard, who had scored 88 runs without losing his wicket against the Australians for Barbados the previous week, should have gained the captaincy. They were to have their words forced down their throats.

As Morris' fitness or unfitness to play was not known until the Test was about to begin, Johnson told Favell he would open himself with McDonald if he won the toss. When word came from the hotel that Morris would not play, Favell would have none of this offer of his captain's.

'I'll take strike,' he said, and in the first ten minutes of the Test cracked four splendid boundaries. All of Australia's first ten batsmen except Benaud batted well. The team's two opening bowlers—Miller 137, and Lindwall 118—topscored and Ron Archer, its other new ball bowler, got 98 (a triple contribution of 353 to the mammoth and forbidding total of 668).

Brought back to bowl at 140 for 3, Miller dismissed Weekes 44 and 'Collie' Smith 2 to make it 143 for 5. Worrell was run out 16 at 147 for 6. For reasons difficult to understand Ian Johnson then replaced Keith by Lindwall, whereupon Atkinson 219 and Depeiza 122 produced an all-time Test record seventh-wicket stand of 347 to make it 494 for 7. When Atkinson came off at 504 for 9 he lay exhausted on the dressing-room table for 20 minutes. Then he led his men back on to the field.

After play that evening in the Australian dressing-room Miller called to his captain and teammates, 'Come over here. You can all hear this.' Confronting Johnson and the grouped team, Keith said: 'I've bowled my heart out for you time and again in the heat and sun on this tour "Johnno", and today when I take two wickets in two overs, two vital wickets, you take me off. Don't expect me to keep slaving out there when the going's tough from now on.'

'Is that all you have to say?' retorted Johnson.

'Yes.'

'Meeting's closed then except, Keith, that I'd like you to come back with me in my car to the hotel.'

Later, on board the S.S. *Rangitane* during our voyage from Jamaica to New Zealand, I asked Johnson what occurred during that ride back to John Goddard's Hotel.

'I just told him I'd knock his bloody block off if he spoke to me like that again in front of the team.'

'What did he say?'

'Nothing.'

'He's got a pretty good reach, rather like *Jack* Johnson's. Weren't you taking a big risk?'

'No. I did quite a bit of fighting with professionals as a youngster and Keith knew. He's also cooled down.'

I checked up on Johnson's account of the incident with Keith later on the voyage. He just grinned.

The West Indies first innings 510 left them 158 behind and Australia's second innings 249 increased the deficit to 407; Ian Johnson top-scoring with 57.

The consistent Walcott's second innings 83 of 234 for 6 saved his team from defeat and it was now 2–0 to Australia with only one Test to go. History had been made. The West Indians, at long last, had been defeated in a series conducted in the Caribbean.

Understandably attendances at the anti-Atkinson protests of the African League had dwindled during the Fourth Test in Barbados. Atkinson had bowled and bowled and bowled during his team's ordeal on the first two days, had then scored that 219 of the still world record seventh-wicket Test stand, and led his men by magnificent example in the field. In all he delivered 84·2 overs, 30 of them maidens, to have 7 for 164 for the match.

After a drawn game against the Windward Islands at Grenada and an innings-and-219-run victory over the Leeward Islands at Vivian Richards' birthplace Antigua, the game against a Combined XI at Montego Bay was washed out and the Australians came, still undefeated, back to Kingston for the final Test.

In this Miller scored 109, his third century of the series, and took 6 for 107 and 2 for 58 to bring his Test batting average to 73·16 from 6 innings (147 highest score, 439 runs) and his Test bowling analysis to 188·2 overs 37 maidens 649 runs 20 wickets at 32·45.

Neil Harvey 7/1/204/650/108·33 was the only Australian batsman to surpass him and Lindwall the only other bowler to take 20 wickets on either side.

Miller figured in three of Australia's nine century partnerships. These three contributed 224 to Australia's cause in the First Test, 206 in the Fourth Test, and 220 in the Fifth.

Examine the records of a century of Test cricket and you will find few, if any, all-round performances of this magnitude—certainly none achieved under such torrid conditions by a fast bowler at the age of thirty-five.

Australia passed the 500 mark four times in its first innings in four of the Tests—scoring 519 for 9, 600 for 9, 668, and 758 for 8.

Nobody can claim that the opposition was weak. And, from

mid-March to mid-June, Miller was the outstanding performer in a series which produced the still-extant record of 21 individual centuries (Walcott 5) and the still-extant record of 16 century stands.

In the final Test Walcott scored 155 and 110 of the West Indies 357 and 319, to make his series figures: 10/155/827 at 82·70.

Australia's 758 for 8 declared in the final Test contained no less than five centuries—Harvey 204, Archer 128, McDonald 127, Benaud 121 (the first 100 in 78 minutes), and Miller 109.

It was a proud and happy team that boarded the S.S. *Rangitane* at Kingston and steamed through the green hills bordering the Panama Canal to Panama City, then down the Pacific to Wellington, before flying home to Australia from Christchurch.

And its captain, as well as its vice-captain, can take a great deal of the credit for its unexpected and still-astonishing performance during which it was undefeated and, for the loss of 60 wickets, scored 3200 runs.

As Field-Marshal Lord Wavell wrote in his biography of Field-Marshal Viscount Allenby (Harrap): 'The part played in a great victory by organisation, preparation and inspiration behind the lines seldom receives proper recognition in military history, which is apt to concern itself solely with the more spectacular movements and clashes of the campaign itself.'

Johnson, behind the lines, and Miller, in the forefront of the fray, had proved a superb combination.

23
The 'Dust Bowl' – England 1956

Following Miller's magnificent, probably unprecedented, all-round performances in the West Indies, including his inspiring captaincy on the last three days of the First Sabina Park Test, controversy as to whether he or Ian Johnson should lead Australia in its quest to regain the Ashes in England in 1956 began to crescendo even during what remained of the Australian winter immediately preceding the Melbourne Olympic Games.

Australia has been described as 'Six States doing their darndest to avoid developing into a nation'. There is copious justification for this claim. From July to October 1955 the traditional interstate rivalries and jealousies again began to raise their seemingly-insatiable heads.

Though born and reared in Melbourne Miller had come to be regarded there as a New South Welshman, not as an Australian, by an extremist and irrational minority. In South Melbourne he was considered a renegade. The controversy provided ideal material for the Sydney and Melbourne media, especially for their Press.

Melbourne, its *Herald and Weekly Times*, its *Age*, its *Argus*, and its pink-paged *Sporting Globe*, was solidly behind Johnson. Melbourne was, and is, a solid city. Sydney, its *Sydney Morning Herald*, its *Daily Telegraph*, *Sun*, *Daily Mirror*, and its three Sunday papers, was firmly behind Miller. Had not New South Wales under his captaincy regained the Sheffield Shield in 1953–54 and retained it in 1954–55?

The Sheffield Shield competition, especially those 'Battles of the Roses' between New South Wales and Victoria, meant much more to Australian sports followers in the mid-1950s than they do today.

In 1955 Queensland had not begun its campaign to 'buy' the Sheffield Shield by importing Greg Chappell from South Australia, Jeff Thomson from New South Wales, and Allan Border from New South Wales. New South Wales had not come to Neil Harvey's rescue by finding him reasonably promising employment in Sydney, as it did after the 1957–58 Ian Craig tour of South Africa. South Australia had not imported Gary Sobers from Barbados or Barry Richards from Natal in desperate bids to regain the Shield it had won only twice in the past twenty years.

For the most part the Australian States, like Yorkshire in England, had mainly relied upon locally-developed players.

Most vehement and persistent campaigner in Sydney for the promotion of Miller to the national captaincy was that ruthless old gipsy of a cricket and Rugby League writer Jim Mathers. Mathers, ironically enough, was Victorian born. Even more ironically he had represented Victoria at cricket in the 1920s.

Those Australian Test stars of the 1930s Bill O'Reilly and Jack Fingleton, who were now expert commentators for Sydney papers, also lent their support.

I was writing for the Sydney *Daily Telegraph* and *Sunday Telegraph* then and Kerry Packer's father Sir Frank was aiming to offload some of my expenses in Britain by syndicating my copy to the Melbourne *Argus*.

Though I was already booked on the S.S. *Himalaya* for the voyage to England Mathers, who was not, claimed in the Sydney *Daily Mirror* that my continued support for Johnson was attributable to the fact that my chance of covering the tour depended upon that *Argus* syndication. This was not so.

My reasons for supporting Johnson's candidature were based upon admiration of his contribution to Australia's success in the West Indies. How could a captain whose team had just created cricket history be displaced—even by the Australian Cricket Board, whose selectors had dumped Bradman after one Test match in 1928, Clarrie Grimmett after he had taken 44 wickets in a Test series in 1935–36, and Miller (the world's finest all-rounder) from the 1949–50 tour of South Africa?

But, in my view, there was more to it than this.

I doubted among other things whether Miller really wanted to lead the 1956 Australian side to England, whether he would be prepared to make the off-field sacrifices such leadership would entail, whether he might deliver a speech in one of Britain's provincial cities to rival that unforgettable one he had produced for the mayor and citizens of that 'famous' but elusively-named New South Wales country town.

'There is an awful lot of cattiness in cricket,' Keith has always contended. 'Realising its existence was the reason, perhaps, why, towards the end of my career, I liked to get away from the team when I was not playing. Putting chaps continually together is the easiest way in the world to court friction. If you go away whenever you get the chance, you come back to them and the job fresh.'

On the other side of the scales was the question whether Johnson, judged on sheer cricketing ability, was entitled to selection for Australia. But that was something for the national selectors to decide—not the Board. If Johnson failed to gain selection Miller, as vice-captain of Australia in 1954–55 and captain of N.S.W. from 1952 to 1956 was the obvious choice.

Miller, even now, a quarter of a century later, will tell you he never really coveted the Australian captaincy. But I feel this can be attributed to the nonchalant attitude he has always adopted when questioned about matters like this; can be attributed to what might, for lack of a better label, be called his mock modesty. 'I couldn't have cared less' or 'I didn't give a stuff,' he will tell you. But I very much doubt this.

Certainly Keith added fuel to the controversy when he began that Sheffield Shield summer of 1955–56 by scoring 164 of a New South Wales total of 440 against Queensland at Brisbane at the end of October; followed this with 7 wickets for 12 in one innings against South Australia in Sydney in mid-November; and scored 128 against Western Australia at Perth early in December.

To this stage of the season Victoria had yet to play a Shield match. When it did so against Queensland in Melbourne on 9 December Johnson's contribution as bowler and batsman was modest in the extreme.

The eagerly-awaited confrontation between the two candidates, the Victoria–New South Wales game at the M.C.G. over

Christmas, was rained off after Victoria 277 (Johnson 20, Miller 3 for 69) had New South Wales 124 for 3 (Miller yet to bat, Johnson 1 for 33).

Forced to retire hurt for 59 in the return game against Queensland at the S.C.G., Miller was unavailable for the second N.S.W.–Victoria match at Sydney in late January. Captained by Richie Benaud, New South Wales tightened its hold on the Sheffield Shield by defeating Victoria by 75 runs and went on to retain the trophy with 22 points to Victoria's 20.

For New South Wales Miller headed the season's batting and bowling averages with: Batting—6 innings, 1 not out, 164 highest score, 403 runs at 80·60; Bowling—94·3 overs, 274 runs, 19 wickets at 14·42. For Victoria Johnson scored only 147 runs at 21·00, but topped that State's bowling averages with 22 wickets for 458 at 20·81.

Despite these statistical discrepancies Victorian influence prevailed. Johnson was re-appointed captain, Miller vice-captain, and Victoria's delightful and efficient Bill Dowling and Leo Rush, M.B.E., were entrusted with the management of the 1956 side.

Victoria, after all, had produced ten Australian cricket captains (six of them from the one club, South Melbourne) and New South Wales only five. And, since the second World War, it has furnished in Menzies, Holt, Gorton, and Fraser four of our seven Prime Ministers. They have a flair for getting their own way down there in the 'Queen City of the South'.

Maybe it was as well for him that Miller was not appointed captain. As we shall see he had enough crucial decisions to make off the field that summer, decisions concerning his own future.

In March–April of 1956 the guardians of English cricket began analysing Johnson's team. Apart from himself and Miller, this comprised Ray Lindwall, Ron Archer, Peter Burge, and Ken Mackay (of Queensland); Richie Benaud, Jim Burke, Ian Craig, Pat Crawford, and Alan Davidson (of New South Wales); Neil Harvey, Colin McDonald, and Len Maddocks (of Victoria); Gil Langley and Jackie Wilson (of South Australia); and that arithmetical genius John Rutherford (of Western Australia). Ten of these players had toured the West Indies in 1955.

One of the most interested Englishmen was our old friend George Oswald Browning (alias 'Gubby') Allen, who had refused to bowl 'Bodyline' for Jardine in 1932–33, who had done a great deal as M.C.C. captain in 1936–37 to heal the ill-feeling created by Jardine, and who had figured in that 'handling the ball' incident at Lord's in 1945.

After an in-depth appreciation of the Australian side Gubby laughingly laid wagers in London that England would retain the Ashes. Despite our Caribbean victories he even gave generous odds.

A pillar of just about everything pillarable at the M.C.C., Allen was also the proprietor of a London stock- and share-broking firm. He was related to England's 'Mr Cricket', our other old friend Sir Pelham Warner. Altogether he was a stimulating and for the most part jovial companion—an amalgam, shall we say, of Geoff Boycott and Denis Compton with a dash of Don Bradman thrown in.

In May of 1956, during the English Cricket Writers' Club dinner at London's Skinners' Hall, Gubby cornered his England and Middlesex colleague Walter Robins, 'Do you know, Robbie,' he said, 'if I'd devoted to my sharebroking business half the time I've spent helping English cricket, I'd be a millionaire by now?'

'Yes, and think of all the good you'd have done for English cricket,' quipped Robins—to our considerable amusement.

It was after Australia had drawn the Trent Bridge and won the Lord's Test of 1956 by 185 runs—Miller (28 and 30, and 5 for 72 and 5 for 80)—that we chipped Gubby about those wagers of his.

'You must be worried, old man?' we said.

'Worried? Of course not. You won't win a Test up north,' he retorted. 'England will be leading two–one when you get back to The Oval.'

'What makes you say that, Gubby?' we asked.

'You won't get another wicket like this one at Lord's, not at Headingley or Old Trafford.'

So far the Australians, ten of whom had shared in those triumphs in the West Indies, had won only three games on this tour. They had beaten only Cambridge, Oxford, and England. They had drawn against eight county sides—Worcestershire, Leicestershire, Yorkshire, Notts, Lancashire, Sussex, Northants, and Kent—and the Marylebone Cricket Club. And they had been the first Australian side since 1912 to be defeated by a county—by Surrey by ten wickets at The Oval.

Beginning the tour at Leicester with a commanding 281 not out of 694 for 6, Miller had scored only 203 runs from his ten other innings before the Lord's Test—57 not out of these during that calamity against Surrey (for whom Jim Laker had taken 10 for 88 from 46 overs in the Australians' first innings and 2 for 42 from 25 overs in the second) and 92 of them against Northants.

Benaud, 160 against Worcestershire; Burke 123 against Leicestershire; Colin McDonald 195 and Peter Burge 131 against Notts; Lindwall 116 not out against Cambridge; Harvey 225 against the M.C.C.; McDonald 122 against Oxford; and Mackay 113 not out against Kent had scored centuries. But none of them except McDonald had been at all reliable on the rain-softened wickets in the inclement weather. England was experiencing one of the wettest summers on record after an abnormally dry spring.

Bowlers, they say, win matches and, with 14 of the 31 first-class games played, only Benaud 27, Johnson and Archer 26 each, Crawford and Miller 24 (16 of Miller's in the two Tests) had taken more than 20 wickets. Lindwall, who had ricked his back on a golf course, had taken 13.

The Australians had to concede there were grounds for Allen's confidence regarding the outcome of the Leeds and Manchester Tests. What they could not understand was why he seemed so confident England would win both of them. They were soon to discover.

It was following the ten-wickets defeat by Surrey, one suffered after Ian Johnson, in a gallant but futile attempt to emulate his counterpart Jim Laker's 46/18/88/10, had over-bowled himself to produce an analysis of 60·3/12/168/6 and scored 0 and 6 with the bat, that the London *Daily Mirror*'s Brian Chapman, the *News Chronicle*'s Crawford White, and the *Daily Herald*'s Charles Bray, supported by Australia's Jack Fingleton in the *Sunday Times*, advised Johnson to stand down and allow Miller to lead Australia in the remaining Tests.

This advice was repeated after Australia's unfavourable draw in the Nottingham Test in which Miller took 6 for 127 and Johnson 1 for 55. Miller's 10 for 152 and 58 runs in the Lord's Test, in which Johnson scored only 23 and delivered but four wicket-less overs, only served to sharpen their quills, despite Australia's impressive victory.

In the games between the Second and Third Tests Johnson contributed no runs and took only two wickets at a cost of 141 runs. In the second game against Yorkshire at Sheffield he posted himself at Number 10 and did not bat, and gave himself only nine overs and took none for 11. Left-hand spinner Jackie Wilson, from 27 overs, took 3 for 40.

Against Gloucestershire at Bristol Johnson scored a duck and did not bowl in the county's first innings while Wilson took 7 for 11, and gave himself only one over in the second innings while Wilson was capturing 5 for 50. Against Somerset at Taunton Johnson again did not bat and his bowling analyses were 23/8/56/1 and 13/3/82/1. He did not play against Hampshire, the game before the Third Test.

During or just prior to the Lord's Test Keith Miller's friend Max Aitken, son of Lord Beaverbrook, approached him with a most tempting offer. He asked him to write a book for syndication in the London *Daily Express* at the end of the tour and to become that newspaper's roving sports commentator and columnist during subsequent European summers. Keith was a natural rover.

Australia's *Sporting Life* magazine, for which he had worked under Johnnie Moyes, had ceased publication in 1954. Since then Keith had spent most of his time touring the West Indies and Australia with national and New South Wales teams. The next Test series was scheduled for 1958–59 when he would be rising forty.

The prospect of following the sun around by spending the Australian summers in Sydney and the European summers in Britain naturally held great appeal. So did the money offered by Aitken on behalf of his father 'The Beaver'. Miller engaged Reuter's cricket correspondent Reg Hayter to help him with the book *Cricket Crossfire*, and accepted the offer.

Keith's decision was also influenced by the increasing pain he was suffering when bowling as a consequence of that wartime injury to his back and his doubtful knee. Before this 1956 tour of England began he had obtained a certificate from a Harley Street specialist stating that he should not bowl except when he felt fit to do so.

Often, I understand, one of the discs at the base of his spine would slip out of position while he was bowling and Keith would push it back into place with his thumb during his return to his mark. He had done this during the West Indies tour but in the cold English climate he kept the certificate in his hip pocket and, according to Ian Johnson, produced it as a kind of leave pass from time to time.

That is why Johnson gave Keith only 77 overs before the Trent Bridge Test. In this he delivered 52 overs to take 6 for 127. He did not bowl at all between the Trent Bridge and Lord's Tests. At Lord's he delivered 70·1 overs to take 10 for 152.

It was because of his knee injury, however, that Miller was omitted from the games against Yorkshire, Gloucestershire, and Somerset which followed the Lord's Test. As acting captain he gave himself only 25 overs in the prelude to the Leeds' Test, the game against Hampshire at Southampton.

'Through sheer necessity,' Keith later explained, 'I had been bowled into the ground at Lord's—Ray Lindwall being unfit and Pat Crawford breaking down in the match and being on the casualty list. During England's second innings I knew I was in for some trouble with my suspect knee. It began to hurt and after the game was over I was given ten days off. The knee puffed up and I had a fair amount of fluid drained from it.

'At first I thought the knee would be OK. I tried a few overs at Southampton in the game against Hampshire, which was the last fixture before Leeds, but I knew then that I was not fit enough to bowl in the Test.

'When we travelled up to the Test, Bradman, who was covering the Tests for the London *Daily Mail*, met me in the lounge of the hotel at Harrogate in which we were to stay. He asked how I was. I told him I would not be fit to bowl. "When you get out there you will feel different," Don said.

'That was a familiar piece of Bradman technique. He had tried a similar approach when I was not up to bowling in the Lord's Test of the 1948 tour.'

Maybe Gubby Allen knew something, I began to think. Maybe he had consulted the same Harley Street specialist as Keith for his own muscular problems which, unhappily, were to have this once-lively fast bowler on crutches before another decade?

England made some changes in its side for the Third Test. The most controversial was the restoration to the batting ranks of the 44-year-old Cyril Washbrook, who had represented England last in 1951. Another significant move was the replacement of fast bowler Brian Statham by left-hand spinner Tony Lock.

England's selectors, who included Gubby Allen and former Glamorgan captain Wilfred Wooller, must have drawn a line at dropping Yorkshire's 'Frightening' Fred Trueman on his home ground—especially after he had taken 7 for 144 (twice dismissing Miller) in the Lord's Test. But the fact that they had settled for only four bowlers (Trueman, Trevor Bailey, Laker, and Lock) suggested they were banking their main hopes (and Gubby those wagers of his) mainly on spin. And this on the ground where Bradman had scored 334 in 1930, 304 in 1934, and 103 in 1938; where Bill Ponsford got 181 in 1930; and Charles Macartney 115 in 1921 and 151 in 1926.

The Headingley pitch prepared for this vital Test of 1956 never quite descended to the condition it was to reach during that mysterious attack of 'fungus fusorium' in 1972. But on it Laker and Lock between them were to take 18 wickets for 194 from the 137·4 of England's 170·4 overs they delivered.

All was not plain sailing for England, however. Gubby's ulcers, if any, must have been troubling him when England, having won the toss, lost Cowdrey 0, Peter Richardson 5, and the giant Oakman 4, to Ron Archer and was 17 for 3 before you could even think. Then in came Washbrook to join his captain Peter May.

In their *Test Cricket—England V Australia* Ralph Barker and Irving Rosenwater say, 'Four days before the game the Leeds wicket was under water but at the start it looked good.'

Nevertheless, as we have seen, the fast-medium Ron Archer, gaining considerable lift and moving the ball off the seam during the first hour, had struck thrice. Johnson anxious to have the faster and more penetrative Miller join Archer when Lindwall, still far from peak fitness, grew tired, strolled across to Keith in the covers.

'I was disappointed,' said Miller 'at not being able to lend a hand in the attack at Leeds, particularly when Ron Archer had got three England wickets down for only 17. Yet if I had bowled then I might have put myself out for the rest of the tour. I reckoned it was too high a risk to take.' Maybe had Sir Robert Menzies been there to persuade him, as he was on that first morning of the Melbourne Test of 1954–55, Keith might have chanced it?

But Ken Mackay (the 1956 Cosier) and Benaud took over the attack and May 101, and Washbrook 98, steered England to 204 before at 6.25 p.m. five minutes before stumps, May played what Ralph Barker has described as 'a tennis shot' at a high full toss from Johnson and was caught by Lindwall at fine-leg.

Night watchman Tony Lock 21, helped Washbrook, Insole, and 'Barnacle' Trevor Bailey on to 248 for 7. Bailey and Godfrey Evans added 53 before Lindwall, bowling at nearer full pace, took three quick wickets to have England all out 325 after 167·4 overs.

By this time bare patches had appeared on the recently-flooded pitch. Even on the second day Benaud had made deliveries turn quite sharply. Rain on the Saturday and Sunday deadened the pitch and on the Monday Miller, who had dropped a chest-high chance at cover off Washbrook when 44 of his 98, did his utmost to make amends during a fight with Benaud to avoid the follow-on.

But McDonald who had scored 449 at 64·14, Harvey who had scored 650 at 108·33, and Archer who had scored 364 at 60·66 in the Tests against the West Indies only twelve months previously, had now contributed 17 runs between them and Australia, at one stage 69 for 6, were all out for 143 (Burke and Miller each 41, Benaud 30).

Seven batsmen had collected ten runs between them and Laker 29/10/58/5 and Lock 27·1/11/41/4 had Australia out for 35 runs less than their initial goal.

In the follow-on Miller, batting at the fall of the second wicket at 45, and Harvey struggled desperately against Laker and Lock. They had Australia 143 and 93 for 2, 89 behind at the close of the fourth day.

The final day was 50 minutes old when Miller's two-and-a-half-hour struggle for 26 runs ended at 108 for 3. Harvey resisted for 270 minutes altogether for 69, but Burge 5, Benaud 1, Johnson 3, Mackay 2, Archer 1, Maddocks 0, and Lindwall 0 not out, could contribute only twelve runs between them. And this time Laker's analysis was 41·3/21/55/6 and Lock's 40/23/40/3.

England had won by an innings and 42 runs. With two Tests remaining the series stood at one match each.

Those perhaps over-eager Australian critics, who claimed immediately after the Test that some over-patriotic Englishmen had instructed the Headingley curator to 'cook' the pitch, would have found it difficult, in view of the ministrations of the Almighty, to prove their case. What we and, no doubt, the English hierarchy did discover was that of Australia's batsmen only Jimmy Burke 41 and 16, Neil Harvey 11 and 69, and Miller 41 and 26, had revealed the technical ability, determination, and concentration required to withstand top-class spin bowling on a turning wicket. And that none of these three had given signs of being able to conquer it in the way the immortal Victor Trumper had done almost throughout that halcyon English summer of his in 1902. Allen was now bubbling with confidence.

During the fortnight before the Old Trafford Test the Australians played only one match, a very favourable draw under the leadership of Lindwall against Middlesex at Lord's. In this game Ian Craig, experiencing another disappointing tour, found some form while scoring 27 and 67 not out against an attack which contained the excellent off-spinner Harold Titmus.

During that Lord's game Chapman, Wellings, and Bray, again supported (possibly inspired) by Jack Fingleton in the *Sunday Times*, renewed their campaign to have Miller take over from Johnson. During it Sydney Press tycoon Frank Packer, who was planning the imminent introduction of television to Australia, flew into London for talks with the executives of the B.B.C.

Learning from his friend Lord Beaverbrook that Miller had either signed or was about to sign a contract with the London *Daily Express*, Sir Frank decided to invite Keith to become senior summertime sports commentator on TV Channel Nine in Sydney. If Keith gained the Australian captaincy all the better for Beaverbrook and Packer, of course. And the higher the fees in Keith's contracts, one would imagine.

But on the eve of the Old Trafford Test when the Australian selectors Johnson, Miller, and Gil Langley, sat down to choose their team it was Miller who broke an embarrassing silence. 'I think Ian Craig should come in,' he said. Langley and an obviously relieved Johnson nodded their agreement. Craig was given Peter Burge's place and discussion ended.

Miller later was to say, 'Privately I felt that Ian was not a "form selection" for the Manchester Test. On the other hand, I did not think it wise to change skippers in midstream.'

Over to the English camp.

On the Tuesday afternoon prior to the Test T. S. (Stan) Worthington, who had helped Wally Hammond to add 266 for the fourth wicket against India at The Oval in 1936 and was now Lancashire County Cricket Club's coach, invited me out to meet the Old Trafford curator, Bert Flack.

Flack was examining his pitch. Under a thick mat of greenish grass the surface looked more than a little rough and, even on that Tuesday about 40 hours before the Test was due to begin, it was brown and criss-crossed with cracks.

'This pitch won't last three days,' I said.

'Yes it will,' replied Flack. 'It's the strip where South Africa totalled 521 for 8 against us and Denis Compton scored 158 and Peter May 112 here last summer. *I'm not going to cut the grass.*'

'That's quite a different matter then,' I replied—greatly relieved.

But Worthington and I had hardly left the ground before two of England's selectors Gubby Allen and Wilfred Wooller walked out to examine that wicket. I had not met Wooller but John Fitzgerald, the Australian Associated Press London-based sports correspondent of the 1950s, had told me of an incident that occurred before the game between Wooller's county, Glamorgan, and Pakistan in Wales in 1954.

Fitzgerald, endeavouring to ascertain whether Glamorgan or the Pakistanis would bat first, approached the Pakistani captain A. H. Kardar as he was returning to the dressing-room after the toss.

'Who won the toss Mr Kardar?' he enquired.

'I don't know, but Glamorgan will bat first.'

'What do you mean you don't know who won the toss?'

'He tossed the coin. It fell on the pitch. Wooller picked it up before I could look at it and said "We'll bat".'

W. G. Grace's favourite old trick!

Soon after Allen and Wooller left the field at Old Trafford that Tuesday afternoon (24 July) of 1956 I was astonished to see Bert Flack approaching his pitch with a lawn mower. I was more amazed as I watched him shave the grass to the roots.

My astonishment knew no bounds a few minutes later when I learnt England's selectors had omitted Trueman—Trueman, who had taken 7 for 144 against Australia at Lord's and 2 for 40 at Leeds. Here was clear indication that England was to rely on spin.

Over to Keith Miller. 'On the first Thursday morning of the Test the pitch was already showing cracks—*cracks*, *mark you*—before even a ball had been bowled. Yet on the practice pitches the day before we had batted on wet, dead turf. We inspected the twenty-two yard strip in amazement and within a few overs of the start the boys were talking in terms of being back in London by Saturday night.

'The umpires were Frank Lee and Emrys Davies. I walked over to Frank and said, "I think three days will see this through. You'll be paid for two days you won't have to work." Whereupon Frank answered, "That's funny, I had just said to Emrys, 'This game will go about three days' and Emrys replied, 'I was going to say the same thing to you.'"'

'But for the rain the game *would* have been over in two and a half days. The first ball I bowled on the opening morning sent up a puff of dust when it pitched—the writing on the wall could not have been larger. And significantly when we played Lancashire early in the season Len Maddocks, our wicketkeeper, was taking balls from Alan Davidson chest high standing halfway back to the fence. Now this Test pitch was red in colour, yet the surrounding areas were blackish, I heard that marl had been put on a month before, even weeks before the match. Now that's much too late to "marl" a wicket. The marl merely provides a surface layer and does not mix with the normal soil unless well watered. In this case the pitch was parched and the surface marl very quickly flaked and cracked so that it readily responded to spin.

'I felt sorry for the groundsman. He had so much publicity that he became a world figure overnight. He confided to me one morning, "I'm fed up with it. They won't even give me five minutes to cut my throat."

'Even if Australia had won the toss, England would have won

the match. Whenever we got on a real turning wicket we bowled like old girls.'

And batted like ballerinas, Keith might have added.

I was covering the Test series you may remember for the Sydney *Daily Telegraph* and *Sunday Telegraph* and, most fortunately, for the Melbourne *Argus*. I was also covering it for the London *Daily News* and Manchester *Evening News*.

I began to publish what I knew about the preparation of that pitch and to ask a series of questions aimed at discovering just who had been responsible for the instructions given to the curator. England had a longstanding reputation for preparing wickets to suit itself. Was it doing so yet again? If so, clearly all the evidence pointed to those two England selectors who had prevented the unfortunate Flack from leaving that thick mat of grass to help shield the surface and prevent the widening of those cracks. And I said so.

Both the London *Daily News* and Manchester *Evening News* published every word I wrote. So did the Sydney *Daily Telegraph* and *Sunday Telegraph*—on the Friday, Saturday, and Sunday of the Test.

But my chief Frank Packer had been reading those comments and questions of mine in the London *Daily News*. He had cabled his editor 'King' Watson in Sydney and confirmed that they had also been appearing in his own papers. Packer also had been wining and dining with a few of his cricket-loving London cronies. Most of these knew I was his cricket writer. They began asking why he employed such 'a shockingly bad sport'.

On the Saturday night of the Test we dined as guests of the Lancashire County Cricket Club. One of the committee, who was sitting at my table, volunteered that the club had nothing to do with the final preparation of the Test pitch. 'Somebody,' he said, 'has gone over our heads.'

I continued my interrogations in the London *Daily News* and Manchester *Evening News* on the Monday. I did so because former England captain Walter Robins and googly bowler Ian Peebles had told me in the foyer of Manchester's Midland Hotel that morning, 'Keep it up. You're on the right track.'

It so happened that just after they had spoken to me I received a cable from Sydney. It was sent by my editor at the Sydney *Daily*

Telegraph 'King' Watson and read, 'You are to make no more comments about the Old Trafford wicket. Confine yourself strictly to the play.'

This did not cover my Melbourne *Argus* copy, I decided, thankfully, and began to send separate cables to Melbourne.

England in the meantime had scored 459 (Peter Richardson 104, Colin Cowdrey 80, the re-enlisted Reverend David Sheppard 113) by 2.10 p.m. of the second day. Towards the close of the first day, however, one delivery from Richie Benaud, who like Ian Johnson does not dig the ball into a pitch as both Laker and Lock do, turned sharply from the legside and kicked high over May's right shoulder.

One had no need to be a Balthazar in ancient Babylon to read the portent of this. Had Australia been batting, both Laker and Lock already would have been making the ball 'bite'.

Between the England and Australian first innings the Old Trafford ground staff came on to the pitch armed with what were described as whisk brooms. They seemed more suitable for the witches scene in Macbeth. Within seconds the groundsmen and brooms were invisible from the Press box—enshrouded in clouds of dust. That was when some Fleet Street genius gave the wicket its unforgettable tab, 'The Dust Bowl'.

Ian Johnson had instructed Flack to use only the lightest of rollers. This must have smoothed the surface of the dust for Colin McDonald and Jimmy Burke put on 48 for the first wicket against Statham and Bailey, and then Laker and Lock before Laker had McDonald caught by Lock at leg slip and Lock, gaining his only wicket for the Test, had Burke caught by Cowdrey without addition to the score.

Australian batsmen had, indeed, developed an extraordinary ineptitude against accurate spin bowling since it was regarded as 'fruit for the sideboard' by even average Sheffield Shield players during the 1930s. But there must be some satisfactory explanation for the dismissal of nine of them for 37 runs from 16·4 overs by a bowler who two years later in Australia took only 15 wickets from 127·6 overs in the Test series of 1958–59. And who in the 1948 series had taken 9 for 472 at 52·44 and in the 1953 series 9 for 212 at 23·55 on English wickets.

Australia, trailing by 375 on the first innings, followed-on with 65 minutes of that blackest of Fridays remaining. Again those whisk brooms, again that lightest of rollers, again those palls of dust.

And again there was at least a nucleus of an opening stand. But when McDonald, at 28 for 0, retired with a knee problem, Harvey struck a full toss from Laker meekly to mid-wicket and Cowdrey held the chance.

Rain permitted only 45 minutes play on the Saturday—that rain that was needed to bind the marl to the main surface of the pitch. During those 45 minutes Burke had fallen, caught Lock bowled Laker, for 33, at 55 for 2. On the Monday conditions were so unpleasant that only 19·2 overs were bowled. Further rain fell during the night and at lunch of the final day (the Tuesday) McDonald and Craig were still together on a now slow, unresponsive pitch. Each of them had been batting for more than four hours.

Just before lunch the sun came out on the sodden pitch and 15 minutes after the interval Laker got Craig lbw for the second time. The youngster had contributed 38 in 260 minutes of mostly immaculate defence. But Mackay caught Oakman bowled Laker 0, Miller bowled Laker 0, Archer caught Oakman bowled Laker 0, made it 130 for 6—or 245 behind with more than a session and a half to go. Laker, with 15 wickets in his bag, was level with Hedley Verity's record, one achieved at Lord's in 1934 (and considerably the more economical of the two).

Benaud and McDonald stayed for 75 minutes until tea, though Laker and Lock had made an experimental switch of ends.

During the tea interval I was handed a clipping from a London morning paper. It contained a cabled quote from an editorial of the Monday morning in my parent paper the Sydney *Daily Telegraph*.

Prophets are seldom without honour, save in their own country, it has been said. Well, this clipping read, 'Sometimes our correspondents are apt to get too close to their work and lose their sense of perspective, especially when overseas. This is what appears to have happened to our cricket writer at Manchester.'

For the first and last time in my cricket-writing career I decided to abandon coverage of a Test match and try to obtain an interview with that character Bert Flack. Bert had been on and off the field for much of the day applying and removing the covers. He was out in the middle right now. I told Sir Leonard Hutton's 'ghost' writer of my intention. 'You'll need a witness and Len's filed his last piece for the day. I'll come with you,' he said.

As we reached the end of the turreted, red-brick Members' Pavilion we intercepted Flack when he was leaving the field.

'How is it, Flack, that you can always make a wicket that suits the home team?' called two (probably Yorkshire) spectators.

Here was heaven-sent manna down with the last shower.

There was to be more.

'I does what I'se told. Makes the kind of wicket they wants. The Press gives me hell and then I has to clean the bloody papers off the ground,' replied Bert.

'Can I quote you on that, Mr Flack?' I asked.

'On that and a heap more if you wants to,' Bert replied.

'No, that will do fine,' I said, wrote out his words, got him to sign under them and Sir Leonard's 'ghost' to witness his signature.

It was too late for the London *Evening News* or even the Manchester *Evening News*. 'The best plan for you to adopt,' volunteered Sir Leonard's 'ghost', 'is to prepare your story for Australia and hold it till 3 a.m. Just before you cable it, release the part containing Flack's statement to Reuter's and Australian Associated Press. Then it will appear in every British morning paper and every Australian morning paper except, probably, the Sydney *Daily Telegraph*.' No wonder he later became editor of a London newspaper.

McDonald was out, caught Oakman bowled Laker, to the second ball after the tea interval of that final Tuesday. He had scored 89 in 337 minutes of most admirable defiance. The ball was turning perhaps more sharply now than at any other stage of the match (which is saying something) and Australia, 205 (Benaud a lonely 18 in the middle of the list), had lost by an innings and 170 runs. They trailed, as Gubby Allen had forecast and wagered they would, two Tests to one with one to play.

Jim Laker finished with the still, and probably eternal, record of 19 for 90, Lock with 1 for 106. Lock had turned the ball *too* sharply and kept beating everything. Laker had wisely allowed the wicket to do the work.

Said Ralph Barker and Irving Rosenwater in their account of

the Test: 'The game was so full of paradoxes as to defy rational analysis.' Said Australia's sporting captain Ian Johnson: 'When the controversy and the side issues of the match are forgotten, Laker's wonderful bowling will remain.'

Wrote Keith Miller: 'Laker's figures against us that season were so fantastic that, looking back on them, they seem almost unbelievable. In three innings against us (counting his "all ten" at The Oval in May) he took 29 out of 30 wickets to fall. We simply had no answer; but then, in all honesty, did the preparers—or perpetrators—of those Oval, Leeds, and Manchester wickets?'

Flighting the ball well Ian Johnson had bowled superbly and most unluckily in this Test; David Sheppard was missed stumped by Maddocks yards up the wicket off him early in his knock of 113 and Godfrey Evans at least twice near mid-wicket on his way to 47.

The Australian captain delivered 47 overs, 10 of them maidens, to take 4 for 151 in England's one innings. He also found it necessary to exercise the brand of discipline he had administered in the West Indies to stifle a protest against the condition of the pitch by several members of his team. Nonetheless the demands for him to stand down in favour of Miller for the final Test grew more intense, both in England and Australia.

The Australians, with both Johnson and Miller on deck, drew the return game against Surrey unfavourably at The Oval. Under Johnson's leadership they beat Glamorgan by an innings and 11 runs at Swansea—Ken Mackay 163 not out, and Ron Archer 148, scoring centuries in their first innings 408 for 4 declared. Johnson delivered 53 overs to take 5 for 82.

Under Miller's leadership the tourists 424 for 4 declared (Burke 194, Harvey 145, and Miller 46 not out) beat Warwickshire by an innings and 127 runs at Edgbaston. Again under Miller's leadership Australia, 146 and 183 for 3 declared (Ian Craig 76 and 64 not out), beat Derbyshire 111 (Lindwall 7 for 40) and 161 (Miller 5 for 29) at Derby.

Back at Old Trafford the Australians under Johnson lost seven wickets for 86 (Statham 6 for 27) against Lancashire before rain washed out the match. At Southend again under Johnson they totalled 349 (Craig 66, Miller 59, Alan Davidson 75) to beat Essex 154 and 183 (Miller 5 for 78 all told) by an innings and 12.

The only changes in the Australian team for the Fifth Test were the inclusion of Alan Davidson for Mackay and of Langley for Maddocks. England brought in a brave (some said reckless) Denis Compton (following an operation for the removal of his knee-cap) and 'Typhoon' Tyson in place of Oakman and Bailey.

Australia still had a chance to level the series. But Peter May won the important toss, his fourth for the series, on the morning of 23 August.

Having accepted the offers of both Lord Beaverbrook and Frank Packer, Miller knew this was to be his last of 29 Tests against England. So far in 28 he had batted 47 times for 1443 runs with three centuries and a highest score of 145 not out at an average of 32·5; he had bowled 5345 balls, 215 maidens, for 1802 runs and 82 wickets at 21·9; he had held 19 catches.

Taking performances in Anglo-Australian Tests as a yardstick—the criterion recommended by Johnnie Moyes—we find that only M. A. Noble (1905 runs at 30·72 and 115 wickets at 24·86 from 39 Tests) and George Giffen (1238 runs at 23·35 and 103 wickets at 27·09 from 31 Tests) have scored more than 1000 runs and taken more than 100 wickets for Australia against England. No other Australian player has achieved a 'double' which compares with Miller's eventual 1511 runs at 33·57 and 87 wickets at 22·40 against 'the Mother Country'.

Both Noble and Giffen captained Australia against England. Miller had not and realised now on the eve of his finale that his chance had disappeared.

Whatever Keith will tell you I know that he dearly wanted to achieve this honour. I also know that he would never have wanted to do so if it involved forsaking his allegiance to his captain—displacing even a man he had never really liked and believed had never really liked him. I know that Keith has no regrets today about his decision to refrain from joining the campaign to unseat Johnson in 1956; a campaign that, most probably, would have succeeded had Keith lent it his support.

Instead Miller went into that final Test of his against England determined, despite his age and his nagging injuries, to make an all-out effort to help level the series at two-all.

He knew Australia would need both runs and wickets from him if it were to win. He knew that to score an adequate number of runs he would have to conquer Laker, as he had done at Headingley in the Fourth Test of 1948 when joined by the 19-year-old fledgling Neil Harvey following the dismissal of Morris 6, Hassett 13, and Bradman 33, at 68 for 3 in chase of 496.

On that occasion the 28-year-old Miller, 'sweeping and driving Laker for 6s and playing a stream of strokes' had set an example which Harvey followed while they were adding 121 in 95 minutes to clear the decks for an eventual recovery to 458 and an eventual Australian victory by the amazing margin of seven wickets.

But Laker with 39 wickets already behind him in the 1956 series, 39 wickets at the extraordinary average of 9·07, was now an enormously greater obstacle. And Miller was eight years older.

'Every time we struck Laker on a spinning or wet wicket in 1956 he was a great bowler,' said Keith after the tour. 'We tried to attack him and got out. We tried pushing and prodding, ignoring runs. We still got out. We had no answer.

'In The Oval Test I changed my technique altogether against Laker. I decided to go forward to him. I found that by this means I greatly diminished the risk of being leg before wicket and also eliminated the fear of being caught in the short-leg trap. This fear of being snapped up by one of the leg-trap fieldsmen was constantly with us. It became almost an obsession. The England close fielders were splendid, with Lock absolutely brilliant.'

In England's first innings 247 at The Oval Miller delivered 40 overs, 22 more than Lindwall and 12 more than Archer, to take four wickets (those of opener Peter Richardson, Number 3 batsman the Rev David Sheppard, and Evans and Laker) for 91.

Then, batting from 47 for 5 on a rain-damaged pitch, Miller joined Harvey. When Harvey left for 39, scored in two-and-a-half hours, at 90 for 6 Keith batted on with Benaud 32, to add 43, and with Lindwall 22 not out, to add another 48. His 61 of 155 had taken Australia to 202 for 9 and it was Statham, not Laker, who dismissed him.

So far, with half the Test to go, Miller had been Australia's, indeed the game's, outstanding player. To the delight of his millions of English admirers, the ageing and wounded 'Lion in Summer' was going out fighting in the land where, eleven years previously, he had made his spectacular international debut; where he had caused England's 'Emperor of Games', Charles

Burgess Fry, to write 'Here is a young cricketing Alexander; a player and a personality who will set out in search of new worlds to conquer in the years following the Hitler War and establish a unique niche for himself in the annals of Test cricket.'

Like Mowgli's old friend, the wolf Akela, he was making one last spring from the Council rock.

And Fry, who died on 7 September 1956 at the age of 84 was there at The Oval to watch.

In England's second innings 182 for 3 declared, Miller took only one (David Sheppard's) wicket from 22 more overs at a cost of 56. But it was he who, after McDonald 9, Burke 1, and Harvey 1, had fallen for the addition of only five runs, partnered young Ian Craig 7, and his captain Ian Johnson 10, in stands that saw Australia home to a draw; it was he who stood undefeated with Richie Benaud at the end as his country, 27 for 5, faced yet another disaster.

This time Laker had taken 7 for 94 (not 19 for 90) for the match to finish the series with 46 wickets at 9·60—figures which only England's greatest of all bowlers, Sydney Barnes, 49 at 10·93 from *four* Tests against South Africa in 1913–14, has excelled.

Miller had fought with might and mane but England, as Napoleon and Hitler had found, can be hard to beat.

Ian Johnson graciously stood down to give Miller the honour of leading the Australians on his last appearance on his favourite and most successful ground, Lord's, against the Gentlemen of England on the day following the Test. But that most ungentlemanly English climate ended proceedings after Miller, batting at Number 8, somewhat ungracefully hit his wicket facing, of all bowlers, John 'Butterfingers' Warr with his score 18 of 226 for 8.

Bradman bowled Hollies 0 in his last Test in England in 1948; Miller hit wicket bowled Warr on his last appearance at Lord's.

Johnson and Miller amicably shared the leadership in the five remaining games in England and Scotland and at the completion of the tour Miller 29 innings, 6 not out, 281 not out highest score, 843 runs at 36·65; and 430 overs, 97 maidens, 980 runs, 50 wickets at 19·68, emerged as third on the batting and second on the bowling averages.

In the Tests his figures were 10 innings, 1 not out, 61 highest score, 203 runs at 22·55; and 205·1 overs, 44 maidens, 467 runs, 21 wickets at 22·38. They made him fourth in the batting and top of the bowling during a series which, for the first time since the five-Test series were begun in England in 1890, failed to produce a century from an Australian batsman.

On their way home the Australians played one last Test against Pakistan at Karachi and three against India at Madras, Bombay, and Calcutta.

Though Miller scored only 21 and 11 in his last Test innings at Karachi, the 21 came from a total of 80 and was the top score. Owing to injury he was unable to take part in the Tests against India, of which Australia won two and drew one.

During July of that long late-April-to-early-November tour of England Miller and Johnson had received the insignia of the M.B.E. from the Queen at Buckingham Palace. Later a youngster produced a book and asked Keith for his autograph.

Keith was about to sign when the horrified lad exclaimed 'Not there!' Noticing that the page he had chosen contained the autographs of Sir Donald Bradman and Sir Leonard Hutton, Keith turned deeper into the book.

He was only an M.B.E.

'Where shall I sign, my boy?' Keith asked.

'Here,' the lad said, turning to a page designated 'Miscellaneous'.

'It is about time I got out of the game,' Keith thought. And he did—immediately upon his return to Australia.

Rosewall was 42 years of age then. Two years had passed since his annihilation by Jimmy Connors in the 1974 Wimbledon Singles final. But he was still plugging along the arduous and monotonous professional tennis trail which Lew himself had abandoned in his late thirties to establish his Campo de Tenis.

It was not as if Kenny needed the money. He was authoritatively reputed to be an American dollar millionaire several times over. And yet only early in 1980 did he announce his retirement convincingly enough to dispel doubt that he was doing yet another 'Nellie Melba'.

At last the player who perhaps came nearer than anyone to becoming a violinist with a tennis racquet had called it a day.

What has all this to do with Keith Miller? you will be asking.

'Plenty,' I reply, for when Keith retired from competitive cricket at the age of 36 in August of 1956, he had plenty of places to go.

Firstly there was a book to be written, a book contracted through Sir Max Aitken, Lord Beaverbrook's journalist son, to be serialised in the London *Daily Express* and syndicated worldwide. Keith had persuaded Reg Hayter, cricket correspondent of Reuter's Agency, to help him with this and it was ready for serialisation and syndication soon after the end of the 1956 Australian tour of England.

Keith did what, if one directs one's mind back to 1930, may be called 'a Bradman' about the articles. And, like Bradman, he was fined by the Australian Board of Control for breaching the clause in his tour contract which forbade commenting for publication until a stipulated period after the end of the tour.

The book *Cricket Crossfire* was published by Oldbourne Press in 1956. I well remember entering a famous Fleet Street bar in late September of that year and encountering an exceedingly worried Hayter in its far corner.

'What's troubling you, Reg?' I asked.

'That bloody Miller promised to be here at 3 p.m. It's now 4.30.'

Keith must have arrived—eventually. The book appeared almost on schedule.

That book and those serialised articles from it were only part of the contract Keith made with Aitken. The more important part was an agreement that Keith should be engaged by the *Daily Express* in the English spring of 1957 as its most highly-paid and prominently-featured summer sports writer for a renewable period of five years.

This contract and its commitments dovetailed conveniently with Keith's recent agreement with Sydney tycoon Frank Packer to become sports editor and top sports telecaster on his pioneering T.V. channel in Sydney during the Australian summers ahead.

From 1956 onward Keith would be following the sun around each year, enjoying the best of both hemispheres, but still domiciled in Australia because of his spacious and comfortable home a few hundred metres back from Sydney's popular Newport Beach. His wife Peg decided that Newport all year round would be preferable to England all year round and Keith found a flat for himself from each May to September in London.

Miller's determination to maintain his premature retirement from cricket suffered a brief but spectacular setback, however, during the English summer of 1959.

Succumbing to an invitation to represent that old 'enemy' county, Nottinghamshire, against Cambridge University he scored 62 and 102 not out at the age of 39, and possibly won over some of the characters who had hooted him so vociferously during the Trent Bridge Test of 1948.

During the English winters when Marylebone Cricket Club teams toured Australia, the West Indies, and South Africa he accompanied them as the *Daily Express* correspondent. During English summers he was given an almost *carte blanche* choice of Britain's most famous sporting events—the cricket Tests, the Epsom Derby, Ascot, Aintree, the British Open Golf Championship, even Wimbledon (despite that setback in 1949 at Roy Minnett's tennis Sundays at Manly) to cover.

Once when, following a visit to Moss Bros in Covent Garden, he arrived at Epsom to cover the Derby in top hat, morning suit, and accessories, the *Express* camera man snapped him. The resultant photograph was captioned 'Killah Dillah Millah' and displayed across two columns of the front page.

Fleet Street legends have it that London's most celebrated journalists live an almost fairy-tale existence. I have heard stories of how Geoffrey Green, *The Times*' soccer correspondent, once covered a football international played between England and Sweden in Stockholm with the help of a radio and telephone from an island in the Baltic, of how he was congratulated on 'the finest piece of reporting he had ever produced'. I have been told how famous Fleet Street cricket writers have 'covered' Test matches at Leeds and Manchester from pleasure yachts on the Costa Brava and Cote d'Azur. But when I tackled Keith on this subject, he vehemently denied he had ever transgressed in this fashion.

Partly, no doubt, why Keith held down that England summertime job of his with the *Daily Express* from 1957 until 1973. Then he was caught up in the general retrenchment policy introduced in the Beaverbrook Empire. Surprisingly, Keith was not so successful with his 1956 television engagement with Sir Frank Packer.

24
Following the sun around – 1957–81

From memory it was at his mountainside tennis camp and bar-restaurant in southern Spain in July of 1976 that Lew Hoad expressed his concern to me about the future of his tennis 'twin' Ken Rosewall.

'"Muscles" just won't know what to do with himself when he retires from competitive tennis. That's partly why he's kept going as long as he has,' Lew said.

Keith will confirm that the times when he feels most relaxed are when chatting with his closest friends over a schooner of beer in a club lounge or at a hotel bar. He has always kept himself well acquainted with current events, has an inquiring and constructive mind, and a dry sense of humour. All this and his much-travelled life, his almost continuous association with interesting and famous people, have made him a stimulating and informative conversationalist.

He is also something of a radical on many subjects, especially the administration of sport.

These characteristics, it was thought, would help ensure his success as a TV personality on Sydney's Channel 9. But they were not enough to counter certain disadvantages. Keith, even in 1956 in his middle thirties, was an extremely shy and self-conscious character. He had always found difficulty in knowing just what to do with those most expressive and restless hands of his. And television is a cruel media.

Indeed, Keith's original problem with TV reminds me of a

story of an American, an English, and an Italian prisoner-of-war who were subjected to a physically painful interrogation towards the end of the second World War.

The American went first and endured six hours of torture before submitting and revealing portions of what his tormentors were seeking to learn. The Englishman lasted seven hours. 'I gave up in the end,' he confessed to the American. 'I gave up because I realised the Italian would spill the beans, tell them all they wanted to know.'

'Well, all I can say is he's held out for a remarkably long time. Why, he must have been in there for four hours, at least,' the American rejoined, glancing at his watch.

At this stage the Italian emerged, looking very much the worse for wear.

'What happened Giuseppi? Congratulations. You've been in for over four hours,' called the American.

'They tied my hands behind my back. I couldn't say a word,' Giuseppi explained.

Maybe Sir Frank Packer should have tied Keith's hands behind his back during the late 1950s when he strode upon the television stage. But neither he nor his underlings thought of this idea and Keith and Channel 9 soon parted company, by mutual consent. It was not until 1977 when Keith began helping to telecast Test Cricket for the Australian Broadcasting Commission under the genial wing of the competent Norman May that he became a success on this media.

So much so that when he learnt Keith was not to be a member of the team of commentators engaged to cover the Anglo–Australian and West Indies–Australian Tests of 1979–80 for TCN 9, a certain Mr M. Brabham, of Epping, New South Wales, dispatched the following letter to Australia's *TV Times*:

'For heaven's sake, TCN 9 Sydney, hire or buy Keith Miller for next season's coverage of Test cricket. It's going to be bad enough having to endure advertisements every two minutes during play. But to hear Bill Lawry and Keith Stackpole trying to comment the rest of the time will turn many off viewing.

'How many other people have enjoyed Miller's sharp, witty comments during Test matches? Come on Channel 9, if yours is the only coverage of cricket next season, make sure it's decent.'

From what I have gathered, Keith had no wish to join the Kerry Packer menagerie.

Miller is successful as a journalist because he possesses that invaluable and indefinable attribute known as news sense. Thanks to his cricketing travels through Britain in 1945, 1948, 1953, and 1956, he also had all the contacts he required.

And these contacts were not confined to cricketing circles. Wherever he had travelled throughout the world Keith had indulged his passion for horse-racing and gambling. Long before he arrived in London in 1957 he could count among his close friends such prominent racing identities as champion jockey Lester Piggott, Australia's 'Scobie' Breasley, who was to ride the winners of the 1964 and 1966 Epsom Derbies and more than 2500 other winners of important races in England, Ireland, and France. Also the Queen's jockey Harry Carr.

Keith was also well known to such racehorse owners as Lord Rosebery, the Ali Khan, and the Duke of Norfolk. In the racing game he would have no difficulty in gathering whatever inside information and news he needed 'straight from the stable'.

He had also become a devotee of England's national winter game, Association Football, once even declared he found it an even more attractive code than 18-a-side 'Australian Rules', at which he had excelled in his youth.

Having neglected no opportunity of watching the FA Cup finals at Wembley during his cricketing visits to Britain he could count such soccer luminaries as Sir Stanley Matthews, Billy Wright, Sir Stanley Rouse and his long-time friend comedian Tommy Trinder, who had acquired his own football club, among his contacts, and they were readily available for news, advice, and quotation.

The coverage of tennis presented no problems for him during the Wimbledon Championships each June–July. Australia's Lew Hoad, Ken Rosewall, Adrian Quist, Neale Fraser, and Rod Laver were regular visitors there and Keith was a close friend of England's Fred Perry and knew America's Jack Kramer, Pancho Gonzales, Vic Seixas, and Tony Trabert well. Turning to big golf he had such celebrities as his friends Peter Thomson, Kel Nagle, Arnold Palmer, Gary Player, Bobby Locke, and the 'Big Bear' Jack Nicklaus to call upon.

His sports editor naturally took full advantage of his new columnist's and commentator's fame and popularity. Keith became a familiar figure on great occasions at Wembley and Wimbledon, Epsom and Ascot, St Andrews and Birkdale, as well as at Lord's, Trent Bridge, Edgbaston, Headingley, Old Trafford, and The Oval.

His early interest in classical music was further developed in England by Sir Neville Cardus, pianist Benno Moisewitch, and the leader of Manchester's Hallé Orchestra, Sir John Barbirolli. Sir John had written the foreword to one of Keith's books, *Gods or Flannelled Fools?* On many an evening Cardus and Keith adjourned together to the former's London apartment and listened to the recorded concertos of their favourite composer Ludwig Beethoven—and particularly to that *Emperor Concerto* which Keith, not surprisingly, preferred above all others.

Soon after he had moved into his London flat in Earl's Court, or Kangaroo Valley as it was becoming known because of the crowds of Australians billeted there or thereabouts, Keith began to develop an interest in the theatre. As a result he met impressario Jack Hylton.

Hylton had an ocean-going yacht and invited Keith to sail with him across the Bay of Biscay to Gibraltar and along the Mediterranean to Spain's Costa del Sol and Costa Brava, to France's Cote d'Azur. Yes, it was a grand life.

Returning to Sydney each Australian spring Keith found less demands upon his time—that is until he became an executive consultant of Robert Sangster's Australian Soccer Pools in the late 1970s. But he was happy to be back home with his wife Peg and their four sons, Bill, Peter, Denis, and Robert and he divided the daylight hours between sunbaking on the beach at Newport, working in the garden, repainting his home, and visiting the races, especially the picnic meetings at Gosford.

For the greater part of the 1960s and early 1970s, however, he was rarely to be seen at the Sydney Cricket Ground, even during Test matches. The defensive kind of cricket played under the leadership of Bobby Simpson and those 'Captains Outrageous' Bill Lawry and Ray Illingworth, held little appeal for him. Especially following that excitingly tied Test of 1960–61 between Australia and the West Indies.

But he did drive from Newport to watch a young fast bowler named Dennis Lillee make his SCG Test debut against Ray Illingworth's England in February 1971.

After England had won the Test and the series, Keith, Colin McCool, and I adjourned for drinks to the M. A. Noble Pavilion bar.

Most of the English and Australian players were either celebrating their victory or drowning their sorrows with champagne in their dressing-rooms in the adjoining old *Showboat* Pavilion. We were surprised, therefore, when a tall, dark, and powerfully-built young man still in his flannels approached and then quietly and respectfully, asked, 'Could I have a moment with you, Mr Miller?'

'Of course, Dennis,' Keith replied, recognising the newcomer as Dennis Lillee.

'I won't trouble you for long. I just wondered if you have Mr Ray Lindwall's address—or, maybe his Brisbane telephone number?'

'Yes, I have both of them in my diary. Do you want Ray for any particular reason?'

'I just thought he might help teach me how to become a good fast bowler.'

A pleasingly modest but not over-tactful reply, we thought. Keith might just have been able to help Dennis with this problem himself. But he never batted an eyelid and, after fossicking in those invariably cluttered pockets of his, produced the required information. Dennis Lillee's own autobiography contains a graceful acknowledgment of the help he received from Lindwall during the early 1970s.

But a decade has passed since then and today Keith is again very much back in the public eye—both in Australia and internationally. His work as an executive consultant and public relations officer for Australian Soccer Pools necessitates almost weekly flights from Sydney to Australia's other capital cities. It also involves him in occasional visits to London. His employment as a sports writer for Rupert Murdoch's morning and evening newspapers in Sydney requires him to cast an eye upon international cricket.

Towards the end of 1979 he was in London one Saturday night

to appear on Fred Trueman's *This is Your Life* episode on B.B.C. television, in Melbourne the following Wednesday to present a cheque to the winner of the week's soccer pools competition, and in Hong Kong the following Saturday to take part in a festival staged by the Hong Kong Cricket Club on the occasion of the opening of the enlarged island racecourse.

Finding it difficult to trace the movements of this modern Marco Polo, I rang his home at Newport on the Sunday morning.

A young-sounding male voice replied.

Suspecting rightly that it was one or other of Keith's four sons, I asked, 'Is your father at home?'

'At home? No. That mad bastard's in Hong Kong trying to play cricket.' Despite the obvious affection implied in the word 'bastard', I felt I should rebuke Peter Miller, as it proved to be.

'Don't you feel you should treat your father with a little more respect? After all, he is quite a famous and important person.'

'I only called him a mad bastard because he's taken Mum with him and now we have to do all the cooking,' explained Peter.

The capacious and comfortable Miller home at Nullaburra Road, Newport, I gathered, had become something of a family community centre, one frequented by three generations of Millers.

And this I found to be so. Keith Miller a grandfather! 'God, struth and starve the blood crows,' I found myself thinking. Well, that dark-haired, brown-eyed, attractive, American lass he had met in Boston way back in 1942 deserved a great deal of the credit for all this. She had been lonely at times, during many long times, while her famous husband travelled the world playing and reporting cricket. But she had gained her reward in the long run, as Benjamin Disraeli's beloved wife Mary Ann, and Sir Winston Churchill's equally treasured Clementine, had gained theirs.

And Keith, rising 16 stone but still imposing and attractive of appearance, sits today (when he is in Sydney) behind the huge glass windows at the front of Australian Soccer Pools palatial ground floor premises in Alfred Street North, North Sydney. Sits facing out towards the northern pylon of the Sydney Harbour Bridge with a glimpse of the white sails of a neck of the blue harbour itself as he greets a constant stream of visiting friends with a blue-eyed smile and that characteristically strong and welcoming handshake of his.

No doubt, he remembers the occasion of the August afternoon of 1945 when he hit 120 runs with seven 6s in 90 minutes for the Dominions against England at Lord's; the day in 1956 when he struck a 6 there 'especially for Her Majesty the (watching) Queen'; the nights in 1943, 1944, and 1945 when he flirted with his life while dropping bombs on German airfields; the day at Sydney when he dismissed England's two greatest batsmen Hutton and Compton in one over for no runs to turn the tide of the Third Test of 1950–51 and then, eleven runs later, disposed of Reg Simpson 'just to make sure'.

But the man who came to be called 'Nugget' by his Air Force and cricketing cobbers during the war because originally he had been their 'Golden Boy', does not talk about these memories of his if he can avoid it. He is far more interested, even as he enters his sixties, in the present and the future.

'You'll have to think of slowing down, taking things easier, Keith?' I suggested to him, thinking of all those plane journeys.

All the old fight came back into those sapphire blue eyes as he faced squarely towards me and drew himself to his full height.

'You know me, Richard, I'll never change,' he said. 'And when I do it will be . . .' And he gave that downward gesture with his thumbs that Roman emperors of old used to give in the Colosseum to decide the fate of defeated gladiators.

'Man can be destroyed, but never defeated' wrote Ernest Hemingway some time ago. And I can think of no man to whom these words apply more fittingly than to Keith Ross Miller—originally of Sunshine, Victoria, and now I hope for many long, happy years, of Newport, New South Wales.

KEITH MILLER
STATISTICAL RECORD FIRST-CLASS CRICKET

TEST MATCHES

Batting:

Against	*Tests*	*Inns.*	*Not Out*	*Runs*	*Highest Score*	*100's*	*Average*
England	29	49	4	1511	145 n.o.	3	33·57
West Indies	10	16	1	801	147	4	53·40
South Africa	9	14	2	399	84	—	33·25
India	5	5	—	185	67	—	37·00
Pakistan	1	2	—	32	—	—	16·00
New Zealand	1	1	—	30	30	—	30·00
Total	55	87	7	2958	147	7	36·97

Bowling:

Against	*Tests*	*Overs*	*Maidens*	*Runs*	*Wickets*	*Average*
England	29	757·1	224	1960	87	22·56
West Indies	10	316·5	53	1047	40	26·17
South Africa	9	226	35	632	30	21·06
India	5	72	14	223	9	24·77
Pakistan	1	29	9	58	2	29·00
New Zealand	1	6	2	6	2	3·00
Total	55	1407	337	3905	170	22·97

UNOFFICIAL TEST MATCHES

Batting:

Against	*Matches*	*Inns.*	*Not Out*	*Runs*	*Highest Score*	*100's*	*Average*
England 1945	5	10	3	443	118	2	63·28

Bowling:

Against	*Matches*	*Overs*	*Maidens*	*Runs*	*Wickets*	*Average*
England 1945	5	121	19	277	10	27·70

SHEFFIELD SHIELD

Batting:

For	*Matches*	*Inns.*	*Not Out*	*Runs*	*Highest Score*	*100's*	*Average*
Victoria	10	17	2	965	206 n.o.	4	64·33
New South Wales	42	57	6	2838	201 n.o.	9	55·64
Total	52	74	8	3803	206 n.o.	13	57·62

Bowling:

For	*Matches*	*Overs*	*Maidens*	*Runs*	*Wickets*	*Average*
Victoria	10	65	4	231	11	21·00
New South Wales	42	767·7	104	2618	98	26·71
Total	52	832·7	108	2849	109	26·13

OTHER MATCHES IN AUSTRALIA

Season	Matches	Inns.	Not Out	Runs	Highest Score	100's	Average
1945–46	3	6	1	273	105 n.o.	1	54·60
1946–47 v M.C.C.	4	6	–	151	70	–	25·16
1947–48 v India	2	3	–	171	86	–	57·00
1950–51 v M.C.C.	3	4	–	373	214	1	93·25
1951–52 v West Indies	1	1	–	30	30	–	30·00
1952–53 v South Africa	2	3	–	117	58	–	39·00
1954–55 v M.C.C.	2	3	–	168	86	–	56·00
Testimonial matches	3	6	–	238	101	2	39·66
Total	20	32	1	1521	214	4	49·06

Bowling:

Season	Matches	Overs	Maidens	Runs	Wickets	Average
1945–46	3	29	2	162	6	27·00
1946–47 v M.C.C.	4	58	9	160	6	26·66
1947–48 v India	2	39·3	3	112	6	18·66
1950–51 v M.C.C.	3	43	7	102	2	51·00
1951–52 v West Indies	1	29·1	5	63	8	7·87
1952–53 v South Africa	2	48	10	127	5	25·40
1954–55 v M.C.C.	2	29	1	85	3	28·33
Testimonial matches	3	41	1	198	4	49·50
Total	20	316·4	38	1009	40	25·22

OVERSEAS TOURS (Matches other than Tests)

Batting:

Season	Country	Matches	Inns.	Not Out	Runs	Highest Score	100's	Average
1946	New Zealand	3	3	–	227	139	1	75·66
1948	England	17	19	3	913	202 n.o.	2	57·00
1949–50	South Africa	8	8	1	331	131	1	47·28
1953	England	17	20	2	909	220 n.o.	2	50·50
1955	West Indies	4	6	–	168	39	–	28·00
1956	England	15	18	5	637	281 n.o.	1	49·00
Total		64	74	11	3185	281 n.o.	7	50·04

Bowling:

Season	Country	Matches	Overs	Maidens	Runs	Wickets	Average
1946	New Zealand	3	17	6	21	4	5·25
1948	England	17	293·3	75	686	43	15·95
1949–50	South Africa	8	121	22	338	27	12·51
1953	England	17	269·4	78	625	25	25·00
1955	West Indies	4	70	17	190	9	21·33
1956	England	15	224·5	58	513	29	17·68
Total		64	996	256	2373	137	17·32

TOTAL FIRST-CLASS

Batting:

	Matches	*Inns.*	*Not Out*	*Runs*	*Highest Score*	*100's*	*Average*
Tests	55	87	7	2958	147	7	36·97
Unofficial Tests	5	10	3	443	118	2	63·28
Sheffield Shield	52	74	8	3803	206 n.o.	13	57·62
Other first-class games	84	106	12	4706	281 n.o.	11	50·06
Total	196	277	30	11910	281 n.o.	33	48·61

Bowling:

	Matches	*Overs*	*Maidens*	*Runs*	*Wickets*	*Average*
Tests	55	1407	337	3905	170	22·97
Unofficial Tests	5	121	19	277	10	27·70
Sheffield Shield	52	832·7	108	2849	109	26·13
Other first-class games	84	1312·4	294	3382	177	19·10
Total	196	3673·4	758	10413	466	22·34